SNAPSHOTS

SNAPSHOTS

ENCOUNTERS WITH TWENTIETH-CENTURY LEGENDS

HERBERT KRETZMER

The Robson Press

First published in Great Britain in 2014 by
The Robson Press (an imprint of Biteback Publishing Ltd)
Westminster Tower
3 Albert Embankment
London SE1 7SP
Copyright © Herbert Kretzmer 2014

ISBN 978-1-84954-717-8

10 9 8 7 6 5 4 3 2 1

A CIP catalogue record for this book is available from the British Library.

Set in Adobe Garamond Pro by five-twentyfive.com

For Sybil

CONTENTS

◇◇◇◇◇◇◇◇◇◇◇◇◇◇◇◇◇◇

ACKNOWLEDGEMENTS

◇◇

The articles in this book appeared originally in the London newspapers *Daily Sketch*, *Sunday Dispatch*, *Daily Express* and *Daily Mail*. I thank Associated Newspapers and Express Newspapers for their kind permission to reprint them.

Thanks are also due to my wife Sybil for her unfailing help in putting the book together, and to my daughter Danielle for the cheerful manner in which she undertook the complicated business of seeking out and clearing all the photographs between these covers.

Thanks, too, to Clive Hirschhorn and Alice Peacock for their valuable advice and assistance.

I DREAMED OF SATURDAY AFTERNOON

This is a book very largely about stars and celebrities, not all of them admirable. One or two proved to be positively hateful. Yet they all had one thing in common: they possessed an aura that made them unique in a way that mattered. And, of course, all were famous.

I caught the fame bug early. I was about eight years old when I was allowed to see a movie for the first time. It was a musical called *Gold Diggers of 1933* and featured a batch of wonderful songs and, I recall, an ambitiously staged finale – 'My Forgotten Man' – which pleaded the cause of the neglected American veterans of the First World War.

I was transfixed. I loved the lilt and lurch of the songs, the free and easy dialogue, the gorgeous girls with their lip-gloss, tight blonde curls and endless legs. I walked home in a state of euphoria. I had seen a promised land.

My revelatory encounter with *Gold Diggers of 1933* took place in Kroonstad, a one-horse town in the central flatlands of South Africa, where I was born in 1925. (The town was actually named after a horse called Kroon who had pulled its rider to safety out of a swollen river.) Kroonstad boasted one high school, one winding river flanked by weeping willows, and a single cinema called the Empire, though few people called it that, favouring the quaint South African term 'bioscope', pronounced 'bye-scope'.

My mother, an immigrant from Eastern Europe, had decreed that my brothers and I could see one film every Saturday afternoon, giving us each a sixpenny coin for the entrance ticket, plus a penny for sweets from Mr Perry's shop next door. You could buy a lot of different sweets for a penny back then.

That single visit to the 'bio' as we called it, and my introduction to Hollywood glamour, changed my life. I couldn't wait for Saturday afternoon to come around. Whether it was smiling chorus girls or the antics of the Marx brothers, I knew I wanted to belong to a world that gave so much pleasure and enjoyment. Indeed, I was so passionate about my weekly visits to the Empire that, if my mother wanted to punish me for any reason, she would, in what I perceived to be an act of calculated cruelty, cancel my next visit to the 'bioscope', inducing gasps of disbelief.

In all I saw about fifty movies a year, thus feeding an addiction shared by millions of my generation across the English-speaking world, a freemasonry of obsessed young geeks who eventually knew the names, not only of all the leading stars, but all the lesser, supporting players whose faces and voices became as recognisable and familiar to us as those of my own family, teachers and neighbours.

Even today, across a reach of three-quarters of a century, I could, without difficulty, reel off their names by the score –

Edward Everett Horton, Hugh Herbert, George Zucco, Guy Kibbee, Franklin Pangborn, Herman Bing, Eric Blore, Mischa Auer, Beulah Bondi, Billy Gilbert, Grant Withers… These were my heroes and I wanted to know more about them. What were they really like? What made them who they were? Clearly I was star-struck, and as I passed out of my childhood and teens and became an adult, I was eager to become a part of their world.

I grew up and left my riverside hometown to become a newspaperman as well as a lyricist, first in Johannesburg, later in London, where I live today. Along the way, I spent about a year in Paris, playing the piano in a St Germain-des-Prés bistro in return for a hot evening meal and trying to write a novel in a Left Bank garret (but couldn't stand the solitude). As a journalist I interviewed, over the years, hundreds of actors, writers, prizefighters, singers. For eighteen years I reviewed plays for the London *Daily Express*. As a lyricist I wrote songs for films, stage, television and the pop music market, achieving considerable success with lyrics for Peter Sellers and Sophia Loren ('Goodness Gracious Me'), for the French singer Charles Aznavour ('She') and, finally, to my surprise, hitting undreamed-of heights by providing the lyrics for the still-running stage behemoth *Les Misérables*, created originally by Alain Boublil and Claude-Michel Schönberg.

But it was newspapers that gave me my start in show business.

Constrained by unforgiving Fleet Street deadlines, the interviews that I did for the pieces I've included in this selection seldom lasted more than 60 minutes. Some were completed in half that time. These are indeed snapshots, but an image caught on the run can often reveal more than you'd get from a considered studio portrait.

All magazine editors know that a famous face on the front cover, particularly that of a young and desirable female, will stimulate circulation. No great mystery there. Everybody loves a star and wants to be drawn nearer to the unknowable secrets that lie at the heart of stardom, distancing the legend from the commoner.

From my parents, who arrived in South Africa from Lithuania in the early years of the twentieth century, I learned civility and table manners. But it was the movies and the stars who appeared in them who taught me how to behave in a wider society; how, for instance, to conduct oneself at a party, what to wear, how to ask a girl to dance, how to withstand the taunts of school bullies. In such matters one could expect little practical help from parents who themselves were strangers in a strange land, coping with unfamiliar challenges and whose command of the English language was sometimes shaky.

In many ways it was Hollywood that guided and educated me by providing new and powerful mythologies. Let me give you one illustration of this. When John F. Kennedy was assassinated in Dallas on that fateful Friday in 1963 I was called on within an hour to create a song about the event to be included in the edition of *That Was the Week That Was* due to be aired on BBC television on the following night.

How does one write a song about so shattering an event? How does one avoid bathos and sentimentality? The answer, wholly inspired by the movies, came to me during the night. I would write a song in the American Western tradition, a song that might have been written a century ago, which made no specific reference to JFK. The components – Wild West, shoot-outs, high noon – would be totally familiar to a modern audience from dozens of Hollywood Westerns.

A young man rode with his head held high
Under the Texas sun
And no one guessed that a man so blessed
Would perish by the gun
Lord, would perish by the gun…

My confidence in the use of the Western metaphor was not misplaced. It was immediately understood. Within a few days the song, called 'In the Summer of His Years', was recorded by a dozen American vocalists including the great gospel singer Mahalia Jackson. Thank you, Hollywood.

As you will see, there are very few businessmen, scientists or military men in this book. The majority of people I've included are, in the broadest sense, entertainers and celebrities who have spent their lives in the white glow of fame. They stand out in the crowd. That is what has intrigued me about them. They are the shining exceptions to the rule.

It has been my pleasure and privilege to get to know them, if only for a moment.

Herbert Kretzmer, London
AUGUST 2014

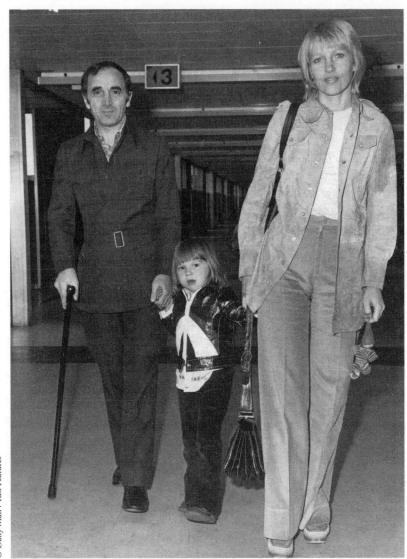

Charles Aznavour and wife Ulla with daughter Katya

CHAPTER I

CHARLES AZNAVOUR – TROUBADOUR

*"Teenage songs are one of the few things
that make me laugh."*

*Though he is considered the embodiment of Frenchness, Charles Aznavour is in
fact a proud Armenian without a corpuscle of French blood in his body. Full
surname: Aznavourian. Born in Paris on 22 May 1924, he is the son of a Left
Bank restaurateur of modest means. Aznavour dropped out of school at the age
of nine, already set on a career as a performer. In 1946 he came to the attention
of Edith Piaf who arranged for him to accompany her on her world tours as an
aide, secretary and occasional songwriter (but never, he says, as her lover). Now
he has taken her place as the mirror in which the French see subtly reflected their
national preoccupation with the game of love. When I interviewed him for the
first time in 1965 he was virtually unknown in the English-speaking world. I met
him in what was once a seventeenth-century granary in the village of Calluis, a
fast forty-minute drive west of Paris. His rooms are spacious and their furnishings
massive. He is served and sustained by a host of secretaries, housekeepers, butlers,
chauffeurs, hangers-on, horses and dogs. Aznavour writes his own songs and
lyrics and sings them in a foggy, throbbing voice with a marvellous melancholy
about it, an instrument for transmitting rage, regret and longing. Only France,
among all the countries of the world, breeds voices like his.*

C harles Aznavour speaks good English, but not good enough, he thinks,
to entertain the British. 'In America they don't care. America is a land
of immigrants. It is a country full of people who speak bad English.'

Charles Aznavour did not smile when he said that. There is little laughter
in his songs.

'People tell me I never smile,' he said. 'But I smile inside. I am not a sad
man. It is hard to make me laugh. I do not find comic what everybody
finds comic.'

Even in repose one can sense a fire burning in him. He is a witness of life.
And death. One of his songs – titled '*Qui?*' ('Who?') – is the statement of
a man twenty years older than the young girl he loves. Who, the lyric asks,
will take my place when I am gone? To whom will you show your moments
of folly?

> '*Qui prendra ta bouche? Qui prendra ta couche? Et m'enterrera pour la seconde fois?*'
>   'Who will take your mouth? Who will take your bed? And bury me for the
> second time?'

'I write songs about love and life,' Aznavour told me.

> 'I sing about the ordinary, the everyday things. I am successful because I tell
> about the real feelings of real people. I am ordinary, like them. They recognise
> in my songs what they themselves cannot express. Yes, many of my songs are
> about the problems of men growing old, about love affairs when we lose our
> young years. I continually find myself thinking about these things.'

Aznavour paused for a silent moment. 'I am going to be forty-one next
month,' he said.

> 'I began to write songs about growing old when I was only twenty. I have
> always had, and never lost, the realisation of how very brief life is. The prob-
> lems of youth are superficial. Teenage songs are one of the few things that
> make me laugh. The boys are always crying because they have lost their little
> girls. It is all nonsense. They can't mean what they say.'

As we talked in Aznavour's ballroom-sized living room numerous bespectacled little men, performing unexplained functions in the household, came
padding in respectfully with papers for Aznavour to sign. He scrawled his
signature with a red felt-tipped pen.
    'The secret to remain young,' he said to me, 'has to do with the ability to
be surprised. Youth is nothing but surprise and enthusiasm and curiosity.
Jean Cocteau was a young man at seventy-seven years. To begin again … to
start again … that is the only exciting thing in life.'
    He reached for a document giving details of a recent French poll, which
named him the most popular entertainer in the country. 'I am number one in
France,' he said factually, without any discernible conceit. 'The work is done
here. It is finished. This is the year I want to capture America. The world is large.'

One of Aznavour's dogs, a full-grown Great Dane, which probably weighed as much as his master, loped into the room and sat adoringly at Aznavour's feet. The singer scratched the dog's head.

Outside, a cluster of workmen were building an open-air dance floor in his garden. Others were repairing the glass dome enveloping his swimming pool. Fantailed pigeons cooed and slithered on the rust-coloured tiles of the house. The telephone never stopped ringing. Berlin, Rome, New York.

'I was poor once. Father was a singer and Mama was an actress. It was ordained, therefore, that I should go on to the stage. That's how it is with Armenians. I made my first appearance when I was nine. I can write songs anywhere, anytime. If I need a song I sit down at the piano and write it.' He reckons that he has written between 600 and 700 songs.

He has filled his house with objects of religious art, not because he is a religious man ('I am like many others who doubt') but because these objects were created by men who did not work for money. 'These objects have a purity I admire and envy. Today we don't know any more who are the real and the false painters. Everything is for money.'

One day Aznavour wants to perform in England. He has turned down British television offers because 'all they want of me is just one or two songs. It is impossible to explain myself in a couple of songs. I have a feeling that England is a very far country from France. I deplore it but I cannot change it.'

On his piano he has scribbled the beginnings of a new song called 'Carnival'. 'My favourite song,' said the number-one music man in France, 'is always the last song I have written.'

10 May 1965

Nine years later, in 1974, Charles Aznavour's song 'She', with a lyric by Herbert Kretzmer, rose to number one in the English charts and introduced the French singer to the English-speaking mass audience that had hitherto eluded him.

Recovering from a skiing accident that broke a skinny leg last January, Charles Aznavour limped awkwardly into the Arrivals area at Heathrow.

He was instantly lost in an anxious huddle of promoters, managers and public relations men. Little Charles (only 5 feet 5 inches and not an ounce of fat on him) had a gentle, melancholy smile for each. Although he was shorter than the scrum that surrounded him, he dominated the place with his self-assurance and quietness.

He has grown accustomed to fame and money. He stays cool. In Britain for a concert at the London Palladium last night, and a date in Wakefield tonight, Aznavour was travelling with his third and final wife Ulla and their entrancing three-year-old daughter Katia, who knows all Daddy's songs. Riding from Heathrow to their Park Lane hotel with the family in a chauffeur-driven Daimler, Charles told me that he was a changed man.

I had first known him in 1965 as an urgent go-getter, working around the clock, scurrying between recording and film studios, eager to earn money, eager for fame. He projected an irresistible energy, but it was not easy to warm to him.

'For years,' he said, 'I wanted to be the first Frenchman in France, the first Frenchman in the world. Coming from way down I naturally wanted to go way up.' For Aznavour it was a rare Napoleonic confession. 'In the process I lost the value of little things, the things of friendship, of people … or perhaps they weren't lost at all, only put away in a corner of my heart.'

Aznavour is at the peak of his career. He will never retire.

'Nobody ever retires,' he said, 'not even Sinatra. I've never met anybody in this business who can stop. Show business is a drug and we are all addicts. There is always a little comeback in us somewhere.'

Aznavour made his name and his fortune writing and singing songs of aching sadness, like the sombre '*Hier Encore*' (which became in English 'Yesterday When I Was Young'), which voices the regret of a mature man facing up to the wasted chances of youth, the slow approach of physical frailty. ('There are so many songs in me that won't be sung…')

For years the themes of age and lost opportunity have obsessed him. Now he gives the impression of a man who has come to terms with his life. 'Breaking my leg was the best thing that could have happened. For five months I couldn't sing, I couldn't go anywhere. It forced me to go into myself, to talk to myself. I'm more open than I ever was. I spend more time with my friends now, and we talk about little things, or nothing. More people call me Charles now rather than Monsieur Aznavour. That is the big change, and that is the way it will go on. I don't go out to win any more, just to work.'

Fifteen minutes later we were drinking champagne in the Grosvenor House Hotel in a suite overlooking Hyde Park. Charles is at the window with his wife. 'This is the greenest city in the world,' he tells her in French. 'Parks give London its poetry.'

He sits down again. 'You can age without growing old. An old man is a man who has given up questioning and accepts everything. To be young one must remain inquisitive, dissatisfied, and never accept anything just because it's established by law, or fashion, or because people love it the way it is.'

He paid the waiter from a crumpled wad of French francs. 'There is no bad money,' said Charles Aznavour. 'Paper is paper.'

13 MAY 1973

Charles Aznavour, true to his word, did not retire; he celebrated his 90th birthday in 2014 with a series of worldwide one-man recitals, which he performed with barely diminished vigour. Since June 2009 he has been the permanent representative of Armenia to the United Nations in Geneva. A statue of Aznavour stands in Gyumri in Armenia. Bing Crosby, on his last ever album, included Aznavour's lament for lost youth, 'Yesterday When I Was Young'.

Lionel Bart pictured during rehearsals for his West End play *Why the Chicken?*

CHAPTER 2

LIONEL BART –
ON THE DAY *OLIVER!* OPENED

◇◇

"I was happier when I was playing washboard
for Tommy Steele."

Born Lionel Begleiter in 1930, youngest of eight children of an Austrian Jewish tailor, he grew up in Stepney, London. His youthful ambition was to be a painter, but a natural, unforced talent for popular melody soon revealed itself. He wrote the early hits of Cliff Richard, Tommy Steele and Anthony Newley. In 1959 he wrote the lyrics (to Laurie Johnson's music) of the Mermaid Theatre's inaugural production Lock Up Your Daughters. *Bigger things were to follow…*

The most successful British songwriter since Ivor Novello and Noël Coward is a small, dark ex-slum dweller with a chip on his shoulder, three cars in the garage, and an income of something like £50,000 a year. His name is Lionel Bart. It is an easy name to remember, and that's the way Bart likes it. He writes songs that are easy to remember, too.

Some envious rivals decry Bart as 'dead commercial', but any of them would trade their teeth for his common touch and royalties. It is practically certain that, at some stage in the past few years, you have hummed or whistled a Bart melody ('Fings Ain't Wot They Used T'Be', 'Livin' Doll', 'Little White Bull') without giving a second thought to the identity of the author. Lionel Bart has won so many Ivor Novello Awards (the Oscars of British songwriting) that the annual prize-giving event at the Savoy has become known, ruefully, as 'Bart's Benefit'.

Just three nights ago he staged a triumphant invasion of the London stage for the third time in 1960 with the opening of *Oliver!*, a musical based on Dickens' *Oliver Twist*, for which Bart wrote the book, music and lyrics.

He lives today in a plush mews house near the South Kensington tube station (which he never uses) and has found solace in the ownership of expensive automobiles.

I called to see him at his home some hours before the curtain went up on the first night of *Oliver!* He was extremely nervous about the prospects of the show.

'I tell you straight, mate,' he said. 'If anything goes wrong on the stage tonight, I'm going to walk out of the theatre and wander around Trafalgar Square until it's all over.'

Eleven hours later Bart stood backstage at the New Theatre being kissed, backslapped and hand-pumped in a delirium of congratulation after one of the most ecstatic first-night receptions London has witnessed since *Oklahoma!* came to town.

Bart accepted the idolatry with a succession of quick, nervous grins. Perspiration filmed his forehead. He glistened like a garden gnome after a shower. But all this – and the banner-waving press notices next morning – still lay ahead of him when Bart and I talked in his mews flat...

He drank a cup of hot tea and stubbed out a half-smoked cigarette. Success has turned him into an anxious man.

'I am always worrying about what comes next,' he said. 'It's a dodgy lark, I tell you. Some people get dizzy with success. Not me. I get apprehensive. That's the word...'

Bart rubbed the side of his nose with his knuckles. It is a long, thin nose that is poised over his mouth like a permanent exclamation mark. 'The phone never stops ringing,' he mock-complained.

'I am inundated with offers. People want me to write songs for shows, songs for films. It's a headache deciding what to take on, what to turn down. I have just rejected a Hollywood offer to write all the songs for Elvis Presley's next picture. Everything I do must be bigger and better than anything I have done before. That's my kick, mate.'

The ivory telephone rang at his elbow. Bart spoke into the mouthpiece. 'Who wants seats for the show? Lord Whom? OK, tell him he can have two.'

Bart replaced the phone, lit another cigarette, juggling with a heavy silver table lighter, which was reluctant to ignite. 'Where was I?' he said.

'Basically I'm successful because I never write into a void. I always know just who I'm writing a song for. When I write a Tommy Steele song, like "Handful of Songs", I write it specifically for Tommy and nobody else. It works better that way, mate. It really does.'

Lionel Bart talks in a soft sandpaper voice with more than a suggestion of a lisp.

He comes from London's East End, a notable crucible of Jewish artistic talent. 'I was born,' he told me, 'in a maternity home we called Mother Levy's.'

'I was the youngest of eight children – four boys and four girls. We were all of us brought up in one tiny slum near Petticoat Lane. Sometimes I was neglected, being the youngest. Other times, I was loved to distraction. When I was twelve my old man gave me a fiddle as a present. I gave it up after six months. It was hopeless. I still can't read a note of music. Can't play a note, either. When I compose a song I just hum it into a tape recorder. Then somebody else puts the dots down on paper. What's the difference, mate? It's working out, isn't it?'

As a Jew, Bart has had to brave prejudice and stupidity on his way to the top. But unlike Frankie Vaughan, whose manly shoulders seem to be free of any chips, Lionel Bart carries in him an inborn caution and a sharpened awareness on matters of race and social conscience. He agreed that most musical shows from the days of George Gershwin and Irving Berlin to the present era of *West Side Story* and *Guys and Dolls* were written by Jews.

'I feel that all life is a search for love, a desire to be loved. And nobody is more guilty of this vice of needing to be approved of, than minority groups like Jews and Negroes. That is why they make such brilliant entertainers. They need all that approval, all the applause. It's a kind of love, isn't it? People like me who come from the gutters of the East End, we haven't got time for all that surface chi-chi like *Salad Days* [a musical about a magic piano by Julian Slade]. We have seen too much that is real.'

Bart now plans to go into hibernation for a year. His major project for the next year is a massive folk opera, conceived on the scale of *Porgy and Bess*, which will describe the life of London's East End under bomb fire. The show, ready in 1961, will be called quite simply *Blitz!*

Bart writes songs with remarkable speed (maximum time per song: sixty minutes) but claims that he needs days and months, even years, of thinking the song out before he reaches the point of creation.

He would not describe himself as a happy person. 'I was happier,' he said, 'when I was playing washboard for Tommy Steele in the early days, and loafin' around Soho with fifteen bob in my pocket.'

Now when he sits in his £4,250 Mercedes Benz convertible (registration plate LB 4), Lionel Bart knows that he has come a long way. But he knows something else too, that at twenty-seven he is just beginning.

3 JULY 1960

With three consecutive hit shows to his name, the unstoppable Bart now turned his attention to an epic musical that, he boasted, would dwarf its predecessors. Conceived on the scale of grand opera, Blitz! *would re-tell the story of the German air raids on London in 1940. It would be a tribute to the fighting spirit of London's East End.*

A few minutes after 11 o'clock last Tuesday morning, in his little mews house in South Kensington, Mr Lionel Bart reached for a fat pencil and scribbled ten words of a song lyric on a large sheet of white paper.

'No more bunking over walls,' he wrote, 'Duty calls, hallelujah, duty calls!' He underlined the words and sat back. Another Bart musical was done.

After six years of planning, four months of actual writing, *Blitz!*, to be presented in London in the spring of 1962, was in the bag. *Oliver!* had a successor.

Yesterday Mr Bart was still pretty wound up about the enterprise. The expected elation following the completion of a big show had not materialised. He paced the floor like a small, nervous ant-eater. 'Man, it's finished. But it's just beginning. Now we start pulling it to pieces.'

Blitz!, he told me, was the biggest thing he had ever attempted.

'The story covers, like, the whole canvas of the German air raids on the East End,' he said. 'It takes place in the Underground shelters and in Petticoat Lane. The leading lady is a big Cockney Jewish mama. I already got someone in mind. Real matriarchal. She'll be wild.'

The story goes back to Bart's own roots. Born within a shout of Petticoat Lane, he was a ten-year-old awaiting evacuation when the bombs began to fall. He saw London burning.

It is no coincidence that both *Oliver!* and *Blitz!* are spelled with exclamation marks. Bart likes to think in superlatives. He describes his new show as something the size of *Porgy and Bess*.

'Folk opera!' he says. 'Orchestra of thirty-five! Cast of sixty! Maybe seventy! Twenty-five songs, plus seven repeats. The second act came fast. Finished it in ten days. When it flows, man, it flows.'

Bart jumped up from his chair. Then sat down again. He is full of quick, unexpected moves. 'I'll tell you,' he said. 'The show is full of kids. Listen…' He rested his lean, tanned hands on his knees and sang an appealing little song at me called 'Mums and Dads'. He sang it with a soft, childish voice, dropping aitches all the way. 'I think it'll go,' he said.

The most successful British songwriter alive was unknown two years ago, hanging around Soho, churning out tumpty-tum ditties for guitar-strumming boy wonders. Then came the stage shows – *Lock Up Your Daughters*, *Fings Ain't Wot They Used T'Be* and *Oliver!* – three hits in a row. The money began to roll in, and the publicity stories began to roll out. The buzz was fuelled by Bart himself, who, despite occasional protestations of humility, is a man who dearly loves to see his name in the papers. Not one in ten thousand, I suppose, could name the writers of *Irma La Douce* or *Espresso Bongo* or *The Music Man* [all musicals running in the West End at the time]. But everybody has heard of Lionel Bart.

The buzz is not always complimentary. Bart has something of a reputation for conceit and arrogance. Bart is not unaware of this.

'Man, what do they expect me to do? I can't be a nice guy to the whole world. I can't recognise everybody in the street. I have no delusions of grandeur. I'm not an intellectual like Peter Ustinov. I'm just a simple guy. They just don't know what the pressures are.'

Another attitude towards Bart seeks to nail him as a copy-cat composer. A Bart tune, say his critics, is an old tune tricked up to sound new.

Bart says, 'Listen, mate. *Fings* is deliberately derivative of the Thirties. And *Blitz!* will be deliberately based on the musical mood of the Forties. The wartime songs … You've got yourself a good popular song when the audience can almost feel the next note, the next lyric. I want my songs to sound familiar.'

By adhering to such simple rules, Bart has made a fortune. He says he cannot estimate his income. 'I've got a mental block about figures. At school, when the teachers wrote sums on the blackboard, I kind of blanked over. I don't add up my money. I just use it.'

But certain things of his boyhood remain with him. These are the things he has poured into *Blitz!*

'I wanted to do something particularly British. Something that owes nothing to American influence. What I remember of the war is the wonderful blitz spirit. It didn't matter if you were Jewish, or black or yellow. You had one common enemy. You laughed at the same jokes. You sang the same songs. It shouldn't be necessary to have bombs dropped on our heads before we learn to live with each other and love each other. I hope *Blitz!* says that. I think it does.'

30 SEPTEMBER 1961

Blitz! had a respectable, but hardly sensational, run of 568 performances. It contained no outstanding hit songs and is seldom revived.

Songwriter Lionel Bart is about to write a musical based on the legend of Robin Hood. The show will not follow the party line about the merry outlaws of Sherwood Forest. 'It is going to be a naughty show,' Lionel Bart told me in conspiratorial tones. 'A very naughty show. Robin Hood is a con man, Maid Marian a nympho and Little John an abject coward. You might describe it as a satirical girlie show that is definitely not for the family trade.'

I was talking to Mr Bart in his newly acquired house off the Fulham Road – a rambling, twenty-five-roomed mansion with minstrel galleries, carved stonework and stained-glass windows, not to mention a hand-painted mural of the Battle of Agincourt, and seven lavatories, one of them done up as a panelled throne room.

'I'm on a big medieval kick,' Mr Bart explained. 'Both my next two musicals are set in medieval times. First, the Robin Hood bit. Then a massive spectacular about the Hunchback of Notre Dame in which every line of the dialogue will be sung by up to 100 voices. There will be,' Bart added as an afterthought, 'no orchestra.'

He talked about the Robin Hood musical, commissioned by a company headed by Peter Sellers. 'We are calling the show *Twang!!* with two exclamation marks. On the posters we shall have an arrow quivering in a tree. The show will be subtitled "The Misadventure of Robin Hood".'

Mr Bart and I took lunch in his spacious study. Between courses he threw back his dark, earnest head and sang me a couple of numbers from *Twang!!* The first song was titled 'Locksmith For The Lady', and will be sung by a line of leggy girls encased in iron chastity belts by their husbands, who have gone off to the Crusades. The main burden of the song is concerned with the determination of the lonesome wives to secure the services of a locksmith to liberate them from their frustrations. Mr Bart followed up with another song in which the wives, now emancipated and unlocked, sing a ditty proclaiming their immediate availability. The title of this song is self- explanatory: 'Thou Hath It Made'. Both songs were pithy, wittily rhymed, and promise well for the rest of *Twang!!*

'What we are doing in *Twang!!,*' said Mr Bart, 'is to satirise the Crusades, the attitude of the Church and, above all, human gullibility, which can turn an outlawed con man like Robin Hood into some kind of heroic saint.

Personally, I find con men very colourful,' he allowed. 'They are, and have to be, chameleon characters, and that is very good theatrically.'

Robin will be played by James Booth, veteran of con men roles.

Twang!! is being written in a hurry. Mr Bart started work on songs a fortnight ago. He says he will have the entire first draft of the show written in another week or two. 'In one single night last week I wrote four new songs. That's the way it comes sometimes, in a kind of flood. I can't always write music that way, of course; I have to enjoy doing it. It has to be a labour of love, not a love of labour. I can't sweat on lyrics. If I write a song, and it is basically a good song, and for the moment I cannot find a good line or a good rhyme, I don't beat my brains out. I just let it go. It will come later, maybe during rehearsals. The thing to do is not to panic.'

After *Twang!!* and the Hunchback musical, Mr Bart plans to stop working altogether and take a year or two off to relax and recuperate. He said: 'I haven't stopped working for eight years. I now receive about a dozen projects a week. I turn them all down.'

Mr Bart looked pleased and calm and assured. The world is knocking on his heavy oak doors. He can afford to be choosy.

6 MARCH 1965

Twang!! was a famous disaster. Lionel Bart rashly tried to save the show by trading his Oliver! royalties. He spent the next twenty years, more or less, lost in a stupor induced by drugs and drink, though he occasionally surfaced to announce grandiose new musicals, which existed only in his head. His only 'hit' (you could hardly call it that) in twenty years was Happy Endings, a thirty-second advertising jingle for Abbey National featuring Bart sitting at a piano, singing to children.

Lionel Bart died of cancer in 1999 and was cremated at Golders Green, London.

Jill Bennett and John Osborne

CHAPTER 3

JILL BENNETT – DRAGON LADY

"Ours is a dangerous, very precarious marriage."

Jill Bennett, a fine English stage and film actress with a somewhat forbidding presence, was born in Penang, Malaysia on Christmas Eve, 1931. She trained at RADA and began her stage career at the Shakespeare Memorial Theatre, Stratford-upon-Avon, in 1949. She was the fourth wife of the playwright John Osborne. Before that, Jill Bennett was the live-in partner of actor Godfrey Tearle, many years her senior. She was later married to writer Willis Hall. When I met her, Jill Bennett had been married to John Osborne for eight years.

I suspect that most men in her audiences are secretly a little afraid of actress Jill Bennett. On stage and screen she frequently projects an embittered, impatient personality, certain of her values, contemptuous of fools and frauds. When her husband John Osborne's play about an explosive marriage, *Watch It Come Down*, opens tonight at the Old Vic, Miss Bennett will be at it again, curling her lip in disgust and scaring the audience.

Offstage and off-duty, Jill Bennett hardly lives up to her image as a dragon. Aware of her forbidding reputation, she disclaims it.

'People think I'm cool, sharp, abrasive. Actually, I'm a lump of jelly inside, prone to every variety of nervous rash. My husband says he married me because I was the wittiest woman alive. I thought, oh, my God, it can't last … one simply can't go on telling jokes the whole time. I would like to play a soft, loving, romantic and kindly woman one day. I'll be much better at it. It'll be easier to do. But very few male playwrights are actually interested in women. They don't write for us because they are scared and bewildered by women. Lots of homosexuals write wonderfully about women because they're really writing about themselves.'

She sipped milk-less, sugarless tea from a plastic cup. We were in her dressing room in the Old Vic. Jill Bennett was surrounded by her small, travelling collection of lucky talismans. She held up an old teddy bear called Sir Teggy, chief among her mascots.

> 'I've had Sir Teggy longer than I've been alive. My mother bought him in Penang two weeks before I was born. Sir Teggy is bolshie, vile, unpleasant, but if I don't take him along everywhere he'll never forgive me. He's got earrings now and gone all poofy.'

She laid Sir Teggy down fondly. But her superstitions cannot cure her of a chronic dread of appearing in public. 'Standing out there' – she nodded in the direction of the Old Vic stage – 'doesn't get any easier. I'm quite likely to come out in a rash. I feel I've got every disease known to man. It's terrible, really. Nureyev said he was driven by fear. I know exactly what he means. I thought I'd get over it as I got older and wiser. Instead I get more muddled, more stupid and more afraid.'

Her strength, she says, derives from her cautious but seemingly secure marriage to John Osborne. But secure is not a word she would choose. 'Ours is a dangerous, very precarious marriage,' she said. 'And I wouldn't be without it for the world.'

> 'John has tried to give me confidence. He allows me to make a fool of myself and gives me the right to fail. I never think of him as my husband. He's my best friend. I was a real mess when I met John. We were friends for a very long time before anything blew up between us. I was in love with someone else at the time. I first saw John at a grand dinner party at Ken Tynan's. John sat next to me and, since he was a vegetarian, he pointed at his food and said: "Do you want my meat?" It's the first thing he ever said to me. He also said I have a wonderful profile, which stunned me, because it's awful. I don't think I said a word. I was out of work and wearing a borrowed dress. I worshipped him as a writer. I'd seen all his plays two or three times. Of course it's an extra pressure to be in a play by one's husband. You want especially to succeed for the sake of someone you love and admire.'

Jill Bennett is an accomplished actress and will no doubt demonstrate it again tonight in the Osborne play about a marriage she describes as 'a dangerous game between two very intelligent people'. That description also appears to sum up her relationship with the playwright.

'I find people are getting nicer all the time. The world's in such chaos, smaller things have greater value. In that way I particularly like actors. They are unselfish, elastic, brave and fearful.'

I like Jill Bennett ... and will never be frightened of her again.

24 FEBRUARY 1976

The ten-year marriage of Jill Bennett and John Osborne eventually turned sour. Their corrosive public quarrels and evident hostility were for years the stuff of theatrical gossip and folklore. Of Osborne, who famously hated his own mother, Jill Bennett once said: 'Never marry a man who hates his mother because he'll end up hating you.' Jill Bennett, who suffered from depression, committed suicide in October 1990, aged fifty-eight. Her ashes, together with the ashes of her friend the actress Rachel Roberts, were scattered on the Thames in London by director Lindsay Anderson.

Time & Life Pictures / Getty Images

Irving Berlin in his office

CHAPTER 4

IRVING BERLIN – GOD BLESS AMERICA

"I think to be a good songwriter you've got to be
a kind of ham."

The great American songwriter Jerome ('Ol' Man River') Kern said famously that 'Irving Berlin has no place in American music – he is American music.' Berlin (born Israel Beilin on 11 May 1888 in Russia) must be numbered among the foremost popular songwriters of the past century. He wrote some 1,500 songs beginning, more or less, with the brash, exuberant 'Alexander's Ragtime Band' (1911), which I regard as the first-ever all-American song which owes nothing to European musical precedent. Almost alone among modern songwriters, he writes both the words and the music of his songs. His body of work includes celebrated screen musicals like Easter Parade *and* There's No Business Like Show Business *and stage hits like the all-conquering* Annie Get Your Gun. *A fervently patriotic American, Berlin wrote 'God Bless America' (1938), which over the years has become an alternative national anthem. In both world wars Berlin tirelessly travelled many thousands of miles, leading uniformed entertainers in his self-written revues like* Yip Yip Yaphank *(First World War) and* This Is The Army *(Second World War).*

Berlin's biggest hit remains the perennial 'White Christmas'. George Gershwin called him 'the greatest songwriter that has ever lived'.

The American songwriter who wrote 'Oh How I Hate To Get Up In The Morning' slept in his London hotel bedroom until lunchtime yesterday. Hours earlier Irving Berlin had flown in from the US. Tomorrow he will see his youngest daughter, Elizabeth Irving Berlin, married in London to Edmund Fisher, son of celebrated ornithologist James Fisher.

Last night, spruced up, shaved and willing to talk, Irving Berlin beamed good will and benevolence in all directions. He appears to be a happy and chatty man, giving the lie to the reputation for curmudgeonly reticence that had preceded him to Britain.

'I am a ham,' he confessed, with no pretence at humility. 'I think to be a good songwriter you've got to be a kind of ham. The same with actors. You must like to show off what you do. You must like to be a success. It's not ego … wait a minute, it is ego. It's the same in any business.'

He talks in a soft, throaty voice. Songwriter Sammy Cahn once told me 'to hear Irving you've got to hug him'. Irving Berlin's conversation is as simple as his songs. He is an ordinary man with an extraordinary gift; and he does not seek to sound cute or quotable.

'The reason I write simply,' he said, 'is that I just wasn't clever when I started.'

'I have never been a smart aleck. I could not read music and I couldn't play the piano in any key except F. Matter of fact, still can't. By the time I had sharpened the tools of my trade I found that I wrote simple songs because that's how they came out of my head. I didn't try to change anything. A certain emotional something went into the songs and I never tried to analyse it too much. It is often the unselfconscious thing that makes a hit. You can become too clever.'

Ten years ago he retired from songwriting. He was already rich and famous beyond measure and expectation, and had achieved a rare immortality in his own lifetime.

'Retirement,' he said, 'made me sick… I mean that. I got really sick.'

'I suffered severe bouts of depression. I worried about everything when, really, I had nothing to worry about. I tried to take up painting, but I was no good at it. I felt that I had to be as good a painter as I had been a songwriter. I hope that doesn't sound conceited, but it's the truth. I'm not a kid any more. Last May I celebrated, or didn't celebrate, my seventy-fifth birthday. I didn't have to prove anything to myself any more. It takes a very rare person to retire gracefully, especially if he has been a success. I had no hobbies. My only hobby is songwriting. So I went back to work.'

Berlin, at seventy-five, says he is as busy as ever. He is writing ten new songs for a Hollywood film called *Say It With Music*. They will be songs in the true Berlin tradition.

'I know,' he said, 'what I can do. I know where I want to go. Age has nothing to do with it. They say Irving Berlin is seventy-five and Noël Coward is pushing sixty. So who's counting? I don't think of myself as any age. I write songs for people. There are lots of old guys writing songs today. You've got to stay healthy. That's all.'

Irving Berlin, I report with pleasure, looked very healthy to me.

13 SEPTEMBER 1963

Irving Berlin, despite the good cheer displayed in the interview above, was not a widely popular man. (During the Second World War, when the US Air Force began daylight bombing raids on the German capital, songwriter Harry Warren complained: 'They bombed the wrong Berlin.') Irving Berlin died in his sleep on 22 September 1989, aged 101, survived by three daughters.

Bob Boothby

CHAPTER 5

BOB BOOTHBY – THE MAN WHO MIGHT HAVE BEEN PRIME MINISTER

"I am not, I am afraid, a humble man."

A man of tremendous self-confidence, Robert Boothby was born on 12 February 1900 in Edinburgh, Scotland. His life was privileged and bountiful – Eton, Magdalen College, Oxford. He made a powerful impact on viewers in the early days of British TV as a debater and panellist. A Falstaffian figure, genial and clubbable, his often scandalous private life was effectively covered up by editors and colleagues who enjoyed his wit and his whisky. The Queen Mother referred to him as 'a bounder, but not a cad'. The MP and author Ludovic Kennedy claimed that Boothby fathered at least three children by the wives of other men.

The short, dark man with a square moustache and a swastika armband sprang to his feet, clicked his heels, raised his right arm and shouted, 'Heil Hitler!' There followed a moment of fluster and confusion. First to recover was a young British MP who had just been ushered into a Berlin hotel suite to meet the Führer in 1932.

The MP jumped to attention, raised his own arm and bawled, 'Boothby!'

History does not record Hitler's reaction to this brief encounter with the Hon. Member for East Aberdeenshire. The way Boothby tells it, the Führer was very surprised indeed. Boothby likes telling that story. Vain, but instantly likeable, Boothby has never been able to resist an audience. Television has made him the most celebrated political face in Britain today, with the possible exception of Harold Macmillan.

Fingering his bow-tie, patting his luxuriant mane of steel-silver hair, Robert John Graham Boothby has charmed his way through a countless succession of TV broadcasts, impressing millions with an unstoppable flow of words, all of them delivered in a deep-throated voice that growls and rumbles on like an overlapping series of thunderclaps. No one has heard him stumble or hesitate. He rolls ever onward like a tidal wave, the correct word, the apt expression always within reach. In an age of colourless political mediocrities, Bob Boothby is a florid, fanciful and exaggerated figure of speech.

I met Lord Boothby of Buchan and Rattray KBE at his Eaton Square apartment for what turned out to be a conversation liberally fuelled by Scotch and water. Boothby off-stage is very little different from the bow-tied titan of the TV screen, unapologetically in love with his celebrity status and the sound of his own voice.

'I like being recognised in the street,' he said. 'I like to be told by taxi drivers, "I saw you on the telly."' Boothby patted his tummy with his fingertips – the gesture of a man more than a little satisfied with himself. 'I am not, I am afraid, a humble man,' he said.

He acquired his self-confidence as a boy at Eton. 'I had the most lovely treble voice,' he told me, relishing the memory. 'I had a truly beautiful voice. I led the choir at Eton. I had great vanity. I enjoyed making old girls cry by singing "O, For the Wings of a Dove" before I went back to sucking bullseyes and doing noughts and crosses.'

Aware of himself, aware of his charm, Boothby has utilised his personal gifts to lever himself into public life and high public office. He does not appear to have become cynical in the process, retaining an uncorrupted, youthful delight in life and a boyish lack of snobbery. His elevation to national eminence seems spontaneous and natural. As a result, his bravado seems unobjectionable. Recently he watched a recording of one of his own TV programmes, applauding himself throughout without restraint. 'I really think I was magnificent,' Boothby told me.

The telephone rang on his desk. While Boothby went to answer it, I noted his collection of gramophone records. Beethoven symphonies, Wagner operas, Schubert, Grieg and, more surprisingly, a compilation of dreamy popular ballads titled *Mood for Love*.

Across the room, Boothby was cackling into the phone, 'Go in and win!' he urged the caller. 'Yep! Yep! Read me in the *Sunday Dispatch* next week. I'm damned good!' Boothby laughed deep down, replacing the telephone mouthpiece. Now he stood in front of the empty fireplace and launched himself energetically into a statement of his beliefs and attitudes.

'I have been a lucky bloke in my life,' he boomed. 'Damn lucky! I believe in chance. I believe in fate. My basic belief in life is you must accept what comes your way and make the best of it. There's not a damn thing you can do about it. If you can't be happy, you might as well be dead.' He puffed at a cigarette and reflected on his own charmed existence. Son of a director of the Bank of Scotland in Edinburgh, Bob Boothby went headlong into politics in his early twenties.

For twenty-four years he represented the 50,000 people who live in the herring-fishing constituency of East Aberdeenshire, and he never forgot his parliamentary obligations to the salty folks who sent him to Westminster time after time. A contemporary said of him: 'You have only to mention herrings in the Commons and Boothby immediately makes a speech.'

As a young politician he predicted and warned against the rise of Nazi Germany. ('I talked with Hitler for over an hour and it was not long before I detected the unmistakable glint of madness in his eyes.') With Churchill he urged greater military preparedness to meet the coming threat.

'My life,' Boothby told me, 'has been so terribly full and interesting. Fortune has put me in the path of great men. Churchill! Lloyd George! Birkenhead! Some of them, like Thomas Beecham, William Somerset Maugham and Compton Mackenzie, have become my lifelong friends. I've had enormous fun in their company. I've learned a hell of a lot from them.'

Boothby shook his giant leonine head. A Churchillian gesture. He said:

'There are no longer any real personalities in political life. When I went into the Commons in 1924 there were forty or fifty people of great independence who spoke in their own right and commanded the attention of the whole country. They've gone. All gone. Today you have competent administrators, that's all. If you walk out now into Eaton Square and ask ten people the names of the members of the Cabinet, most of them would stick at Macmillan.'

From another room a vacuum cleaner began its familiar domestic hum. A maid was doing out the Boothby apartment.

Boothby lives the life of a sophisticated bachelor, which he is not. He was in fact married in 1935 to Diana Cavendish, daughter of Lord Richard Cavendish and niece of the Duke of Devonshire. The marriage lasted about a year. Boothby swears he will never marry again. He is a man who clearly relishes his freedom. He loves good food, good whisky, good conversation. He is playfully secretive about what he calls 'my other vices'. 'I've been told that if I were ever to write my true life story, with complete candour and utter honesty I could earn myself a million pounds ... but I would have to spend the rest of my days in Tahiti. Whoever told me that was absolutely right! What's more,' Boothby added, 'I am considering it!'

When he became Rector of St Andrews he shocked sections of the Scottish clergy by urging students to 'Make the most of life … it won't last long.' During the course of a memorable address to college students, he said: 'The purpose of life, as I conceive it, is simply the enjoyment of it. Therefore, I say unto you, enjoy yourselves and be gay. Beware of those who talk of salvation rather than happiness. What kind of God is He that creates a world from which we have to be saved?'

Boothby has been hailed over the years as 'the man in the shadows … the man who might have been Prime Minister'.

His political courage and acumen are unquestioned. He foresaw the trend towards a united Europe. He warned against Munich in the days when Munich was just another name on the map of Germany. Yet, career-wise, Boothby never made the political Big Time.

'It all depends,' he told me, 'on how much you want power. Nobody believes this, but I've never really sought power.'

> 'If I really wanted it, I could have got it. I would have subordinated all my other interests in order to get it. Gone hell bent for it. As Churchill did. As Anthony Eden did. What I have wanted is to be in a position to influence policy, which is quite a different thing.'

His friend, Sir Compton Mackenzie, whom he calls Monty, has made a pact to write Boothby's obituary one day, notwithstanding the fact that Sir Compton is seventeen years older than Bob. I asked Lord Boothby what headline he would most like to see above his own obituary. Boothby stared into his whisky. Then he invented his own epitaph. 'This is the headline,' he said, 'He Was A Man Who Loved Life – And Lived It.'

17 APRIL 1960

Rumour and scandal followed Bob Boothby all his days, yet he appeared to lead a charmed and protected life. It was only after his death that the full extent of his recklessness became more widely known. It had been, for instance, an open secret that he was for many years the lover of Lady Dorothy Macmillan, wife of the Tory grandee and sometime Prime Minister. It was also established beyond doubt that Boothby had been a promiscuous bisexual who kept company with notorious characters like the feared gangsters the Kray brothers, with whom he was openly photographed alongside East End boys of doubtful age and morality. There had also been, early on, some barely covered-up financial shenanigans when Boothby was a young parliamentary minister. When it was uncovered, this

scandal almost certainly put paid to any higher political ambitions he may have once entertained. Robert Boothby died on 16 July 1986.

Arthur Edward 'Scobie' Breasley

CHAPTER 6

SCOBIE BREASLEY – A DAY AT THE RACES

"You've got to know when to ask a horse the vital question."

Back in the '50s and '60s the bid to ride the most winners in a single turf season often developed into a head-to-head between the popular Australian jockey Scobie Breasley and the grim-faced 'boy wonder' Lester Piggott, who was twenty-one years younger than Breasley. It was said that, during a race, when Piggott found his progress to the winning post impeded by Breasley he would sometimes taunt the older man with cries of 'Move over, Granddad!' Towards the end of the 1961 racing season, when the legendary Breasley–Piggott rivalry had grown particularly intense (Scobie eventually winning the title by a single race), I spent a day at the races with the veteran Australian rider.

S cobie Breasley comes down the stairs wearing a brown suit and an aura of unflappable calm. Tanned, leathery, balding fast, he stands on tiptoe at the front door to kiss his wife, May, goodbye and then clambers into the back seat of a £7,000 Rolls-Royce Silver Cloud. The Breasley dogs – an Alsatian named Bing and a miniature collie named Earl of Arundel – set up a clamour of barking as Bruce, the uniformed Aberdonian chauffeur, steers the Rolls out of the wrought-iron gates of Heather Brae, the Breasley home in Putney, London.

It is 10.45 in the morning. Another working day has begun in the life of the forty-seven-year-old Australian horseman who arrived in England eleven years ago, and this year has out-raced every other British jockey except Lester Piggott.

By nightfall yesterday Scobie (real name Arthur) Breasley had ridden 155 winners this year, putting him within easy challenging distance of Piggott, who has booted home 158 winners in 1961. The next fortnight will decide the issue.

Either of them could be Britain's champion jockey this year but they are furlongs apart as personalities. Breasley is a grandfather, benign and shy, devoted to a quiet home life, entranced by his newly arrived granddaughter Zonia. He is a simple man of simple pleasures. Piggott, at twenty-six (he was born on Scobie Breasley's wedding day – 5 November 1935), is dry, uncommunicative and not easy to reach.

Scobie Breasley talks in the raw, loping cadences of the Australian outback. Born in Wagga Wagga, New South Wales, on 7 May 1914, the sixth of seven children of a saddle-wise cattle-drover, he became one of the greatest jockeys of the century. 'As a small kid I was put on to a horse as soon as I could walk. Wonderful animals. Nothing like 'em … I love 'em.'

Piggott, on the other hand, talks in reluctant, unfinished sentences. Partly deaf since birth, he speaks with a slight nasal speech impediment, which does not improve his willingness to engage in banter. Heavier than Scobie, Piggott is aware that increasing weight may one day end his brilliant career. He once said: 'You have got to make the money while you can. There is not usually much left at the end…'

Scobie Breasley's Rolls-Royce whisks along through the autumn morning. 'There's no explaining,' he tells me, 'why one jockey is better than another.'

'It's a question of instinct and feeling. Like a violin player. It's not enough to play the right notes. I can't explain it. Nobody can … It's a mystery, the feeling a man has for a horse. You've got to feel it in your hands, in your brain, exactly when a horse is ready to go. You've got to know when to ask a horse the vital question. Know what I mean?'

The afternoon at the racetrack passes quickly. Between 1.45 p.m. and 4.15 p.m. Scobie Breasley changes five times into new colours. As he walks to the paddock, only the grey hair on his temples shows beneath his skull-hugging jockey's cap.

It does not turn out to be a good afternoon for Scobie. He rides three horses into second place. Between defeats he talks, smiling, with the legendary jockey Sir Gordon Richards and the Duke of Norfolk. Scobie never loses his air of mild-mannered benevolence.

Piggott, who seems too tall for a jockey, walks to the paddock lost in some personal reverie. Phlegmatic and solemn to an absurd degree in one so young, he moves quickly across the grass, a solitary figure. As a boy jockey he had been pitchforked into a tough grown-up world that took few prisoners. Somewhere along the line it would seem adolescence eluded him. He has always been known as being very demanding on his mounts. 'A lazy horse will get little mercy from Lester,' it has been said.

Piggott's usual reply: 'I ride to win. That's what I get on a horse for.'
Shortly after five o'clock Scobie is back in his Rolls, heading home.

'I try to get home every night. I'm a quiet man. I can't remember the last
film I saw. I didn't do so good today, did I? Pity. I would have liked to give the
Duke of Norfolk a win. But I can only go as good as the horse. I can't go alone.
Still, boil it down and what does it matter? I just got a letter from a friend in
Australia. He tells me he's got cancer. Think about that. Is it important that I
rode seconds instead of firsts today?'

Breasley's heavy-lidded, Bing Crosby-type eyelids begin to flutter. 'I won't
need any rocking tonight,' he says. One minute later he is fast asleep. Scobie
Breasley's Silver Cloud – registration SB53 – hums through the dusk towards
London.

21 OCTOBER 1961

*Scobie Breasley died aged ninety-two on 21 December 2006 after suffering a stroke.
In the course of a long career he rode 3,251 winners, 1,000 of them in Australia,
the rest in Britain and elsewhere. As a rider he used the whip more sparingly than
his rivals. He retired in 1990 and lived out his last years in Australia.*

*In 1987 Lester Piggott (nicknamed the Long Fellow), a nine-time Derby
winner, was sentenced to three years imprisonment after being found guilty of
tax fraud of over £3 million. He served 366 days. The following year he was
stripped of his OBE. Piggott, age fifty-one, who had a personal fortune at that
time estimated at £20 million, eventually retired in 1995, having ridden 5,300
winners in a career lasting forty-seven years. He is considered to be the greatest
English flat race jockey of all time.*

Dr Jacob Bronowski

CHAPTER 7

DR JACOB BRONOWSKI –
THE ASCENT OF MAN

"Bruno always likes to see the other fellow win."

Jacob Bronowski – mathematician, biologist, humanist, TV presenter – is a polymath whose landmark BBC TV series The Ascent of Man *(1973) established him as one of the most effective and loved communicators of the television age. He was born on 18 January 1908 in Lodz, Poland. The family moved to Germany during the First World War and thence to England, where Jacob won a scholarship to Cambridge. In 1935 he received a PhD in mathematics. During the Second World War Bronowski worked in operations research, where he developed mathematical approaches to bombing strategies for RAF Bomber Command. After the war he joined a British team researching the effects of nuclear bombing on Hiroshima and Nagasaki. He became familiar to the British public through the BBC TV version of* The Brains Trust *in the late 1950s. Bronowski married Rita Coblenz in 1941. The couple had four daughters. When I met him in 1960,* The Ascent of Man, *which would make him world famous, still lay sometime in the future.*

In a spanking new house, which nestles on the Highgate fringe of Hampstead Heath, a small man with a familiar face removes his jacket. 'The day you become middle-aged,' he says, 'is the day you say of anybody "he's got nothing to teach me".' On the basis of this judgement, middle age still lies far into the future for 52-year-old Dr Jacob Bronowski, scientist, mathematician, widener of horizons, and Britain's newest and most improbable TV star – though he would firmly rebut any such description.

He is a great absorber of information and a great deliverer of it. Dr Bronowski (his friends call him Bruno) is Britain's most visible link between the couldn't-care-less masses and the bewildering world of science. Week after week the bespectacled doctor smiles tirelessly into the cameras, probing the origins of life, explaining with charm and clarity the meaning and purports of nature. He's a man with a mission, a Brains Truster you feel you can trust, our No. 1 telly-teacher, a sort of nationalised Mr Chips.

Now he sits, teeth clamped lightly on a semi-Churchillian cigar, relaxed in his own home. He talks easily. Even his small talk is self-revelatory. 'The only trouble with my Tuesday night *Insight* programmes on BBC television,' he laughs, 'is that they prevent me from playing chess with my friends. They happen to meet on Tuesdays too.' Dr Bronowski utters a tiny tsk-tsk of regret.

Dr Bronowski, director of the National Coal Research Establishment, a former chess champion of Yorkshire, analyses his shortcomings as a player. What he has to say turns out to be a penetrating character sketch of himself.

> 'The top chess players have a number of gifts which have nothing to do with the ability to play chess. The best players have a tremendous will to win. I doubt whether I have this kind of toughness, this kind of brutality, which is needed to win any game. The best players have an enormous devotion to the game. The game is all-absorbing to them. I never felt it was the most important thing I could be doing at the time. What else? Ah, yes. The best players all have a much more subtle understanding of their opponent's psychology than I have. I am deficient in all these things, but especially in the will to win.'

Attractive, blonde, Mrs Rita Bronowski looks up suddenly from her coffee cup. 'You're not a very competitive guy altogether, Bruno,' she tells him. And to me she says: 'Bruno always likes to see the other fellow win.'

Dr Bronowski agrees immediately. 'Good chess players,' he says, 'tend to get very angry when the other fellow makes a good move. I tend to sit back in admiration!'

Rita Bronowski, who married Dr B. when he was a £300-per-year lecturer, sums it up for me: 'Bruno has no professional jealousy. He likes to see the young men coming on.'

Dr Bronowski beams into the fire. This is a man entirely devoid of malice, the softest boiled egghead in the business.

I cannot conceive of Dr Bronowski ever intentionally insulting anyone. His respect for people is such that he will never treat flippantly even the most foolish-sounding questions sent to the BBC for the consideration of *The Brains Trust*.

'Human beings are sustained by respect. We owe one another respect. I always felt when people asked a question they meant something serious by it, and that at least as much thought should go into the answer as went into the question.'

But kindness must not be allowed to compromise personal integrity. When comedian Bernard Braden was suggested as a *Brains Trust* question master, Dr Bronowski considered the innovation opportunist and refused to participate. When a *Brains Trust* viewer submitted a question about interracial marriages ('Would you let your daughter...?') Bronowski detected prejudice behind the query and declined to discuss it at all.

Polish-born Jacob Bronowski arrived in England in 1920 with his parents. At Whitechapel Public Library young Jacob, aged twelve, taught himself English by reading Frederick Marryat's novel *Mr Midshipman Easy* – 'which I still think is a wonderful book'.

The intense dark-haired boy soon became aware of his remarkable mental gifts. His parents were careful not to make too much of his genius.

'My father and mother brought me up to consider that my gifts were quite normal. I never had the idea that being clever was anything special. Even now I have to remind myself that what I find easy to understand other people might find difficult.'

He won a scholarship to Cambridge. A brilliant student, he was already aware that science does not exist in a vacuum, that the object of science was not to produce objects. ('I don't care a bit about all those things going around in orbit.') A scientist, he says, must never cease to wonder. 'Nobody,' he told me, 'can carry on in science who hasn't got this sense that the whole thing is shot through with unseen miracles. This is a real emotion. You get exactly this when you are moved by a great book or a great play.'

Example: At Cambridge he saw *Oedipus Rex* for the first time. The emotional onslaught of the drama so overpowered the eighteen-year-old Bronowski 'that I had to leave the theatre to go and be sick in the lavatory. I never did see the rest of the play.'

For forty years Dr Bronowski has observed the British from within. 'They are a nation of Philistines,' he has decided. 'But tolerant Philistines.'

'They are very careful in their reactions. In Vienna I saw a crowd of students carry Maria Callas shoulder high from the Opera House to her hotel. The British would never do that. It's unthinkable. On the whole, I prefer the

British attitude. It allows a chap to do his work without being swept away by torrents of popular acclaim.'

There was a pause now. Nicole, second youngest of Dr Bronowski's four daughters (no sons), pattered down the stairs. 'Please, Mummy, can I listen to the radio?'

'What's on?'

'The programme where we play detectives.'

'All right.'

Delighted, the child hurried upstairs again. Dr Bronowski stares through the glass wall of his home. The woods beyond were invisible in the darkness. 'We have birds here,' he said. 'I know nothing about birds and plants. When I take my children for a walk in the country I am ashamed of my ignorance.' He excuses himself. 'I was always brought up in towns.'

But there is no excuse, he feels, for the man in the street who is too lazy to absorb the fundamentals of science. This is Bronowski's message; his mission. 'The scientists are inheriting, are conquering the earth. We must learn to speak their uncouth language or we shall sink to the status of the native yokels when the Normans overran this country.'

It is this capacity for lucid expression that gained him his enormous following on television, not least among women.

Dr Bronowski watches television sparingly. He keeps his TV set in another room ('one should never have TV in the main living room'), selecting his programmes carefully, switching off immediately afterwards. His tastes run from the arts series *Monitor* to the Wild West-based *Maverick*. ('What fascinates me about *Maverick* is the card playing. When I play poker I never seem to hold anything better than a pair of Queens.') He was also a devotee of Anthony Newley's experimental TV series *The Strange World of Gurney Slade*.

He said: 'There are about a half a dozen TV programmes worth watching every week. I feel about TV what I feel about smoking. On a good night, one cigar is all you are entitled to ask of the world.'

The fog was rolling over the heath when Mrs Bronowski saw me to the door. She had the last word on her celebrated husband. 'Bruno has a mind that can see round corners.'

11 DECEMBER 1960

The Ascent of Man *was a thirteen-part TV series produced by the BBC, written and presented by Bronowski in 1973. Much of his commentary was unscripted. It*

was perhaps the most impressive solo performance in the history of the medium in Britain. The series traced the progress of the human species through the centuries, through the understanding of science. Bronowski died a year later – 22 August 1974 – of a heart attack in East Hampton, New York, and is buried in London's Highgate cemetery.

Dave Brubeck on *The Ed Sullivan Show* in New York

CHAPTER 8

DAVE BRUBECK – MASTER OF TIME

"Breakin' ice and moving in … that's our kick."

David Warren (Dave) Brubeck was born in Concord, California on 6 December 1920 into a family devoted to music. His mother studied piano in London under Myra Hess. As a pianist and composer Dave Brubeck alienated many traditional jazz fans and critics with his sometimes bewildering cross-rhythms and time signatures ('Take Five', 'Blue Rondo à la Turk') but finally won over most opposing voices. As an undergraduate he set out to study veterinary medicine until one professor protested, 'Brubeck, stop wasting my time and yours.' After graduation in 1942 Dave Brubeck was drafted into the forces, serving in France in General Patton's Third Army. Brubeck formed one of the first US Army bands to be racially integrated. In the post-war years he experimented with various styles and groupings, but it was only when he teamed up in 1951 with alto-saxophonist Paul Desmond that Brubeck found his most enduring voice. In 1954 Dave Brubeck became only the second jazz man to be featured on the cover of Time *magazine. The first, three years earlier, had been Louis Armstrong.*

On a cold night in early winter I called in at a small hotel in Half Moon Street, off Piccadilly, and found Dave Brubeck in bed staring at the ceiling. He wore cream-coloured pyjamas and apologised for meeting me in his sleeping attire.

'Man, I'm tired. I'm just tired all the time.' Brubeck, piano-playing mastermind of the jazz quartet that bears his name, lifted a long-fingered hand from below the warm sheets and raised the bedside telephone. 'I'm not in,' he spoke into the phone, 'I'm not in to anybody. No, wait. If my wife calls from the States, I'm in.' He replaced the receiver. 'Man, the pressure,' he said.

He was in town for a tour. A Brubeck disc called 'Take Five', an intricate composition by Paul Desmond, which deftly featured an elusive 5/4 time pattern, had recently broken through to public acclaim. Brubeck suddenly found himself a pop celebrity in Britain.

Brubeck jumped out of bed and crossed the carpet to visit the loo. Seconds later he returned. He was still wearing his socks.

'It's no surprise to me that one of my discs has become a hit with the kids. It proves what I've always said. The public is a darn sight smarter than we think they are. Television and the press are calculated at too low a level. The good has to be made as attractive and as desirable as the bad.'

He got back into bed, pulling the sheets up to his chin.

Brubeck's detractors claim that his preoccupation with experimental musical forms and challenging rhythms have distorted and eroded the spontaneous spirit which is the essence of jazz. He is impatient with his critics. 'What we are doing,' he explains, 'is breakin' ice and movin' in. Breakin' and movin' in, that's us. That's our kick.'

He had to be a musician. He was brought up in a house with six pianos. From his mother, a devoutly Presbyterian music teacher, he inherited a distaste for strong liquor ('I'm a wine man, sometimes') and a strong taste for Bach and Debussy.

Brubeck married at twenty and stayed married. He told me that he lived with a lyric-writing wife named Isla, five pianos and six children, whose births he celebrated with compositions like 'Kathy's Waltz', 'Crazy Chris' and 'Charles Matthew Hallelujah!'

Appalled by the cruelties he had witnessed during the war, Brubeck became a Catholic, living his life according to a Christian ethic not lightly compromised. He had recently declined twenty-three dates out of a projected twenty-five-concert tour of the American Deep South because impresarios demanded he drop his black bass player Eugene Wright and substitute a white player.

A few months later Brubeck cancelled an American TV show because the programme's commercial sponsor wanted Eugene Wright out of camera range. 'That cost me 8,500 dollars,' Brubeck said. 'More than I used to make in three years.'

I said goodbye to Dave Brubeck, the rancher's son who very nearly became a vet, and left him to sleep out what was left of the cold night.

21 NOVEMBER 1961

Some half dozen years later I met Brubeck again backstage at the Royal Festival Hall. As I stepped into his dressing room after one of his concerts he looked up and, after only the slightest hesitation, pointed at me and asked, 'Did you have to write that about my socks? I don't customarily wear socks to bed.' He had played several hundred concerts around the world and no doubt met thousands of strangers since our single brief meeting on that cold night in London, but he recognised and remembered me on sight. It could only have been because he was still sore about the socks. Dave Brubeck died on 5 December 2012 – a good man who lived a good life.

Yul Brynner

CHAPTER 9

YUL BRYNNER –
THE BALD PHILOSOPHER

"Acting is just a part-time job that got out of hand."

Yul Brynner was born Yuly Borisovich on 11 July 1920 in Vladivostok, though he sometimes claimed a more exotic Mongol-Tartar inheritance. His mother was the granddaughter of a Jewish doctor who converted to the Russian Orthodox Church. Brynner became an actor in his twenties, and shaved his hair to appear in the Broadway musical The King and I, *a stage role he played 4,525 times in all. He also starred in the film version in 1956, winning a Best Actor Oscar. Other starring roles include* The Ten Commandments *(1956),* The Magnificent Seven *(1960),* Taras Bulba *(1962) and the science fiction fantasy* Westworld *(1973).*

The most celebrated bald head on earth rested against the high back of an easy chair. But Mr Yul Brynner, who owns the head, was in no mood to talk about it. Mr Brynner is a stern man who regards his skull as an unsuitable, not to say undignified, topic of conversation.

'I have no vanity about my looks,' Mr Brynner said in a deep, rumbling voice. 'I once shaved my head to play *The King and I*. Later I found it more comfortable to leave it that way. Press agents in Hollywood made a big thing about it. It was certainly not my idea.'

Mr Brynner, with whom I was having breakfast in his London hotel suite, slapped a generous layer of jam on a slice of toast, washed it down with steaming hot tea. His deep-set eyes darted about the room.

'Any number of admirable men have been bald,' he said. 'I might mention Gandhi and Confucius, and…' At this point Mr Brynner appeared to run out of bald, admirable men. 'And lots more,' he ended lamely. He touched a table napkin to his lips in the manner of a royal personage indicating that he had no more to say on the subject.

'This is a late breakfast for me,' he said, reaching for some more toast. 'I have already been out and about this morning visiting some of my favourite pipe shops in London. This is the greatest town in the world for pipe smokers. I love good wood. I am strictly a straight grain man. Good wood, I always think, gives you a kind of aesthetic pleasure while you're having a good smoke…' Yul Brynner's conversation is peppered with references to the delights of good food, good wine and nicotine.

He is uncooperative when questioned about his personal life. 'My passport will tell you that I was born on 11 July 1920, in Sakhilin, in northern Siberia. That's all I really care to say about my life. I never talk about it. My life does not amuse me. It's a bore. It has absolutely no importance in my mind.'

Brynner smiled at me and asked whether I would care for a second cup of tea. He jumped up and poured it for me – a stocky figure in a well-cut grey suit, his head shining like a polished ivory ball in the spring sunlight.

'I don't really regard myself as an actor,' said Brynner, who is one of the most highly paid actors alive. 'I am really a director. Acting is just a part-time job that somehow got out of hand…' His eyes assumed the look of one who has been wrongly judged. 'I do not like the attention I have received since I became a so-called star,' he complained. 'Publicity is not something that is dear to me. I don't enjoy being recognised. Some people think that just because they once bought a ticket to one of my films that they own me! But one cannot go on being a star twenty-four hours a day. You have to be a human being first … a human being.'

Brynner busied himself with his breakfast. 'I am always hungry,' he said. 'As you can see, I am a man of appetite. I am not like other men. I lose weight extremely easily.'

'I spend a tremendous number of hours alone, studying philosophy. I have a Master's degree in Philosophy from Sorbonne University. I study for my own interest and pleasure. I would not describe myself as a religious man, but I am a man of faith. All men have fears, and I am no exception. Fears stem from ignorance. That is why I study as much as I do. At times I am full of fear for the human race. I am also full of fear for myself, as a member of that race. We are all responsible for the world. We always tend to blame others. We say, "Look what they are doing!" But who are they? We are all drops in the same ocean. They are us!'

The hungry philosopher lit a filter-tipped cigarette. For a moment he seemed rather small and middle-aged, like a Russian businessman far from home.

'My job as an entertainer is to make people aware that we are all members of the same human community, all responsible for each other. Executives dread me,' said Brynner, 'because I can be embarrassingly honest. When executives haven't known their jobs I have laughed at them out loud and chased them out of the studio!' Brynner seemed to enjoy the memory. 'But I assure you,' he added modestly, 'that I bow down to people whose opinions I respect.'

Mr Brynner's secretary came in to remind the great man that he had to go to the West End to meet three hundred film critics.

'Three hundred!' roared Mr Brynner, disbelievingly. He reached for a soft hat. 'I wear a hat to avoid recognition,' he explained.

A few minutes later the owner of the most celebrated skull in the world wandered out into the London streets. Nobody recognised the head under the hat. 'You see,' said Brynner, 'it works.'

17 MARCH 1959

Yul Brynner married four times, fathered three children, adopted two. He died of lung cancer on 10 October 1985, on the same day as Orson Welles. Brynner made an anti-smoking TV commercial, released after his death, which he blamed on his tobacco habit ('Whatever you do, don't smoke').

George Burns with Kermit the Frog on *The Muppet Show*

CHAPTER 10

GEORGE BURNS – THE SUNSHINE BOY

"If you wait around long enough, you get to be new again."

George Burns was born Nathan Birnbaum in New York City on 20 January 1896, one of twelve children of a synagogue cantor. Starting out as a child entertainer he became the longest-serving vaudevillian of the twentieth century. As the years passed he became chiefly famous for staying alive until he was over a hundred years old. In America he was known as the cigar-chomping stand-up star of long-running comedy shows on radio and television, usually in the close company of his real-life wife, Irish-Catholic Gracie Allen, who acted as his lovable but dim-witted spouse, a device that allowed Burns to stare fondly at the audience and, between cigar puffs, share his dumbfounded responses to her endless drolleries. After Gracie's death, George Burns got comic mileage out of the subject of his advancing years. ('The girls I go out with these days … even my tuxedo is older than they are.') Burns enjoyed a remarkable resurgence of popularity as he advanced into late life. He appeared in Neil Simon's The Sunshine Boys *(1976) and two years later appeared with distinction in the hit movie* Oh God!, *in which Burns played God.*

Biting on a two-inch cigar butt, George Burns stepped off the Chicago plane while most of London was still struggling out of bed. The eighty-year-old American comedian looked wide awake and amused. Jet-lagged fellow passengers wandered around Terminal Three bumping into their suitcases. But George Burns, despite his years and a loss of a night's sleep, refused to succumb to fatigue. 'After all,' he said, 'some other guy's been driving the plane. I just sat there smoking cigars and having a drink. What the hell's wrong with that?'

This self-effacing no-fuss attitude is a central facet of Burns's character. He does not appear to regard himself as important or even particularly talented.

Of his forty years with his late wife Gracie Allen in the celebrated *Burns and Allen* radio and TV shows, George says modestly, 'I was just Gracie's straight man. She was the funny one. All I had to do was chew on a cigar and stay out of the way.'

Burns remembers Gracie with a touching adoration, still regularly visits her Hollywood grave to talk to her … 'about what I've been doing, about anything at all'.

The airport terminal cleared. Burns jumped nimbly into the back of a massive, cushioned Rolls-Royce. Neat and diminutive (9 stone 11 pounds), he settled back for the drive to Broadcasting House and the first of the series of London engagements. Almost lost in the vast car, Burns resembled a gnome twinkling at the world through outsized horn-rimmed spectacles. For no reason at all, at least as far as I could see, he sang a snatch of an old song ('you're daffy as a daffodil'), kicking out a foot on the last line in the manner of an old vaudeville hoofer.

Last night Burns charmed royalty and the rest of us heading a charity bill at The Palladium in aid of the Migraine Trust. At eighty he is again a world headliner thanks to his Oscar-winning turn in *The Sunshine Boys* opposite co-star Walter Matthau.

'I haven't stopped working,' said the genial octogenarian. 'I've just come back from Australia. This summer I'm touring with Carol Channing. If you wait around long enough, you get to be new again. I stay young by not thinking about it. I never carry anger and I never worry about anything I cannot help. A year ago I underwent open-heart surgery, but I wasn't concerned about it. Let the doctors worry! When I woke up from the operation I applauded the surgeon for five minutes, and here I am…'

'I have a nice life. I get up every morning, do some floor exercise to get my heart going, arrive at my office at 10 a.m. and work until lunchtime. I get to my own table at the Hillcrest Country Club at about lunchtime where I sometimes meet old friends like Groucho Marx, Danny Kaye and Milton Berle. The tables at the Hillcrest are getting smaller. Guys are dying off all the time. There's very few of me left. I play bridge until four, sleep until five thirty, get up, watch the news and have a couple of martinis. I feel a bit like Adolph Zuckor [the veteran Hollywood tycoon who died last week aged 103]. When somebody asked him how it felt to be one hundred and two, Zuckor replied: "I feel just as good now as I did two years ago!"'

Infectiously Burns laughed aloud.

'Yes, a nice life,' he said. 'The thing to do is to stay out of bed. When you get to my age, bed can suddenly seem very comfortable. You can fall in love with your bed. Not me. I still go out with girls. Young girls. They are safe with me. I would like to go out with women of my own age … but there are no women of my own age!'

Again, that hoarse sudden laugh. Laughter erupts constantly in this pleasant, popular man with the grey toupee and cheap domestic American cigar in his mouth. As the Rolls pulled up in the crisp London sunshine outside Broadcasting House, Burns said, 'Remember the song about a foggy day in London? They'll have to change that title.'

He summed up his simple-hearted philosophy.

> 'Listen, I like movies where the fellow gets the girl and the horse wins the race. I don't watch any sad pictures. I haven't seen *Jaws*. There's a fellow doing an impersonation of me in a TV commercial. My agent said we should sue him. I said: "Forget it, things could be worse … I could be doing him!"'

'That's it,' said George Burns. 'I don't work too hard. I take it easy. I don't sweat.'

14 JUNE 1976

Burns vowed to appear live onstage on his hundredth birthday, but in July 1994 he fell down in his bathroom and was not fit enough thereafter to make good his promise. He died on 9 March 1996 in Beverly Hills at the age of one hundred years and forty-nine days.

Matt Busby

CHAPTER II

MATT BUSBY –
THE MAN WHO LIVED

"I just wanted to stay in that oxygen tent and die there."

Legendary football manager Sir Alexander Matthew (Matt) Busby was born in a two-roomed pitman's cottage in Bells Hill, Scotland on 26 May 1909. Matt's father was killed by a sniper's bullet at the Battle of the Somme in 1916. He started his football career, aged seventeen, playing for Manchester City on a one-year contract at £5 per week, but it was as the longest-serving manager of Manchester United (1945–69) that Busby will be remembered. His youthful team of players (the so-called 'Busby Babes') won the League in 1956 and 1957. But tragedy was waiting in the wings. On 6 February 1958 the team was on its way home from a European Cup Tie against Red Star Belgrade when the aircraft crashed on the runway at Munich. Twenty-three passengers were killed, including eight Man United players and three Club officials. Duncan Edwards, one of the team's stars, died from his injuries a fortnight later. Two other players were never able to play football again. Matt Busby spent eight weeks in hospital and barely survived the crash.

More than a thousand days have passed since that calamitous February afternoon when an airliner picked up speed along the tarmac at Munich airport, refused to lift and tore into the buildings looming in the fog beyond. More than a score of passengers died in that horrific accident, including eight 'Busby Babes' of the Manchester United Football Club.

Nobody who was in Britain that night will forget the wave of shock that swept the country. Nor is anyone likely to forget the man who lived – the man who lay, silent and suffering, under a transparent oxygen tent in a Munich hospital.

Matt Busby, miraculously, is alive. He has rebuilt his team of footballers, and today lives a quiet life in Manchester.

That life is forever changed. His body has mended. His smile is as sudden and warming as ever, but there is a hurt in Matt Busby that will never be calmed.

For this indestructible man, tears are always near. 'Deep down,' he said, 'the sorrow is there all the time. You never really rid yourself of it. It becomes part of you. You might be alone, and it all comes back to you, like a kind of roundabout, and you weep…'

He reached into his jacket pocket and busied himself filling and lighting his pipe.

'The first time,' he said, 'was when I went to the football ground at Old Trafford after the accident. I don't know. I just looked at the empty field and I tell you I have never in all my life felt such a terrible vacuum. And so I cried, and afterwards I felt better for the tears, because I had forced myself to go back there. It was something I'd done, something I'd conquered. The first rung of the ladder…'

At one time, it seemed to him, death would be a wonderful relief. He wanted, even prayed for, the end to come. 'It was at these times,' he said, 'when I gradually began to become aware that some of my boys must have been killed. I did not know for certain, I just knew something dreadful had happened. I was in that tent, barely alive myself. Twice I had been given the last rites of the Catholic Church. I just wanted to stay inside that tent and die there, rather than come out of it and learn the truth. So I prayed for the end to come quickly. I have never said this to a living soul before…'

But Matt Busby's will to live was stronger than his longing for the release of death. 'Strange,' he said, 'how you hold on, the things you clutch at. In the middle of it all I found myself seeing visions of the ones I loved most in the world. Then I would fight back.'

Matt Busby spoke slowly, with hesitancy. This son of a miner has never been a glib man. He is a man of action and judgement. Around Manchester he is a beloved figure.

Many men would never have flown again. Matt Busby's decision to do so is typical of the man. It needed a year of faith and fear before he was able to force himself into the metal confines of an aircraft once more. He said: 'I swore I'd never fly again. Once, at the hospital in Munich, they wheeled me on a stretcher into the sunshine of the veranda. As we left the door I had the sensation of flying again. Before I knew it I was screaming. They had to hold me down.'

Busby lapsed into a silence. Then he said:

'There was something else. Something that made me fly again. One of the teachings of the Roman Catholic faith, as I understand it, is that your life is in the hands of God … that when your time comes to go you must be ready and prepared, for you will surely not escape it. Why then, I asked myself, was I avoiding the air? Was I so uncertain of my trust in God? So one day I flew again. It was only a short hop, from Manchester to Rotterdam. But it was long enough. Every second of that flight was like an endless torture. Along the runway I actually relived the whole crash, saw the whole thing. I have flown many times since, but it hasn't got much better. A kind of terror will always remain with me.'

Busby feels deeply that because he has been spared death he must somehow justify his survival by using the days that remain to him rebuilding what was so cruelly destroyed. 'It is the object of life,' he said 'to build … to create. At Munich, when I knew the worst, I understood at last that to pray for death, as I had done, was wrong and cowardly. I knew that somehow I must succeed again for the sake of those who had died. Otherwise my life would have no meaning.'

So Matt Busby dedicated himself to rebuilding his life and his team. That is one of the legacies of the Munich accident. There are others. He has never again been able to trust in the permanency of anything. He has never again been able to celebrate fully his team's victories on the football field. He is only too aware that one fatal circumstance, in the span of an eyelash's blink, can engulf exultation in tears.

'I keep thinking to myself,' he said, 'about what we had once built at Old Trafford.'

'Everything was going so well. Success was in our blood. All gone in a second. Just like that. This has had a permanent effect on me. I find myself waiting for the next blow to fall. I am apprehensive all the time. I'm not saying I'm the best Christian who ever lived, but I attend to my duties and go to Mass and Confession, and the Church is a very great solace to me. I want to be – and try to be – a better man than I was before the crash, but I don't think I am.'

Matt Busby's pipe had long gone cold in his hand. He moved awkwardly in his seat, stretched his legs. 'I am as well as I shall ever be,' he said. 'I have even begun to sleep reasonably well again, and that's a blessing.'

He looked at me across the floor of his living room. 'I'll tell you something,' he said. 'When it is quiet like this, sometimes, I see them all again, my boys, doing the things they used to do, laughing and joking and running around. Sometimes, do you know, I still see them playing…'

5 DECEMBER 1961

Matt Busby died of lung cancer on 20 January 1994, aged eighty-four.

Billy Butlin

CHAPTER 12

BILLY BUTLIN –
KING OF THE HOLIDAY CAMPS

"We have to push harder than the big blokes."

As a messenger boy working for a Canadian department store, young Billy Butlin spent a vacation in the store's summer holiday camp. The experience changed his life. In later years Butlin would establish a chain of holiday camps, hotels and villages across the face of Britain, urging thousands of families to enjoy cheap and cheerful vacations where their every wish would be catered for, from three meals a day to a free, round-the-clock round of fun, games, supervised children's playgrounds, dances, celebrities and bathing beauty contests. Butlin had noticed that English seaside landladies had traditionally required their guests to quit their lodgings between meals. The Butlin philosophy encouraged them to stay on site and enjoy themselves. The first Butlin camp opened at Skegness at Eastertime 1936, officially inaugurated by celebrity-pilot Amy Johnson, the first woman to fly solo from Britain to Australia. The Skegness camp, instantly successful, was followed by others. Post-war austerity Britain had never seen anything like it. The larger camps served 200,000 meals a week. Overnight, it seemed, Butlin became a household name and a national institution.

His name – William Edmund Colbourne ('call me Billy') Butlin – is plastered on hoardings, painted on concrete, spelled out in lights, stencilled on canvas tents. Billy Butlin's compulsion to proclaim his identity whenever and wherever possible has been apparent ever since he owned his first hoop-la stall, forty years ago, in a travelling funfair. Even then he insisted that his shirt-sleeved assistants display the big letter 'B' stitched in red on their breast pockets. Butlin's the name, and don't you forget it.

Most people today who go to his string of vacation villages (and many who don't) think of Butlin as a beer-drinking, genial cheerleader who just happened to hit on a good idea about family holidays. Butlin encourages this public perception of himself. Advertisements for his camps invariably include a drawing of Butlin himself, chortling, chuckling, bubbling with almost insane good cheer. A perfect picture is presented of every child's favourite, sweet-toting uncle. The truth is, however, that Billy Butlin – like anybody else who is liable to earn something like £1 million in a good week – is a complicated figure, in whom aggression, pride and ostentation are balanced by unexpected feelings of inferiority.

When I called to see him at his Oxford Street office the other evening, I found him garrisoned defensively behind the biggest desk I have seen in England – a billiard-table-sized hunk of furniture that had once belonged to Herr von Ribbentrop at the pre-war German embassy in London.

Speaking softly, and betraying his lack of schooling by dropping his aitches like confetti in June, Butlin told me about his life. His father, the son of a Gloucester clergyman, had fallen in love with the daughter of a travelling showman. Both families had objected to the union. The lovers married and ran away to Cape Town, where Billy was born, his birth coinciding more or less with the arrival of the twentieth century.

Billy was an only child. A lonely child. His loneliness has always stayed with him. It is the key to his personality and his success. He is driven to surround himself constantly with happy people, people enjoying themselves, people who are grateful to him for giving them respite from their monotonous lives.

In conversation Butlin is apt to be genuinely shy and diffident. The revealing quotes begin to come…

> 'Had I been one of a large family I might not have been so successful. Right at the heart of me there is a small lump of loneliness, which is a sort of driving force for what I do in life. I can cure it only when I am watching happy people and sharing their contentment.'

It is twilight. Billy allows himself a whisky, stepping across his office to fetch the bottle from a cabinet.

He is a neat, compact man (5 feet 7 inches), and his healthy plumpness tends to make him appear shorter than he is. Like a lot of short people, from Napoleon to Jack Hylton, Butlin is aware that some of the more aggressive aspects of his personality may be a compensation for his stockiness.

'All short people feel that they have to work a bit harder than the big blokes,' he said. 'They have to be more kind of pushful, y'know? I don't like the word aggressive. I was the youngest Canadian soldier fighting in France in the First World War. Sixteen I was. When things look 'opeless, I think of those days and say: "Well, it's a hell of a lot better than it was."'

A suggestion of a moustache bristles on Butlin's stiff upper lip as he continues. 'What rankles with me sometimes is my lack of education. I only went to school for three years.'

His pale-blue eyes stare at me across Ribbentrop's vast desk.

'I keep wanting to prove to myself that I didn't need an education, that I could do what I want to do without a college degree. That is why I like challenges, why I like doing things that people say I can't do, or I musn't do.'

Butlin left South Africa when he was ten, immigrated with his parents to Canada. His father died, and Billy went to work to support his mother. He knew the pride of the poor, and still does.

Like many under-educated people he half-envies, half-distrusts the verbal fluency of the well schooled.

'I don't like people who do a lot of talking. I don't speak very well. It stops me getting on my feet. There is a kind of shyness in me. I'd rather pay someone to go up into the limelight on my behalf ... just as long as the name Butlin is given credit.'

After the First World War he came to England on a Canadian cattle boat with £5 in his pocket. He joined a fairground, soon had his own stall, his own staff. Today he owns holiday camps, hotels, construction companies, amusement parks. More than 50,000 people a week spend their summer holidays under his cheerful banner, paying an average £13 10s each for the privilege. That adds up to something like three-quarters of a million pounds a week from his holiday camps alone.

Like many successful men he is disinclined to talk about his failures. 'I tend to refuse to admit that I'm losing when things are bad,' he told me. 'My failures don't exist for me. I suppress them completely.' He prefers to dwell on his successes, on his need to be known, named, admired. The public address system at his camps is called Radio Butlin. How he loves that name!

In 1959 he married Norah, the woman who had been known as 'Mrs Butlin' for twenty-three years. She was, in fact, the sister of Butlin's real wife Dorothy, who had refused consistently to divorce him until her death in 1958. A great amount of public understanding and sympathy blessed the long-delayed legal union of Billy and Norah – a testament to the popularity of them both.

But Billy's popularity is misleading. He is very much a closed book, even to those nearest to him. He constantly puzzles his own directors with sudden, lone-wolf decisions. A close associate told me: 'I've known Billy for twenty-five years and learned nothing more about him in all that time.' Billy himself told me: 'I've never felt I'd like advice from anybody. I like to think things out alone.'

He is bluff, gritty, candid. In a competitive age he is a giant-killer. His personality is complex and isolated, but his formula is simple. He will be remembered as the tycoon who made his millions by liberating the masses from the irksome annual chore of having to make a personal decision about their leisure time.

The Romans believed in bread and circuses. Butlin believes in soda pop and roller-skating rinks. He has made his mark on history by adhering to the most simple and most profitable formula of them all:

Give the people what they want.

13 MARCH 1960

Butlin retired, for tax reasons, to the Channel Island of Jersey, where he occupied himself with charity causes and where he established several hotels and a small holiday village. He suffered a heart attack in 1977, ushering in a period of severe ill health. Stomach cancer was diagnosed in 1979. Butlin died a year later and is buried in the cemetery of St John's church, Jersey.

A Butlin's poster

Truman Capote

CHAPTER 13

TRUMAN CAPOTE – DAZZLER

"If I stay in London too long I become physically ill …
I disintegrate."

Truman Capote (born Truman Streckfus Persons in New Orleans, Louisiana, on 30 September 1924) wrote his first novel, the semi-autobiographical Other Voices, Other Rooms *(1947), when he was only twenty-three. The book was an instant sensation, critics acclaiming the young author's precise, exquisite style. Harry Halma's photograph on the book jacket, according to Capote's biographer Gerald Clarke, 'caused as much comment and controversy as the prose inside'.*

Long before this glittering debut, Capote had been abandoned by his parents and lived a restless, rootless childhood, being raised by a succession of relations. He was a silent, withdrawn boy whose introverted behaviour caused him to be seen as abnormal by those entrusted with his care. Truman was even sent to a psychiatrist who, he declared later, 'naturally classified me as a genius'. Among Capote's most successful books were Breakfast At Tiffany's *(1958), subsequently filmed with Audrey Hepburn as Holly Golightly, and* In Cold Blood *(1966), a 'non-fiction novel' about the real-life multiple murder of a prosperous Kansas wheat-growing farmer and his family. Capote had spent at least four years researching* In Cold Blood. *The book made millions for Capote, earning the contempt of English critic Kenneth Tynan, who accused Capote of delaying publication of the book in the ill-concealed hope that the two killers would eventually be executed, which they were, providing the book with a neat climax. 'Does the work come first,' asked Tynan, 'or does life?'*

L ike many others I became aware of Truman Capote when I read his first novel *Other Voices, Other Rooms*, a slim volume famous not only for its content but for its cover photograph, which depicted a wan, melancholy and apparently consumptive figure stretched out on a chaise longue. When he suggested that we meet in the Dorchester bar I expected to find an exhausted, distant youth who had written all his books in the shade of bayou creepers in the old South. Nothing of the kind. Truman Capote turned out to be a perky little chap (5 feet 3 inches) who looked somewhat like a budgerigar, talked with a lisp and was keen on a jabber over a drink. He wore, from the ground up, a pair of light-fawn suede shoes, fastidiously laced, a skin-tight blue suit, a polka-dot bowtie and an outsized red carnation in his buttonhole.

As soon as our drinks were ordered and delivered, he was off and running, a real gossip. The film of *Breakfast at Tiffany's* – had I seen it, well, never mind, he didn't blame me, ha ha – had nothing to do with his novel, but mind you, Audrey Hepburn was an absolute doll, wasn't she?

Truman ('call me Truman', he insisted when I greeted him as Mr Ca-po-tee) glowed with cheer and talked up a storm. He told me he was a very slow worker, put in a four- or five-hour working day, yet averaged only fifteen pages of manuscript a month. He wrote his books in Switzerland, which he pronounced Thwitzerland. He wrote the first draft of his books in pencil, in a meticulous, diminutive script; then he transferred these notes to a second notebook with a fountain pen. He typed the result on yellow paper, then completed the process on white paper, all the while listening to recordings of Bach, his favourite composer.

He told me that he lived and worked alone on a splendid alp – 'thplendid alp' – except for a bulldog named Charlie and a couple of cats. One was an Irish Kerry Blue named Kelly; the second was a Greek alley cat named Mau Mau who was 'quite fabulous ... the Greta Garbo of catdom'.

He did not regard himself as an educated man. He had dropped out of school at sixteen and still could not with any confidence spell words like 'perceive'. He would never master the multiplication tables and could not, to this very day, recite the alphabet.

'Can't do it, can't get through the alphabet,' Truman said. 'I had the most insecure childhood of anyone I know. Divorced parents, living with this relative, then that relative ... ghastly, all of it.'

He kept a mental list of things he hated. The city of Paris figured high in the list. 'Last year I drove 150 miles out of my way to avoid even the outskirts of Paris. The Parisians do not like me and I do not like the Parisians. Then I discovered something: Parisians hate everybody, including each other. They are unkind, mean and stingy. All the nice people in Paris want to kill themselves ... and the rest ought to!'

Truman laughed so hard at his quip that his tortoise-shell spectacles became dislodged, falling half way down his nose; he pushed them back into place with the tip of his little finger.

He maintained a second home in Brooklyn, and took a two-week vacation in Venice every year. 'Venice is too rich; like eating an entire box of chocolate liqueurs in one go. I cannot bear it for too long.'

Another city he cannot visit for too long, he said, was London, which he saw as a 'delicious, great, big, soggy steak and kidney pie … if I stay here too long I become physically ill … I disintegrate.'

All in all, he had decided, Switzerland was the one place where he could live and work in peace. In Switzerland, he said, he was able to stay 'out of trouble'. He took care, he said, not to hob-nob with the movie crowd around Klosters. Truman threw up two small clean hands in mock horror. 'That is Hollywood Thwitzerland?' He made it sound like hell on earth.

24 NOVEMBER 1961

The chase after social success and celebrity fatally undermined the once-promising life of Capote, who turned to drugs and drink in his later years.

His last book was the unfinished Answered Prayers, *a vicious semi-disguised assault on the wealthy, sophisticated Manhattan society women who had hitherto felt flattered to be part of Capote's court. He died of liver cancer on 25 August 1984 at the Bel Air home of Joanne Carson, former wife of TV host Johnny Carson. Capote's death was famously described by writer Gore Vidal as 'a good career move'. Norman Mailer praised Capote as 'the most perfect writer of my generation'. Capote himself wrote: 'Life is a moderately good play with a badly written third act.'*

Leslie Caron on the movie poster for *Gigi*

CHAPTER 14

LESLIE CARON –
A PRIVATE WOMAN

"You can always guess the private life
behind the face of a star."

*Leslie Claire Margaret Caron was born in Boulogne-sur-Seine, France, on
1 July 1931, the daughter of American dancer Margaret Petit and Claude
Caron, a French chemist. She was spotted early in her ballet career by Gene
Kelly, who cast her in his upcoming MGM musical* An American in Paris
*(1951), replacing a pregnant Cyd Charisse who was due to play the role. Other
successes followed:* Lili *(1953),* Daddy Long Legs *(opposite Fred Astaire, 1955)*
and Gigi *(1958).*

L eslie Caron dislikes nightclubs, dancing, popular music, publicity stunts,
television. 'There are so many things to do,' she said.

> 'There is so little time to do them all. I've never heard a Tommy Steele record
> in my life. I have not seen him on the stage, television, films or anything. Elvis
> Presley? Well, maybe I heard one of his records somewhere a long time ago,
> I'm not sure.'

She ran a small hand through her cropped reddish hair and seemed unre-
pentant. Now a resident Londoner, she lives with her husband, the youthful
(still in his twenties), eminent theatre director Peter Hall, in a neat, white
house in Montpelier Square, a serene backwater a mere hundred yards away
from the traffic jams of Knightsbridge.

She is a quiet woman, seldom interviewed, a contained, elfin figure
who occasionally emerges from her private world to dazzle moviego-
ers in iconic screen musicals like *An American In Paris, Lili,* and the

newly completed film most likely to conquer the West End in 1959
– *Gigi*.

When I met her this week, she looked windblown and a little pallid.
She led me to the study for tea, clicking a string of chunky beads,
which hung down to her waist. She walked with a slightly bobbing
lope.

The study was furnished as if history had come to a halt in 1910. 'I dislike
modern things,' she said. 'I like to surround myself with the things of past
cultures. I feel very insecure in the very present world.' (French-born, she has
yet to master the English language in all its complexity.)

The marriage of the Halls seems successful, so far. If, however, it
had turned out a failure, according to Caron, her unhappiness would
have revealed itself on the screen, cut short her career, destroyed her
ambition.

She seemed eager to press this point. 'Well, look,' she said,

'I honestly wouldn't even care for my career if I didn't enjoy an interesting
and happy private life. I'm not at all ambitious in that way. If I was personally unhappy, it would show in my films. There's nothing sadder than to see
someone who appears lonely on the screen. You can always guess the private
life behind the face of a star. Movies don't lie! I would rather play with my
babies than do anything else. When I made *Gigi* in Hollywood last year I
took my baby son, Christopher John, with me. He was three months old.
The whole family came, too. This week I'm going to Hollywood again. I'm
taking my French nanny and both babies. Peter will join us there. We move
as a family...'

Later she spoke of her fears. 'I have one terror in my mind. I live in physical
terror of atomic weapons. Weapons are invented, and they are always used
... always.'

Perhaps that is why she surrounds herself with the trappings of a past
free of threat. Maybe that is why the wide-eyed waif with the world at her
dancing feet remains just an old-fashioned girl.

1 JANUARY 1959

Despite good intentions Caron married and divorced three times. Her
marriage to Peter Hall lasted nine years, and ended when Warren Beatty was
named as co-respondent. From 1993 to 2009 Caron ran a provincial hotel
and restaurant some 70 miles south of Paris. She appeared in approximately

fifty films during her career. Her autobiography, Thank Heaven, *appeared in 2010.*

Leslie Charteris arrives at the airport

CHAPTER 15

LESLIE CHARTERIS – THE MAN WHO INVENTED THE SAINT

✕✕✕✕✕✕✕✕✕✕✕✕✕✕✕✕✕✕✕✕✕✕✕✕✕✕✕✕✕✕✕

> "I wanted to show off. I did abominable things,
> like wearing spats."

Leslie Charteris, born in Singapore on 12 May 1907, wrote and sold his first crime novel during his first year at Cambridge. His third book, Meet the Tiger! *(1928), introduced a character named Simon Templar, alias The Saint, an idealised, modern Robin Hood figure whose heroics ('headache of cops and crooks alike') would sustain Charteris over an entire lifetime. He wrote several other things (screenplays, translations), but basically all his creative energies were devoted to the further adventures of The Saint. Eventually the Saint books would be created by ghostwriters, with Charteris supervising and editing their work. In 1932 Charteris moved to Hollywood, where he joined the payroll of Paramount Pictures. Always adventurous, he wrote a food column for a glossy US magazine, was an early Mensa recruit, and travelled on the maiden voyage of the German airship* Hindenburg *to New Jersey a year before the gigantic craft went up in flames. In the '60s Roger Moore (and later Simon Ogilvy) kept The Saint tradition alive with a well-received television series.*

The last thing I expected Leslie Charteris to be was Chinese. But the creator of Simon Templar, alias The Saint, is indeed the son of Dr S. C. Yin, a Chinese surgeon who lived in Singapore, and his English wife. Charteris's full name is Leslie Charteris Bowyer Yin.

'The Yins,' he explained, 'were Emperors of China from about 1760 to 1120 BC, otherwise known as the Shang dynasty; I am their direct linear descendant. I learned to speak Chinese and Malay from native servants before I could speak English.'

I had driven out to meet Leslie Charteris at a hotel in Maidenhead called Skindles. The hotel, on the river, is a '30s place with a '30s name. Leslie

Charteris is a '30s man. He is tall, with Asian eyes and an alert, athletic gait. He seemed shy and defensive at first but presently loosened up and seemed disposed to talk about how much he had loathed his life as a boy in an English public school. He had been sent there after travelling around the world with his parents three times before his twelfth birthday.

> 'My years at public school here in England were the unhappiest of my life. I have never taken kindly to discipline; I hate to be forced to occupy myself with things which don't interest me, and I hate all the cruder kinds of physical discomfort. The only time I was ever warm at school was in bed. The theory seemed to be that if boys were warm and comfortable they would be led into lives of sexual vice. And the food was foul.'

Though we met on a chill, rainy day – nobody was out rowing the boats – Leslie Charteris wore an open-neck sports shirt with short sleeves. His feet were bare except for a pair of beach sandals.

'The English school system leaves boys quite incapable of dealing with women in later years,' he said.

> 'Young boys should be exposed to the company of young girls from an early age. It doesn't do them any harm to have crushes. I'll say one thing for my school, though. When I see the horrible lack of education that most American school-children get away with, I am grateful that I had all that education shoved into me.'

When he left school, Charteris told me, he went through a big reaction. He grew a thin moustache, took to wearing vivid green shirts and a monocle. He criss-crossed Britain with a travelling funfair, worked as a barman in Torquay and played bridge professionally in a London club, a game he grew to abhor. 'In those days I just wanted to show off. I did abominable things, like wearing spats.'

At Cambridge he did little except read and write crime novels. Dr S. C. Yin of Singapore was less than pleased. He regarded all writers as rogues and loafers. But Leslie went on writing and, although they were later reconciled by letter, father and son never again spoke to each other.

Between books Charteris went in for tin mining, gold prospecting and pearl diving. He had tireless energies. He earned a pilot's licence. He became a respected bullfight enthusiast and wrote an excellent introduction to his own English translation of the memoirs of the torero Juan Belmonte.

Meanwhile, the Saint books kept coming off the assembly line, exciting popular acclaim and enviable sales. 'Each book took me about two years to think out,' he said, 'and about ten days of high-speed dictation. There have been ten Saint movies so far, but none of them appealed to me. George Sanders was all wrong for the part. He was too surly and too nasty. Ronald Colman would have been ideal in his heyday.'

Charteris married and divorced various wives, became a naturalised American citizen in 1946, settled in Florida and spent his summers fishing and roaming the world with each of his wives in turn.

> 'We just had fun and slaughtered fish. I am addicted to marriage. Reaching maturity is an awfully slow process. One must go on changing for a long time, otherwise you might as well be buried. Religion doesn't enter my head any more than cannibalism; some people do it, but I don't. I don't feel Oriental in any way. I don't think I have inherited any of the wisdom of the East. By education and by environment I come from somewhere in the middle of the Atlantic. What's more, I have renounced all claim to the throne of China.'

26 June 1960

In 1952 Charteris married his third and last wife, Hollywood actress Audrey Long. The couple moved to the United Kingdom. Charteris died on 15 April 1993 in Windsor, England.

Maurice Chevalier at the King's Head, Glasgow

CHAPTER 16

MAURICE CHEVALIER – THE DECEPTIVE SMILE

"I have made a success of everything in my life. Except love."

He was, with the possible exception of De Gaulle, the most famous Frenchman of the century. Nobody could resist Maurice Chevalier and his all-conquering smile. Behind the smile, however, lay a lifetime marked by miserly self-interest, lacking all charity. He was born poor on 12 September 1888, became a professional performer at the age of twelve, was slightly wounded by shrapnel in the opening months of the Great War, taught himself English in a German PoW camp, and was released thanks to the intervention of his mistress, Folies Bergères star Mistinguett. His post-war career at the Folies was instantly successful and he never looked back, becoming a Hollywood star in the mid-30s, co-starring with Jeanette MacDonald in the Rodgers & Hart musical film Love Me Tonight *(1932). (It was common gossip that MacDonald and Chevalier detested each other.) During the Second World War he performed, unwisely, on the official German Radio Paris, and sang for French PoWs in camps inside Germany. Chevalier was cleared of any more serious charges of collaboration by post-war tribunals. The court decided that he had simply 'gone along' with the Occupation. He was hardly alone in this. After the war he rebuilt his career, touring the world, reaching new heights of success with his late-life appearance in the Hollywood musical film* Gigi, *in which he memorably thanked heaven 'for leetle girls...'*

The final, terrible days of Maurice Chevalier moved one biographer – a toughened *Newsweek* correspondent who had covered the Vietnam War – to tears. The French music hall star, whose jutting lower lip and jauntily tilted straw boater were for half a century tokens of an unassailable global celebrity, had withered in his last year into a frail, stooped figure, subject to uncontrollable fits of weeping, haunted by paranoid visions of betrayal, praying daily on his nurse's arm in front of an effigy of his adored mother.

Some years before those final days of torment, I flew to Paris to meet Chevalier, and found a vain, careful old man torn between a desire to go out in glory and a powerful drive to go on making as much money as he could while he could still stand up.

Well attested and beyond dispute were his monumental egotism, chronic miserliness, self-serving moral cowardice during the Nazi occupation of France, which brought in its wake charges of wartime collaboration, which clouded the legend ever after.

I waited for Chevalier in the living room of his white-walled villa at Marnes-la-Coquette, an hour's drive from Paris. It was an airy room, full of light, crammed with exhibits proclaiming the presence of a famous man – paintings by celebrated artists like Raoul Dufy, clusters of silver-framed photographs of crowned heads, military top brass and famed, faded performers inscribed in fawning terms to the great Chevalier.

He was suddenly in the room, walking toward me with the slow rolling gait of a sailor home from the sea, his hands clasped piously just below his chest, his hair thin, shiny and ivory-white. He wore darkened glasses.

He invited me to take a chair, and as he talked it became clear that he was only interested in how to end his career on a triumphant note, how to avoid decline, how to protect his reputation. He did not wish to talk about anything else. 'The time has come,' he said, 'to frame my whole life in a nice way, a clean way.'

> 'It is so rare to survive, to be a little somebody … there must come a time when you compare your face in the mirror with your passport photograph and, if you are an honest man, you know it is time to stop. One must learn to bow out five minutes before the audience stops applauding. One must not run after things when, in truth, they are running away from you…'

I had been warned by Terence Young, an Irish film director who directed the first Bond movie, that it was unlikely that I would be offered as much as a glass of water chez Chevalier. Chevalier's tight-fistedness was the stuff of legend. The memory of childhood deprivation stayed with him to the end. Never the sort of man to reach for a restaurant bill, his resentful nature was forged in the rundown Paris *quartier* where he was raised, the ninth son of a feckless riverside drunk who left home one day and never returned.

A child entertainer, with a special line in foul-mouthed comic patter, Maurice Chevalier was already at twelve a morose, anxious boy, hoarding his wages and passing them on to his Flemish-born mother 'with the touching devotion,' wrote biographer Edward Behr, 'of a retriever returning a stick to its master'. The Parisian novelist Colette met Chevalier in his teens and described him as 'obnoxious, and brutal to little people'.

When I cautiously raised the topic of what I called his 'reputation for thrift', Chevalier did not respond immediately, but a while later, leading me to the garden, he stopped beside an Utrillo streetscape resting on an easel in a vestibule, depicting the Paris slum of Menilmontant. 'I grew up in those streets. We were very poor. I learned to be careful. I am careful still.'

3 FEBRUARY 1968

Chevalier died at home on New Year's Day 1972.

Pet

CHAPTER 17

PETULA CLARK – A SINGER IN EXILE

"French people laugh a good deal less than the English."

Petula Sally Olwen Clark was born on 15 November 1932 in Epsom, Surrey. She started as a child entertainer during the Second World War singing for the troops on radio programmes, sometimes touring with fellow child performer Julie Andrews. Petula was dubbed 'Britain's Shirley Temple'. She was spotted by a film director in 1944, when she was twelve, and appeared in a run of TV and film roles. In 1958 she made a breakthrough appearance at the Paris Olympia, beginning a life-long association with publicist Claude Wolff, now her husband. In 1960 she toured with Sacha Distel (they remained close friends until Distel's death in 2004). She moved to France in the '60s, where she has lived with Wolff ever since. They have two daughters, Barbara and Katherine, and son Patrick. By the mid-60s her career was in the doldrums until she formed a profitable, professional partnership with composer/arranger Tony Hatch, whose 'Downtown' gave her her first number-one record in the US. Petula has never looked back. She starred in two important movies, opposite Fred Astaire in Finian's Rainbow, *and opposite Peter O'Toole in* Goodbye Mr Chips.

The English girl singer who still resembles an underfed child said an unexpected thing: 'Paris still frightens me. Sometimes, I feel like an utter stranger here.' Much has been written about Petula Clark, child actress and vocalist, 'the girl next door' who, at twenty-five, hopped over to Paris to record two songs, married her French recording manager, and stayed on to become a smash with the French and with the world.

In her Paris apartment overlooking the springtime trees of the Bois de Boulogne, a mere horseshoe's throw from the swank Longchamps racecourse, Petula Clark curled her legs beneath her and spoke of her difficulties in coming to terms with the tough, impulsive city that has elevated her to a stardom she never knew at home.

'There are no people on earth,' she said, 'as frightening as the sophisticated Parisian. They are brittle and bright and terribly, terribly chic. It's all a kind of parade, a peacock thing, generated by smart chit-chat, an awareness of new trends, new vogues, and if you don't get its wavelength it's easy to be left out in the cold. It can all be rather tense and alarming.'

This kind of herd behaviour is virtually unknown in London, a city without a café society.

'It scares me,' says Pet Clark.

'I find it difficult to be worldly-wise and witty, to flit from one item of elegant, gossipy chit-chat to another. It must be my English education, but I can't make it. At first it didn't matter to me. I was happy to be living in France with the man I loved, having my home, and all that. Then gradually I came face to face with it. I had to. It is impossible to avoid it. But I am learning all the time, about them, about myself. I don't scare quite as easily as I did. I believe they have realised now that I am not debonair, not prepared to discuss my private life as casually as they do. I'm terribly serious about the personal side of my life. They know that when I arrive at a party with my husband Claude I am going to leave with him, too. My home is my own. This is where we live. This is the way I want it.'

A declaration of independence. For a moment her English jaws seem set against the reckless ways of the naughty French.

In a nearby chair, working on a blueprint for a new sound system for her, Pet's French husband, Claude Wolff, smiled a smile of tolerance and affection.

Pet kept talking about the French:

'What's more, they are so fickle. They can move so terribly quickly to a new crush, like a school of fish. Still, they do create a special kind of excitement. It is because of them that Paris remains the capital of fashion and beauty. And they keep me alive and alert.'

Those who worship Petula Clark's riches and achievements might be less envious if they were aware of the numbing programme of travel and performance that keeps her going, sometimes almost beyond the threshold of physical endurance, through these days of her greatest success. In the past fortnight alone she has performed, been recorded or televised in Lyons, Orléans, Berlin, San Marino, Milan, Poitiers, Paris, London and Los Angeles.

More often than not, Pet travels through the night from one town to another in one of her three shooting-brakes, with her husband-manager by her side. 'Sometimes the days and nights seem to pass without any meaning or measure,' she said.

'Running, running all the time, no time to eat, no time to sleep, getting to the edge of fatigue. Sometimes I can actually hear me speaking to myself in the middle of a song, "What are you doing here on this stage? Why are you doing all this in French? What's it all about?" Once or twice I have even dried up in the middle of the song, even though I have sung it a thousand times. That's the business I'm in.'

It was after midnight. Pet was suddenly seized by an impulse to see her two-year-old daughter Catherine. She invited me along. We tiptoed into the darkened nursery. Pet stood at the cot. Then she kissed her fingers and pressed them to the forehead of the sleeping child. Another daughter, Barra (short for Barbara), is three and a half.

'Poor little loves,' said Petula when we were back in the living room. 'They never hear English spoken at all. You should hear them. "Pazzez moi la cheese, mama." That sort of thing. We have just taken on a new nanny, an Australian. Her chief qualification is that she speaks no French.'

Pet talked longingly of the old life.

'Do you know what I really miss? A jolly good laugh. I don't laugh as much as I used to. French people laugh a good deal less than the English. When the Parisians go to hear a singer like Charles Aznavour, for instance, they don't go particularly to enjoy themselves.

They go for the emotional experience, almost to suffer with him. They get more kicks out of sadness.'

She shrugged. 'They're Latin, after all.'

Despite such hits as 'Downtown' and 'I Know a Place', much of her material is in the more mature tradition of the French chanson. 'One of the songs I sing concerns a girl who says: "Why do they only want to see me smiling? Why don't I have the right to die?" It is a lovely and profound song. I get an emotional satisfaction singing in French that I can't possibly get in England. English pop is trivial. It has to do with the Anglo-Saxon mentality. The

English tend to keep their finer personal feelings to themselves. They don't display them in popular love songs.'

It occurred to me that Pet was now referring to the English as 'they'. She is a woman belonging to two worlds. 'I have two passports,' she said, 'and I am not protected by the British Embassy here.'

At about two in the morning Pet went sleepily to bed. Claude bravely (and speedily) drove me back to my hotel. He told me: 'In the early days it was Petula's crazy French accent that got Paris. Now she is accepted for herself. A lot of people, in fact, believe that she is French. But to me she will always be a very English girl.' Claude smiled and took a corner on two wheels.

12 May 1965

In 1981 Petula Clark starred as Maria von Trapp in The Sound of Music *in the West End, and later as Norma Desmond in* Sunset Boulevard. *She played Desmond more than any other actress.*

In 1968, singing her own song, 'On the Path To Glory', with black singer Harry Belafonte for a US television programme, she took hold briefly of Belafonte's arm. The show's sponsor, Chrysler, mindful of southern bigotry, insisted on a re-take with the two singers standing well apart. Petula Clark and her husband refused to comply and destroyed all alternative takes. The programme is now viewed as a milestone in the story of US race relations.

Petula Clark and Sacha Distel

Cassius Clay (Muhammad Ali) shaking hands with British boxer Sir Henry Cooper.
Boxing promoter Jack Solomons looks on (left)

CHAPTER 18

CASSIUS CLAY – LUNCHTIME IN SOHO

"Float like a butterfly, Sting like a bee,
Your hands can't hit, What your eyes can't see."

A diminutive woman shopping in Soho at lunch-time yesterday noticed a cluster of press photographers waiting outside the doorway of Isow's restaurant in Brewer Street, Soho. Prompted by curiosity she asked one: 'Who are you waiting for?'

'Cassius Clay,' said a photographer.

The lady paused. 'Who's he,' she said, 'when he's at home?'

I salute that anonymous lady with her shopping basket. I salute her ignorance, her innocence, and her resistance to the shrewdly calculated publicity drive that has made 21-year-old American heavyweight Cassius Clay into the most celebrated prizefighter since Rocky Marciano. There cannot be many around like her.

I was over at Isow's restaurant yesterday, where show business and sporty people normally gather daily to eat salt beef and wave at each other, to see Cassius M. Clay in the flesh.

He looked alert, unblemished, well fed. His lips were pink and soft. He sat slumped in a chair, his eyes closed, surrounded by cameramen and sportswriters, waiting for the cameras to start turning, waiting for the questions.

When the big lights came on Clay opened his eyes and started shouting like a wounded bear. It was outrageous stuff, laughable, irresistible. Clay, who is here to fight British heavyweight Henry Cooper next month, is the worst and funniest actor I have seen in a year.

'Henry Cooper is a tramp, a cripple and a bum, who will fall in the fifth round!' roared Clay, his eyes flashing with phoney wrath. 'But if Cooper talks about me, I'll cut him down in three.'

Pleased with his little rhyme, Clay held up a big brown fist and waved it aloft like a child's balloon. 'It ain't gonna be a fight,' he predicted. 'It's gonna be a total annihilation.'

'Are you really all that sore about Cooper,' I ventured to ask Clay, 'or is that part of the act, too?'

'Ugly fighters are lousy fighters and to me Cooper is the ugliest,' said Clay, his nostrils flaring with excitement.

As the cameras continued to flash in his face, Clay grandly announced: 'I don't want to see this Henry Cooper bum in the street. I don't like bums,' he added mysteriously, 'who talk too much.'

I said, 'Cooper will be along in a minute.'

Clay wheeled his head towards me disbelievingly. He said slowly and with emphasis: 'You...must...be...joking. This town isn't big enough for Cooper and me! Man, I could take on Henry Cooper and Ingemar Johansson and Brian London on the same night and finish them all in nine rounds!'

Clay kept talking. He never stops for long. The reporters scribbled furiously.

'The big fighters,' Clay continued, 'see me on the horizon and, man, they fly!'

Clay, descendant of Kentucky slaves, talks with a Southern accent you can spread on a slice of corn bread.

'I know they call me loudmouthed, cocky and loquacious,' Clay shouted. 'I don't care. Just buy the tickets, man. Just buy the tickets.'

Cooper arrived.

'Get that bum away!' Clay yelled with renewed fury. 'What's he doing here?' Clay called over his body-guards, who obligingly held down Clay's arms as he gave a poor imitation of a man spoiling for a fight. 'Get that ugly bum outta my sight,' Clay cried. Cooper grinned.

We sat down to lunch. Promoter Jack Solomons and famous Cockney comedian Bud Flanagan sat between Clay and Cooper. The two boxers shook hands for the photographers.

Clay's eyes sparkled like black grapes. He said to Cooper: 'You...are... in...trouble!' He took a mouthful of ice-cream. 'I nevah eat this stuff if I'm training for a real fight,' he boasted.

Throughout the lunch Clay kept stealing sidelong glances at Cooper, and muttering destructive oaths under his breath. A waiter said of Clay, admiringly: 'He's so cheeky you have to smile at him, don't yer?'

'It's okay,' said Henry Cooper magnanimously. 'He's enjoying it.' Bud Flanagan rose and began to table-hop, working the room. I grabbed the opportunity to occupy Flanagan's empty chair, next to Clay. 'These fists,' he told me, even though I had not asked him, 'are greased lightning!'

I nodded respectfully, but I remembered Ingemar Johansson telling me at breakfast one morning at the Savoy: 'When this fist sends them down they stay down!'

'I'm too quick for Cooper.' Clay said, 'I think too fast. I am the boldest and most popular and prettiest fighter in the world today, and naturally I am going to be champion of the world. I have known this evah since I was fifteen years old. I have known my destiny.' Clay looked at me: 'You are lucky to be talking to me, fella. People all ovah the world want to talk to Cassius Clay.'

I asked Clay if any amateur glory-seeker, jealous of Clay's reputation, had ever challenged him, had ever sought to settle things out of the ring, in private, in pursuit of instant fame.

'Listen,' Clay replied, 'anybody who tries to tangle with me must be crazy. He...must...be...cuh-razy! It would be better for that man to climb into a den full of wild lions...with a dull razor!'

28 MAY 1963

Clay beat Henry Cooper, of course. He beat pretty well everybody he met (fifty-six wins, thirty-seven by KO). He was three times World Heavyweight Champion. He changed his name to Muhammad Ali in 1964; three years later he refused to be drafted in the US Army and was stripped of his titles for four years. ('I ain't got no quarrel with the Viet Cong. No Viet Cong ever called me "nigger".') He is generally regarded as the greatest boxer who ever entered a ring. In 1984 he was diagnosed with Parkinson's disease. He married four times, fathering seven daughters and two sons.

Billy Cotton's show opener 'Wakey, Wakey!'

CHAPTER 19

BILLY COTTON – NOT ALWAYS AS JOLLY AS HE LOOKED

"You had a feeling you were penetrating where few people had gone before."

William Edward ('Billy') Cotton, the celebrated British bandleader, was born in London on 6 May 1899. During the First World War he lied about his age to enlist in the Royal Fusiliers, landed at Gallipoli in the midst of a battle, and learned how to fly a Bristol Fighter aircraft. He made his maiden solo flight when he was not yet nineteen on the day the Royal Flying Corps was officially renamed the Royal Air Force. He was a more than competent amateur footballer, turning out for Brentford Football Club and the Wimbledon squad. He led a successful dance band after the war, gradually changing its appeal to embrace vaudeville and slapstick comedy. He married in 1921 and had two sons, one of whom, Bill Jr, rose to be managing director of BBC television.

Twice this weekend radio and TV audiences will hear Billy Cotton's familiar cry of 'Wakey, Wakey!' echoing through the land. For many Cotton's jubilant cry will be a signal to switch off, or switch over. These will be people unamused by the spectacle of a group of elderly male musicians acting silly, shouting, 'Whoops, dearie!' and cavorting about in skirts and baggy bloomers. For others the cry will be an invitation to surrender happily to the *Billy Cotton Band Show*'s addictive mix of hijinks, sentiment, sweetness and light. Billy Cotton may not be everybody's packet of chips, but he remains unabashed and apparently indestructible, an essential feature of British popular culture.

Cotton started his first band in Brighton more than forty years ago. His musicians tend to stay with the band for decades. Cotton's apple-cheeked singer, fifty-three-year-old Alan Breeze, the most famous unknown singer in the land, has been with the band for thirty years. Working for Cotton is a career and a life sentence. Anybody who hasn't been with Billy for at least a dozen years is considered a new boy.

Cotton himself is a mystery. His fans and followers see him as jolly old Uncle Billy, a beaming Dickensian figure who sprang, fully grown, out of Cockney folklore.

Even a brief conversation with Cotton, however, reveals someone who is not always as cosy as he seems. He's a man, for instance, with a powerful urge to test his chances of survival in conditions designed to bring some lives to a sudden stop. Thus he is addicted to driving fast cars on long stretches of open highway and opening the throttle until the speedometer shivers towards the 150mph mark. Cotton says that speed relaxes him. 'If I was to tense up at speed I'd pack it in tomorrow.'

There is something of the loner in him. He detests back-slappers and loud congratulations. Close-up, despite his boomps-a-daisy TV image, he is a brave adventurer of stubborn pride, and I do not mean ego. Once he marched his band out of a West End nightclub because, he told me, he was expected to bow to the customers as they arrived. 'I couldn't manage it.'

After the war he raced cars, finishing fourth in the 1949 British Grand Prix. He kept a private plane, a Gypsy Moth, at Croydon.

> 'I would drive out before dawn, push the plane out, and climb up to 6,000 feet before the sun was up. You had a feeling you were penetrating where few people had gone before. I used to put my head over the side, clear my throat, and spit out of the plane, look down on London and say to myself, "Share that among you."'

22 FEBRUARY 1963

My Fleet Street editor at the time read my copy in advance of publication and shook his head regretfully when he read that Billy Cotton had spat on London. 'We can't print that!' he said, his voice rising with surprise. I tried to persuade him that it was the only thing worth quoting in the interview, but the editor evidently felt that we had to save Billy Cotton from himself. Thus do national institutions protect each other. I suspect that Billy Cotton privately despised his public – or much of it.

After a stroke, Billy Cotton died in 1969 while watching a boxing match at Wembley.

Billy Cotton and Band acting silly

Fleur Cowles

CHAPTER 20

FLEUR COWLES –
THE WOMAN WHO INVENTED HERSELF

"I don't carry the past with me … never!"

*Fleur Cowles (born 20 January 1908) did not like the sound of her original name,
which was Florence Freidman. She was determined to lose it and, what's more,
to lose the identity that went with the name. With persistence and diligence she
erased or denied any detail pertaining to her humble origins (her father was a
novelty salesman; her first husband Bertram Clapper manufactured wooden shoe
heels). Thus lowly Florence became exotic Fleur. She literally reinvented and
renewed herself, a life-long subterfuge that proved remarkably successful. She had
the charm, talent and ambition to carry it off. She mingled with popes, presidents,
potentates. She seemed to know everybody in the world worth knowing. The writer
Selena Hastings described Fleur as 'monumentally vain'. American humourist S.
J. Perelman lampooned her in the* New Yorker *as* Hyacinth Beddoes Laffoon.
Fleur Cowles married four times.

Birds were singing in the sun-splashed treetops as I swung my car off the
main Eastbourne highway on to the stony farm roads of East Sussex.
May was bustin' out all over and the cattle were standing like statues. A
signpost warned 'Drive Slowly – Tiny Dogs Playing' as I drove the last slow
yards to the country home which already stood in this lovely spot when the
Spanish Armada set sail.

An American ash-blonde wearing massive dark glasses waved me a
welcome from a low-slung lawn chair. This was her home. This was her
hideaway. Her name is Fleur. She is as unique as her name. By any standards
she is one of the more remarkable women living in Britain today.

Fleur – such a pretty name – was once a high-powered advertising executive
in New York. Then she married millionaire media boss Gardner Cowles and
became Associate Editor of the magazines *Look* and *Quick*. Fleur was one of

President Eisenhower's personal representatives at the coronation of Queen Elizabeth II in 1953. Eisenhower, she says, is one of her oldest friends. 'I'm very devoted and grateful to him for his many nice gestures towards me...'

Fleur wrote a sensational book about General Perón and his wife Evita, both of whom, she says, she knew intimately. She clocked up 150,000 miles a year as a foreign correspondent and unofficial US ambassadress. On her way to the Korean War she stayed with her dear old friends the Shah and Queen Soroya in Tehran.

The catalogue of personal achievement and acquaintance is extensive. She published, last week, her latest book, a biography of eccentric Spanish artist Salvador Dalí. She opened, last week, the first one-woman exhibition of her own flower paintings. The show goes to New York in October. Recent guests at her Wednesday cocktail salons in her town flat in Albany, off Piccadilly, include Douglas Fairbanks, Danny Kaye, Labour leader Hugh Gaitskell and Cary Grant, who was best man at her final marriage to wealthy British timber merchant Tom Montague-Meyer. She's a friend of the Duchess of Windsor and Mrs Eleanor Roosevelt.

Enough, already?

She poured a cooling drink for me and we sat talking on the lawn chairs. Her voice is low, soft and mid-Atlantic. She wore casual country clothes – an orange sweater knotted by the sleeves around her neck. She seemed very still and serene, like a boxer resting quietly between rounds.

I mentioned that some of the book reviewers had not been very kind about her Salvador Dalí book. One critic was ungallant enough to refer to her as 'that high fashion dame'. She shrugged. 'The English,' she said, 'dote on eccentrics, but they rather resent them when, like Dalí, they are not English.'

An unseen cuckoo sang in the nearby woods.

She accepted a cigarette from me, saying, 'I never smoke except when I am offered a cigarette. I would take one every minute if it were offered to me. Otherwise, I'd just never remember to smoke...'

Tea was served on the lawn. Two diminutive long-haired dachshunds trotted towards us across the lawn. Behind her dark glasses, Fleur Cowles's hazel eyes crinkled with amusement. She introduced her pets. 'This is Mr McLeod, and this is Mr McGuinness. In my London flat I have a cat named Mr McKassa. The cat is Abyssinian. It's the breed, you know, from which the entire cat family is descended.'

No second-hand breed of cat, I felt, would have satisfied Fleur Cowles. It had to be an Abyssinian. The prototype. The real thing. The elusive cuckoo sang again. Fleur Cowles appeared to regard the sound as a personal challenge.

'I've never seen the cuckoo,' she said. 'They tell me he's the ugliest bird alive. I'm dying to see one now. He's up there right now, mocking me…'

Yes, she had to collect things. Antiques, pictures, eccentrics, friends. When she saw the cuckoo she would be satisfied. That, at last, would be collected, too.

One of Fleur Cowles's favourite words is 'unacceptable'. She used the word to describe idle housewives, the South African apartheid regime and a friend of mine who keeps reptiles for pets.

'Quite unacceptable,' said Fleur Cowles, shivering delicately in the afternoon sunshine.

Hard work she finds most acceptable. She is no stranger to work. Painting, writing, entertaining. What is her secret?

'I can turn off my thoughts like an electric switch,' she replied, 'and go on to the next thing. I don't carry the past with me. Never! I have no real interest in the past. I'm always terribly excited about the thing I'm about to do.'

One of the things she is always ready to do – this was unexpected – is to see a bullfight. She has written about the Spanish national fiesta for glossy magazines. 'I saw my first bullfights in Mexico and always hated them,' she told me. 'Then I became friendly with some matadors and, when I began to see the fights through their eyes as well as mine, I began to appreciate both sides of the debate.'

On her early life she would not be drawn, deftly side-stepping any question that she found 'unacceptable'. She offered tit-bits. 'I sat on Bernard Baruch's lap when I was a child … My grandfather started the Pony Express…' She was ceaselessly polite, though guarded.

Now, she had things to do. 'You must come again,' she said. I left the house as the sun began to dip behind the trees. I drove away from Mr McLeod and Mr McGuinness and the painting, writing Fleur Cowles, age forty-five and still going strong.

As I put the car into gear and rolled away, she was still on the lawn, watching for the cuckoo.

20 MAY 1959

My wife and I spent two brief vacations with Fleur and Tom in their converted fortress in Extremadura, Spain. Conversation would, at some point, inevitably return to the famous people she had known. More than once, usually after dinner, she would bring out and display a collection of crumpled letters written to her by the Queen Mother, whom she sometimes described as her best friend. Fleur Cowles (pronounced Coals) died on 5 January 2009, aged 101.

Marlene Dietrich

CHAPTER 21

MARLENE DIETRICH – FLAME IN THE NIGHT

"There may be something heartbreaking in those letters. You can't just send them a photograph."

Born in Berlin on 27 December 1901, Marlene Dietrich started her career as an actress and singer in the nightclubs and film studios of pre-Nazi Germany. She was catapulted into enduring celebrity by her performance as a heartless vamp in the film The Blue Angel. *By the early '30s Dietrich had become one of Hollywood's hottest stars, celebrated for her high-cheekboned beauty, her taunting, inviting singing voice ('See What The Boys In The Back Room Will Have'), above all for her shapely legs, insured, according to the Hollywood publicity machine, for a million dollars. She hobnobbed with presidents, princes and best-selling writers. During the Second World War she identified herself with the American cause and the democratic values of the Allies, touring war fronts untiringly as a troop entertainer, antagonising many in Nazi Germany who felt betrayed by the Berlin-born superstar. Later, as her Hollywood star waned, she embarked on tours of posh nightclubs and theatres in Europe and America. When she appeared in London's Café de Paris, she was introduced nightly by luminaries like Noël Coward, and Douglas Fairbanks Jr. Fame clung to her, to the end, like a skin-tight gown.*

There is a line in her most famous song about men clustering around her like moths around a flame. An appropriate image, as it happens. The crowd of perhaps 250 waiting outside the Birmingham stage door did suggest, in the dusty half light, a cluster of moths in their dull, sensible clothes and English reticence. They had just seen and heard their heroine performing her familiar repertoire of mostly sad songs; now they waited for the legend to appear among them, close enough to touch.

Some talked in low voices; most said nothing at all. Then, suddenly, a murmur of excitement as the green swing doors opened inwards and Marlene

Dietrich emerged wearing a fire-engine-red trouser suit, crisp and newly pressed, topped off with that fine floss of blonde hair. She was unmistakably a flame, glowing in the night. The moths stirred and shuffled about.

Her friend Ernest Hemingway called her 'the Kraut', describing her as 'brave, beautiful, loyal, kind and generous … every time I have seen Marlene Dietrich ever, she has done something to my heart and made me happy.'

Jean Cocteau defined her as 'a frigate with all sails flying, a figurehead, a Chinese fish, a lyre-bird, a legend, a wonder'.

'Marlene makes blurb-writers of us all,' wrote critic Kenneth Tynan, another worshipper.

For a full half an hour she stands on the shabby Birmingham sidewalk, signing autographs. The crowd has fallen into a fascinated silence. You can even hear her pen swishing and squeaking as she repeatedly signs the name 'Dietrich' with a swift flourish across their glossy theatre programmes. Occasionally, from somewhere, a woman's voice pipes up: 'Mar-leen, you are fabulous.'

Another female voice confides in German, *'Ich bin von Berlin und Wien'* – I am from Berlin and Vienna. Dietrich receives this information with the lift of one eyebrow, but she says nothing. She retains her privacy.

A couple of relaxed but steadfast policemen, one of them very young, stand by in case they are needed. There is nothing for them to do at the moment; the crowd keeps its distance. Dietrich leans back slightly and whispers to me: 'I am astounded how quiet these people are …' Swish-swish goes her pen. 'In America they would be screaming.'

The last of about 200 programmes is signed. Dietrich turns and gently cups one hand over the cheek of the younger policeman. 'When I leave on Saturday you'll be able to get some sleep.' He smiles shyly.

We press forward to a waiting limousine. A fiftyish woman wearing glasses starts forward to embrace her. Dietrich hugs her closely and even kisses her cheek. Another woman cries out, 'Mar-lene, you are super.' Yet another, with tears in her eyes, takes Marlene's hand and kisses it with reverence.

The two policemen lean and shove, clearing a path to the car. Dietrich is in danger of being trapped against the hard edge of the car's open door. But she makes it into the back seat of the limo, me beside her. The door closes. The fingers of the faithful scratch at the car windows. Dietrich rolls down a window, holds their hands, presses their fingertips, all the while counselling them in a low, cool voice. 'Be careful of your feet, don't get run over … mind the car … thank you, be careful…'

Free at last, the car speeds away. Dietrich spins around. She waves and smiles through the rear window.

When we finally lose the crowd around a corner, she throws herself back against the seat agitatedly, clasping her hand before her. She is profoundly moved by the crowd, by their outpouring of love.

More autographs at the hotel. More hugs and kisses and snapshots. I escort Dietrich to her door on the ninth floor of the Albany Hotel. We arrange to meet tomorrow; it is clear that she hates to be interviewed. (She had agreed to speak to me only after I had reluctantly promised her PR man that Dietrich could peruse my copy before publication. She had been much offended by recent newspaper stories written by callous American reporters; she is suspicious of me, of all journalists.)

It is 2 p.m. on the following day. As arranged, I meet Dietrich in her suite, the Warwick, the hotel's grandest, overlooking the soulless, mid-town heart of Birmingham. The star wears black slacks, a billowing silk flowery blouse, shaded glasses. Her manner is polite but remote, a bit of a chilly blast after last night's almost chummy candour at the theatre and on the drive home.

But presently she begins to thaw out. We talk of London and its current crop of West End plays. She speaks with awe of Laurence Olivier and Paul Scofield. How does England produce such great men of the stage? I invite her to list other heroes. Oh, she replies, there are too many – Ernest Hemingway, Noël Coward, Frank Sinatra, the nuclear physicist Robert Oppenheimer, Dr Alexander Fleming, the discoverer of Penicillin.

'Fleming gave me the first Penicillin culture he ever developed. I have it framed in my apartment. When I saw how his discovery saved the lives of soldiers who had lain in the mud for days I felt I just had to see him with my own eyes, if only to see him walking out of his house. As it happens, a meeting was arranged between us, a dinner party, which I cooked. We became and remained good friends.'

A recent recruit to the gallery of men she admired was the Israeli General Moshe Dayan. 'Oh,' said Dietrich, 'he's just dreamy, a very mysterious guy. I don't think you can know him fast.'

Dietrich had been moved to tears by the spirit of the state of Israel. 'I wish I were intelligent enough to describe it. The best, the most alert youth today is in Israel and Russia, and in Poland, too. But the Poles are too poor to have that stamina.'

I remarked that her catalogue of admired people included no women. 'Men are better than women,' she replied immediately. 'They are stronger characters; they have better brains; they are not so muddled in their thinking. I believe it is true that women do think differently. They complicate rather than simplify matters. Maybe it's in the glands. I fancy myself as having more of a male brain than a female brain. I am not easily distracted.'

Dietrich is distracted, however, by astrology.

'My sign is Capricorn. It is not a very good sign, though it is good for organising things. I am compelled to bring order. I can never go to bed if there is disorder anywhere in the house. I sometimes go into my friends' houses and start straightening out their kitchens. I am wonderful for other people. I do their housework. I tend their children. We Capricorns do not have easy lives. We take everybody's troubles on our own shoulders. We ask for it. Everybody plonks it right here.'

She touched her shoulder with a slim, freckled finger.

'We should all learn something about astrology. It does help, particularly in understanding small children before they are old enough to explain themselves. Parents can learn a lot about the inner lives and characters of their kids by understanding their astrological signs and using them as a guideline. In my next life I want to be a man – and an Aquarius.'

Dietrich seemed to view the modern age with bewilderment and regret.

'Nothing good seems to be happening. We all hoped for better things with the end of the Vietnam War, and now it's over, but it still goes on. Can you imagine a more gigantic job than being a parent today? You cannot always sanction young ideas if they are not your own. But if you refuse them you only drive them away; there is no middle way.'

The conversation veers dangerously towards the subject of age. Dietrich becomes offhand and cool. 'My age seems to obsess people. Who cares how old Olivier is, or Scofield, not that I compare myself to those geniuses. As for my career, why I choose to go on, I go only where I am asked. I never look for work. People invite me; that makes it very easy.'

But she has seen many years, and endured much, and has survived with grace. She talks of the friends she has outlived, the constant tidings of death.

'The terrible thing is that they all go, and one has to take it. If you don't want to take it you have to die before them. I have seen so much death. In Italy during the war the men I knew in Bomber Command would not talk about the friends who did not return from the raids; they simply learned to accept that they were

dead and gone and over with. If they had to mourn each lost friend it would
have been too terrible. As a child I was taught to hide sorrow, not to show my
feelings or inflict them on others. The British idea of facing up to disaster is very
close to what we were taught as children in Germany, which was not to make
a fuss. I don't know if it is a good idea to suppress sorrow. It is probably better
to cry and wail, like they do at a Jewish funeral, and get it out of your system
that way. Everything you are taught as a child stays with you. Everything is
implanted, even the kind of things you will admire, the kind of things you will
eat. You cannot change; I cannot change. Mind you, I am not always in the same
mood. Reporters crowd around me at airports and expect me to be something
I am not. If I am gay and nice they say "where's the mystery?" If I just walk by
mysteriously they say "she's not nice". The other day I came off a plane holding a
coat, which just happened to hide my face. The picture captions said that I was
"doing a Garbo". You can't please them, that's for sure.'

I left Marlene Dietrich to get on with her fan mail, to which she devotes two
hours every day. 'There may be something heartbreaking in those letters. You
can't just send them a photograph.'

She shook my hand at the door, polite and enigmatic to the end.

A few days later, true to our bargain, I took my account of our meeting to
the Savoy Hotel in London and called her on the desk phone. 'Please send it
up,' she said in that familiar throaty voice, 'I cannot see you today.' I waited
in the lobby. Twenty minutes later she returned my article, unchanged except
for one word. She had erased 'freckled'. Accompanying the returned article
was a note signed in Dietrich's own hand.

'Thank you so much,' she wrote. 'The only thing I miss is the mention of the
young people who make up <u>Half</u> of the audience. Love, Marlene (in a hurry).'

24 JULY 1960

Marlene Dietrich died, a virtual recluse, in Paris on 6 May 1992, aged ninety. Cause of death was given as renal failure. The funeral service, held at the Church of the Madeleine, was attended by 3,500 mourners. The coffin, draped in the American flag, was transported to Berlin, where Dietrich was buried in the Friedenau cemetery, near her mother's grave and not far from the house where she was born. The inscription on her gravestone reads 'Hier Stech Ich An Den Marken Meiner Tage' *(Here I Stand at the Milestone of My Days). Threats were made by neo-Nazis to desecrate her grave, and it was decided not to name a street after her. But the sheer weight of Dietrich's fame and personal integrity seems to have subdued German resentment. She was eventually given the freedom of the city, a central Berlin public square was named after her, and in 1997 a German postage stamp was issued bearing her image.*

After her death, her many well-attested love affairs, some of them bisexual romances, became part of Hollywood folklore. But she was only married once, to film director Rudolph Sieber, by whom she had one daughter, Maria Riva, who remained close to her mother in her final years in her apartment at 12 Avenue Montaigne. In death, Dietrich's fame remains, somehow, as potent as ever. She is to be found in the line-up of uber-celebrities on Peter Blake's cover of the Beatles' iconic album Sergeant Pepper's Lonely Hearts Club Band.

A German postage stamp featuring Marlene Dietrich was issued on 14 August 1997

Walt Disney on the lot of his studio in California

CHAPTER 22

WALT DISNEY –
THE MAN WHO INVENTED A MOUSE

"Mice frighten me …
you never know where they are going."

*Walter Elias Disney was born in Chicago on 5 December 1901. His surname is
understood to be a version of d'Isgny, a Frenchman who landed in England with
William the Conqueror in 1066. Walt Disney was an early arrival in Hollywood,
turning out animated cartoons in the early '30s, of which the most successful was
Three Little Pigs (1933). Over the succeeding decades Disney became a world
celebrity, a fiercely patriotic American whose spread of movie studios, theme parks
and merchandising outlets combined to make him the head of one of the most
profitable business corporations of all time. He was married to Lillian Bounds
from 1925 until his death in 1966. The couple had two daughters, one of them
adopted. In 1960 Disney's face featured on a US postage stamp.*

He walked into the room looking more like a successful politician than
like Mother Goose. The same toothsome grin, the same brisk moustache. The glossy thatch of dark hair, streaked with silver. The same hint of
stubborn cunning.

But he was Mother Goose all right. Nobody, living or dead, has amassed
a larger financial fortune out of fantasy. For thirty years he has populated the
world of childhood with squeaky-voiced animals, singing puppets, fairy-tale
princesses – a dazzling cluster of demons and dwarfs who have become part
of the mythology of our age.

Sixty years old next birthday, Walter Elias ('Walt') Disney is a genius, a
billionaire, everybody's idea of a favourite uncle, and one of Hollywood's
toughest and most irascible bosses. He is one of the best-known, least understood figures alive, a problem and a paradox – a self-made, hard-headed
business executive who bursts into real tears at family occasions like weddings

and births. He has made millions laugh, yet gave me the impression that he had no real sense of humour himself. He has created a new art form, yet confesses that his own skill with a pen is second-rate.

One day last week, while summer rain drummed at the closed windows of his Dorchester Hotel suite, I sat down with the contradictory Mr Disney.

His welcoming grin soon faded. He looked weary and creased. 'I need a holiday,' he said, massaging his cheekbones with his fingertips. 'I'm the only man I know who has never had a vacation. There's just no time for it. To me, a holiday is having a change of troubles.'

This was no theatrical self-pity. The truth is that Disney, who bosses thousands of employees, virtually runs a one-man-band. And the band never stops playing. Behind his mild, mellow front there is a combination of compulsive drive, unshakeable faith in his own instincts, and hair-trigger impatience.

An employee in Disney's London headquarters – which sprawls over four floors in a building in Pall Mall – told me in a hushed and reverent voice, 'Walt has the moodiness of genius. One minute he is happy and smiling. Then suddenly he is morose and snappy. We never know from day to day …' Another Disney staffer put it more succinctly: 'Walt is a cheerful megalomaniac. If you contradict him, you're out!'

Disney himself commented: 'Everybody in this studio sees me differently. Some of them characterise me as a bogey-man who roars into the shop and tears up everything other people have been working on for weeks. But someone has to say yes and no and stick to it. And that's my job.'

Behind Disney's feverish energy is the galling memory of an impoverished adolescence. Some misguided biographers have guessed that his boyhood was filled with laughter, story-telling and impossible dreams. They guessed wrongly. Disney was brought up in an atmosphere of rough justice, with little to cushion him or his brother Roy against the stark reality of the world. For six years as a small boy, Walt delivered newspapers for his father, rising from his bed at 3 a.m. to trudge through Kansas City snowstorms with his pile of journals.

In his early twenties Walt went to Hollywood, determined to break into the film cartoon industry, already aware he was a one-off original, that he had to hitch his wagon to his own personal star, that he would be only happy working for one company – Walt Disney Inc.

Four years later on a train trip, inspiration hit Walt Disney between the eyes. 'I'm gonna create a new character,' he announced to his wife Lillian as the train jostled through the night. 'Mortimer Mouse.'

'Not Mortimer, dear,' replied Mrs Disney. 'Such an ugly name. What about Mickey?'

Within weeks Walt had rushed out an item called *Steamboat Willie*, a short, jerky flicker that featured a black and white mouse with saucer ears and legs like thin sticks of liquorice. Disney himself supplied Mickey's falsetto voice on the soundtrack. (He still does.)

Mickey Mouse was an instantaneous conqueror, dubbed into fourteen languages. The Germans called him Michael Maus. The Japanese queued to see Miki Kuchi. Spaniards raved over Miguel Ratonocito.

Mickey Mouse went into Madame Tussauds and the *Encyclopedia Britannica*. Mussolini and Field Marshal Jan Smuts of South Africa adored Mickey. Hitler hated him. The Kremlin approvingly praised Mickey as a 'working-class symbol'.

As Mickey prospered, so Walt Disney began to expand the house built on the antics of the immortal rodent. Still only twenty-eight, Walt began manufacturing new cartoons called 'Silly Symphonies'. He hired new hands, built new studios, licensed the manufacture of Mickey Mouse toys, clothes and novelties.

Once Mickey was born, Disney never found time to look back. His output today is unmatched by any film factory on the planet. Cartoons (*Sleeping Beauty*, *Cinderella*), real-life adventures (*Davy Crockett*, *Pollyanna*), nature series (*The Living Desert*, *Vanishing Prairie*), countless furlongs of TV material pour out of Disney's California studios. Theme parks proliferated.

Observing his own avalanche of successes, Disney never lost his head, never 'went Hollywood'. He avoids the social round, preferring to stay at home with his wife, garage workshop and only pet – a black poodle named Lady. ('Mrs Disney doesn't much like animals,' Walt explained. 'She prefers grandchildren.') Acknowledging his debt to Mickey Mouse, he refuses to have any mousetraps in his Hollywood home, even though he told me that 'Mice frighten me … you don't know where they're going.'

To this day, Walt Disney retains the hash-house appetite of his rugged youth. He prefers canned beans to caviar, Irish stew to T-bone steaks.

With the passing years Disney has become increasingly authoritarian, correctly convinced that his own intuition and snap judgements have kept him at the top. Consequently he becomes brusque and crotchety with do-gooders and child psychologists who have criticised him for filling his cartoons and nature films with equal rations of sentiment and savagery.

'Look here,' Disney told me,

'What's the matter with sentiment? What's the matter with sweetness? Dammit, we're all sentimental at heart. We're all ready for a good cry. To be smart today you've got to sneer. Well, I don't sneer. I'm kind of naïve. I'm kinda off-beat in this cynical era. Everybody's hiding inside their shells. When they go home and beat their wives at least they're being honest. I'm often attacked for putting too much horror in my films. Gee, I don't know. Maybe I did overdo the Witch in *Snow White*. But in the original story, you know, the witch was forced to dance in red-hot shoes until she dropped dead. Now, I didn't show that, did I? In my movie she just fell off a cliff – a natural disaster, see? In *Three Little Pigs* I even let the Big Bad Wolf get away! In the original story they cooked him and ate him. How do you like that?'

Disney sipped an ice-cold Coke and chortled angrily to himself, like Donald Duck.

'What's the matter with a few nightmares? Why, I still have nightmares myself. I wake up, kicking off my covers and skinning my knuckles. So what? Everything today, dammit, is so supervised. So many people today are tampering in the lives of children. Thank God my parents let me grow up. They taught me right from wrong and that was it.'

He stood up and said, 'Gee, I don't know ... I can't analyse it.'

Like many self-educated men he trusts his instincts and his common impulses rather than his under-rehearsed powers of reason.

His self-confessed dislike of reading ('I'd rather have people tell me things'), his distrust of child experts and psychologists, his acknowledgement of his own naïveté: these are the hallmarks of a lowbrow who plays his own hunches.

In a revealing moment Disney told me: 'I've never ceased to wonder at the world.'

He is a sixty-year-old child with a child's uncontaminated sense of innocence and astonishment ... and a child's natural sympathy for the living things of the world.

Walt Disney is still playing with toys.

14 AUGUST 1960

In 1966 Disney was hospitalised to repair a neck injury, said to be the result of too much polo. Preparing for the operation, doctors discovered a cancerous tumour in his left lung. The lung was removed. Some three weeks later Disney collapsed, and within weeks was dead of acute circulatory failure. A long-standing urban myth claims that Disney's body was cryogenically frozen to await future resuscitation. Some have said that his frozen corpse lies buried beneath the Pirates of the Caribbean *ride at Disneyland. The first known cryogenic freezing of a human body did not take place until January 1967, more than a month after Walt Disney's death.*

'Uncle Walt' and some of his creations

Sacha Distel

CHAPTER 23

SACHA DISTEL – LIVING THE GOOD LIFE

"It is a very nice feeling … to be a golden boy."

Sacha Distel, named and listed among world celebrities in the lyrics of Peter Sarstedt's famous song 'Where Do You Go To My Lovely?', wanted above all to be recognised and respected as a jazz musician. One of the most accomplished guitarists in France, he performed alongside jazz greats like Miles Davis, Stan Getz, Dizzy Gillespie and Quincy Jones. Another kind of fame got in the way. Not that Sasha is complaining.

Sacha Distel is a dapper, permanently tanned Parisian charmer whose good humour, good looks, sea-green eyes and celebrity status have wreaked havoc in many a feminine heart. Those who have fallen into Distel's arms include Brigitte Bardot, to whom he was briefly engaged; Annette Stroyberg who, like Bardot, was once Mrs Roger Vadim; and the ravishingly pretty Francine Breaud, an Olympic winter sports champion who not long ago hung up her skis to become Madame Distel and appears to be enjoying it greatly.

It may seem odd to introduce this account of my meeting with a professional singer with a summary of his trophies as a lover. Yet why not? Few knew his name until his emergence as the man who was going to wed the coveted Bardot.

Like Cliff Richard in England he retains an ageless, unthreatening appeal, and looks like the sort of boy any mother would be glad to have her daughter bring home to tea. Everybody likes Sasha.

Sitting in the living room of his Paris home – a room of remarkable Englishness (tea on the table, hunting horns and prints on the walls, Portobello Road bric-à-brac everywhere), he immediately distanced himself from the tacky world of French pop music. He is above all that. He is a class act. 'Pop music is in decline here,' he told me.

'You should hear some of the rubbish the French radio has been putting out. You would not believe it. We reached a point here where French disc companies would record maybe as many as 200 singers and groups in a single week hoping that one – only one – might make it. They would record just anybody. It is bizarre, no?'

'All they asked,' he added, 'was that the singers must be as young as the customers. The adoration of youth is universal. To be young today is to be God.'

Distel was dressed in a neat, dark suit, white shirt and tie. His wife came into the room, looking as fetching as a starlet; together they apologised, needlessly, for the quality of the tea we were drinking.

To serve a good tea in the English manner is, I was informed by Distel, considered very voguish among young French entertainers. The Distels appear to be a devoted couple. In Sacha's outgoing manner, in his eagerness to please, not a hint remains of the high-living St Tropez playboy who wooed and won the girls and punched photographers on the nose when their flashlights discomfited Brigitte Bardot.

Though he hasn't lost his taste for speed and adventure (he is driving his third Porsche and is learning to pilot a plane), he radiated the composure of a man who has come to terms with life. The gay young blade has found its scabbard.

He takes himself seriously as an entertainer. He has taught himself to sing fluently in half a dozen languages. Currently, he has best-selling Top Ten hits in France, Italy and Germany.

He spoke of his multiple successes with quiet confidence:

'It never occurred to me that I might fail. I knew I would meet the public. It had to happen. I am only glad it happened so fast. Success, when it came, did not disturb or astound me. I grew up in an atmosphere of variety and popular music. My uncle is Ray Ventura, the bandleader; I led my own Dixieland band at school here in Paris. I used to play the guitar for Juliette Greco. I watched her work every night. I learned the good things and how to avoid mistakes. I did not allow myself to be caught by the fake glamour of sudden success. I have seen too many big stars who become nothing. But it would be a lie to say that I did not enjoy the success. It is a nice feeling, a very nice feeling, to be a golden boy.'

Distel keeps himself in good physical condition, drinks rarely and smokes never. His home in Paris is an expensive town house, in a private square in the very heart of the city, a sudden outpost of calm where we could hear birdsong and the swish of the wind through the chestnut trees in his garden. He has another home in the French Alps where he met Francine on the slopes.

'I like my life,' he said, 'and I intend to go on living it by making a resolution not to chase after every new style, every new fashion in music.'

'That way you only last two or three years. Look at Chevalier and Sinatra and Yves Montand, and Sammy Davis Junior. They go on year after year. They are made to last. These are the people I respect. I want to be like them.'

Distel guarantees fresh material for himself by writing many of his own songs. When Sinatra recorded a Distel original called 'The Good Life', the accolade thrilled Sacha. 'It was like getting the *Legion d'Honneur!*'

Francine came back into the room toting Laurent, her first-born, a wide-eyed, six-month-old who weighs in at just over 20 pounds. 'Say goodnight Daddy,' Francine instructed her infant son in English.

Sasha jumped up to kiss the little fellow on the head. 'I have never heard this baby cry in all his six months of life,' he said. 'Never once. He is a very nice boy.'

Daylight had faded when Sacha saw me to the door. Much remained, he said, to be considered, including the possibility of starring in a French movie biography based on the life of Maurice Chevalier. 'I would like that. He is a big man.'

Sacha Distel stood in the doorway like a man who had at last come home and found peace after many loud adventures. 'One can always progress,' he said. 'One can always do better.'

11 MAY 1965

Distel, by every account, remained loyal to Francine and devoted to their two sons. 'Whatever I want in a woman I can get at home,' he said. In 1971 he had a world bestseller with his recording of the Bacharach–David song 'Raindrops Keep Falling On My Head'. In 2001 Distel appeared in London's West End as the crooked lawyer Billy Flynn in the musical Chicago; *few who saw that show could have known that Distel was already in the grip of the cancer that would bring the curtain down on his charmed life in a French provincial hospital on 22 July 2004, at the age of seventy-one. The Chevalier biopic remained an unrealised dream.*

Luis Miguel Dominguín

CHAPTER 24

LUIS MIGUEL DOMINGUÍN – MATADOR

"We learn with country girls."

Luis Miguel Gonzalez Lucas, one of the best, and best-known, bullfighters of the past century, was born on 9 November 1926, adopted the name Dominguín from his father, a glamorous bullfighter of the '30s. Luis Miguel made his debut in the bullring as an eleven-year-old. In his early twenties he was on the same card as the great Manolete on the fatal afternoon in 1947 when Manolete lost his life to a bull of the feared breed of Eduardo Miura. Dominguín was perceived as a cold, analytical matador whose dangerous tactics, like putting his lips to the horns of a wounded bull, led to justifiable charges of loftiness and conceit. He retired several times. ('I have lost the feeling,' he once said. 'One cannot play with one's life.') He lived a vivid social life, mingling freely with world celebrities and women of outstanding beauty (Bardot, Rita Hayworth, Ava Gardner, among others).

He was personable and articulate. In an interview with Fleet Street journalist Nancy Banks-Smith he shrugged off the charge that bullfighting was cruel, comparing it with pigeon shooting. 'A wounded pigeon is left to die a slow, painful death. But the death of a bull is merciful – in twenty minutes he is dead. I, Dominguín, guarantee it.'

He sat, impossibly handsome and relaxed, smoking lots of cigarettes, in the corner of London's Connaught Hotel lounge. You saw him the moment you entered the place, across the plants and the anonymous huddles of aperitif drinkers. A slim, dark man in an open-necked shirt and cashmere sweater of daffodil yellow, a focal point and a born charmer. Luis Miguel, known as Dominguín.

No other bullfighter in our time except El Cordobes has been more celebrated than Dominguín, who became a professional matador at twelve and ever afterwards, on his good days, seemed to treat bulls with imperious disdain, as if they were large dogs to be played with.

He retired a decade ago, admired but unloved by the crowd, with a reputation in the bullring for remote arrogance. He is a celebrity, an intimate of the famous (Hemingway, Picasso, Cocteau), and of course very rich indeed.

In London yesterday Dominguín met me and talked about his decision, at the age of forty-five, to go back to the bulls next month.

'How to describe it? It is like being with the woman who pleases you most in the world when her husband comes in with a pistol.' Dominguín laughed and raised his eyebrows. 'The bull,' he added, 'is the woman, the husband and the pistol, all in one. No other life I know can give you all that.'

Of course it was the danger, he explained, that provided the kicks. Acute physical risk cleared the mind, brought a man closest to himself.

> 'I feel a need once more to live deeply and feel intensely, as on fight days, any one of which could be my last day on earth. To live this life we all need an imperative motivation, not something to do, but something we must do. Last winter I fought a bull at a charity benefit in Madrid. It was like waking up after being asleep too long. I came alive.'

Dominguín lit another filter cigarette and said: 'This is the moment.'
Like all bullfighters he openly acknowledged fear.

> 'It is worst before the fight, in my dressing room. It is a spiritual fear. You've got to beat it or it will beat you and stay with you forever. In the ring there is only physical fear, not to be gored or killed. It is a lesser fear and I handle it by being professional.'

In the year before he died, Ernest Hemingway, bullfighting's most visible non-Spanish apologist, wrote a famous series of articles for *Life* magazine exaggerating the rivalry between Dominguín and his brother-in-law Antonio Ordoñez, picturing the pair as the two top matadors fighting for the world title.

'About the bulls,' Dominguín told me, 'Hemingway had no idea. Maybe he knew something about bullfighters, but if you want to know about the bulls you must do it to yourself.'

Dominguín in retirement hardly went near a bullfight, but thinks the whole spectacle has become more flashy, less risky, because tourists were filling the bullring who didn't know the difference between making it and faking it.

That's why he has decided to start his own comeback trail in a tourist trap like Palma, on the holiday island of Majorca. 'There I can take it easy,' he said, 'and not feel so responsible. It is like trying out a show on the road.' He smiled. 'We learn with country girls…'

Was he not, like Cassius Clay, perturbed about slower reflexes, declining physical power, reduced getaway speed?

Dominguín held up both hands in a gesture of delight. 'Six months ago I was forty-four years old. Now I've made my decision I feel twenty-five again. If you have illusions you have everything. If you don't have illusions you have *nada* … nothing.'

11 MAY 1971

Shortly after the above interview Dominguín returned to the ring in Majorca, wearing a 'suit of lights' designed for the occasion by his friend Picasso. Dominguín's comeback, however, was short lived. Dominguín married twice. By his first wife, Italian actress Lucia Bosè, he had two daughters and a son Miguel Bosè, now a singing star. Luis Miguel Dominguín died of heart failure on 8 May 1996, aged sixty-nine.

J. P. Donleavy

CHAPTER 25

J. P. DONLEAVY – THE GINGER MAN

"There is something about American society that corrodes one …
Americans are not interested in the long haul."

*Irish-American writer J. P. Donleavy was born in New York City on 23 April
1926. He served in the US Navy and then moved to Dublin after the war where
he attended Trinity College. His first novel,* The Ginger Man *(1955), was banned
and burned in Ireland on the grounds of obscenity, but continues to be a world
bestseller, having sold 45 million copies, and has never been out of print. Other
notable books and plays by J. P. Donleavy include* Fairy Tales of New York
(1961), A Singular Man *(1965) and* The Beastly Beatitudes of Balthazar B
(1968). The Ginger Man, *describing the adventures in Dublin of an American
student, Sebastian Dangerfield, is clearly autobiographical. The novel is listed in
the Modern Library Top Hundred Books.*

'It strikes me,' said J. P. Donleavy, a man of unexpected opinions, 'that the
world is enjoying the greatest time of peace it has ever known. In spite
of the fighting in Lebanon, the bombings and the shootings, if a major war
broke out now these things would pale into insignificant local events.'

Donleavy, novelist and playwright, is peacefully in London for this week's
revival at the Shaw Theatre of his 1959 play *The Ginger Man*, which made
a star of Richard Harris and earned Donleavy a reputation as a picaresque,
roistering affront to religion and good taste. 'One of the most nauseating
plays ever to appear on a Dublin stage,' was one of the kinder comments on
The Ginger Man in the Irish press at the time.

Times have changed, notably in the theatre, and James Patrick Donleavy,
known as Mike, has changed with them. At fifty he has long since renounced
strong drink and brawling, and now lives a life of long silences and monas-
tic self-discipline in a nine-bathroom mansion on his cattle farm in Co.
Westmeath, Ireland, where he started his latest novel just over a month ago.

Donleavy sipped a fresh orange juice – a bearded, silver-haired, impeccably suited figure. He smiled a lot, but his voice seldom advances beyond a murmur. He declares himself delighted to be back in London, 'the world's greatest city'.

Son of an Irish-born civil servant who was 'a spoiled priest and therefore better educated than most emigrants', Donleavy long ago surrendered his US passport for an Irish one.

> 'There's something about American society that corrodes one, and I couldn't live there now. The United States is an impossible place for a so-called serious author like myself whose books build up slowly over the years. Americans are not interested in the long haul. Books have to be bestsellers, up there in the lists. The serious author is wiped out or ignored. I would have been dead a long time ago in America.'

So he much preferred London, a marvellous town for authors, where one could remain isolated and unbothered, taking long walks. Donleavy is an obsessive walker and bus-catcher. 'I can jump on a bus, any bus, ride all the way out to the last stop and get off, go into some strange pub and find a whole life going on inside … like chancing on a religious ceremony.'

His books, based on this kind of apparently random exploration, have made him a well-to-do man. He rises early, takes his breakfast in his workroom, trying to hold back the pressures. He disappears into one of his nine bathrooms ('my ablutions take a long time') and is ready to start writing at about 11 a.m.

'I stay at it as long as I can. I build up slowly. Between 1 p.m. and 3 p.m. I'm usually working at a very high pitch.'

He stops writing between 3 p.m. and 4 p.m. unless he is operating at white heat, 'but it's unwise to have too many of those driven periods…'

The house in Ireland, he tells me, is quite spectacular, with a marvellous indoor pool. It was intended for some Hollywood stars but they were scared off when the troubles came to Ireland. 'It's completely different from the Ireland I knew when I came to Trinity College, Dublin. In those days you carried away your slops in a pail.'

An important section of his readers, he said, were isolated people, loners who somehow hadn't made the grade. In Donleavy's maverick heroes they found mirror images of their own failure and sense of detachment.

Donleavy's eyes are light and frequently betray an inner amusement, contrary to his image as a taciturn recluse. 'Hell, no. I see myself as a kind of journalist, going out and picking up stories. I don't read novels. Instead,

I read newspapers avidly, buying six or seven at a time. Go through them with scissors.'

There is not a vestige in this gentle, polite man of the former amateur boxer whose reputation as a brawler in the pubs of Dublin struck awe into assailants and opponents. 'I used to have terrible fights. People seemed to take exception to my quiet manner and beard. My beard would always do it. I became such a terror that I would be pointed out, respectfully, to big guys in pubs. I enjoyed quite a mystique.'

Donleavy recalled a famous traffic-stopping fight with Irish playwright Brendan Behan (*The Quare Fellow*) in the middle of Fleet Street.

'We were drinking and I tried to cash a ten-dollar bill. This infuriated Brendan. He thought I had waited too long to cash the bill. He grabbed me and pushed me up against the wall. We squared off in the street. I remember cracking Brendan a tremendous, down-swinging right to the nose. He fell down and stumbled about. He wasn't much of a fighter. He was a shrewd, naïve man and a much more serious author than anyone realised. No, I wouldn't describe Brendan Behan as a friend. Rather as a close enemy.'

Donleavy lives now with his second wife, and never goes to church. 'I was raised a Catholic but gave up religion when I was about fifteen, never followed it since.'

As an author he looks after his own contracts and legal negotiations, distrusting all agents and middle-men. 'I have learned to fend for myself,' he says.

Donleavy is still fending for himself, a singular man with a lot of ginger in him.

28 JANUARY 1976

Donleavy married and divorced twice, and had two children. Cared for now by his son Philip, he has lived for years in his crumbling country house in the Irish midlands. Though not a recluse, he is no longer interested in being interviewed. Though still writing, he has published nothing for almost twenty years.

Duke Ellington

CHAPTER 26

DUKE ELLINGTON – MAESTRO

"They get the money and I get the kicks."

Bandleader-composer Edward Kennedy ('Duke') Ellington, born in Washington DC, on 29 April 1899, was among the most significant figures in the history of jazz (although jazz was a word he hated). An eminent Boston critic named him 'the greatest composer of the twentieth century'. Ellington formed his first orchestra in his early twenties and led it (from the piano) until his death. He was always a pioneer exploring untried musical sounds and textures. He wrote more than a thousand compositions, some of them with his muse and creative partner Billy Strayhorn. I met Duke Ellington for the first time in Paris in the early '50s and even got to play a four-handed piano blues duet with him at a Paris party (the Duke was a forgiving man). A dozen years after our first meeting in the French capital, I was fortunate enough to meet him again in London.

Duke Ellington, wilting with fatigue, flew into London after a sleepless and apprehensive night on a plane from New York. He was hungry and he was cold. 'Flying is not one of my great joys, but hell, who wants to sail the North Atlantic in weather like this?'

Within an hour of touchdown he was padding around the swank Albany Suite of the Dorchester Hotel like a woolly brown bear seeking a place to hibernate for the winter. When he found the bedroom he looked disapprovingly at the single bed he found there. Ellington is a big, expansive man who likes big, expansive beds. 'Where's the king-sized bed I had last time?'

The hotel page looked distressed. 'We only have one and Elizabeth Taylor is using it,' he said.

Ellington's eyebrows climbed languidly up his forehead. He ordered breakfast – lemon tea and fried eggs – and fell down on a sofa to await his meal in moody silence.

Tonight in London Duke Ellington and his band open a British tour. This is Ellington's fourth visit to Britain since 1933. In those innocent days British newspapers referred to him as 'dance-tune composer' and a 'Negro bandmaster', and featured bewildering and patronising feature articles about him under such headlines as 'The Soul of a Negro'.

Breakfast was wheeled in and Duke Ellington began to thaw out. Squeezing half a lemon into his milkless tea he recalled affectionately two of his early British champions.

> 'The late Duke of Kent was a pretty fine jazz piano player, did you know? We played a lot of four-hand duets together. Sometimes the Duke of Windsor sat in, too. He turned out to be a swinging drummer. It wasn't just Little Lord Fauntleroy drumming, I can tell you. The Duke of Windsor had a hell of a Charleston beat.'

The door opened. 'I'm the hotel valet,' said the hotel valet.

'I've got nothing here, except what I'm wearing,' said Duke Ellington. Ellington munched away at his breakfast, gaining strength with every bite.

'This jam is the wildest,' he said. He is a prodigious eater. Nothing about him seems to have changed since I met him first in Paris, twelve years ago. His conversation is still peppered with soft-spoken, sardonic self-mockeries. 'I'm just an impetuous upstart.'

He is still given to long periods of silence. He is still unfailingly gracious. The pouches under his eyes are still the baggiest in show business.

At the age of sixty-three, Edward Kennedy Ellington still remains the most dominating figure in jazz and its only true genius. He makes music that is exultant and richly textured. He was ahead of his time when he started. He is ahead of his time today.

He dislikes discussing his music on what he disdains as the 'arty-crafty' level of professional music criticism. ('Such talk stinks up the place,' he once said.)

He told me: 'I don't even know what the word "jazz" means any more. The music has outgrown the word. The cats in my band stay with me because I pay them tremendous salaries. They get the money and I get the kicks.'

He shrugged off the current faddism about the bossa nova. 'It's not new. It's just better known. There are no new rhythms in the world.'

The telephone began to ring. Ellington answered the calls himself, greeting old friends. To a female caller he said gallantly, 'Of course I know your voice, honey – a most melodic tone, matched only by your most melodic contours.'

To another caller he said, 'How am I? Hell, baby, how should I know? It's too early to know how I am.' It was 10.30 a.m. and Ellington looked more tired than ever. A leaping flurry of sleet hit the uncurtained window. Ellington looked happy. 'This is a wonderful and civilised town. My favourite town on earth. Every time I come to London I go home speaking English better.'

He lay on the sofa again.

Thirty years ago he was banned from London's best hotels because he happened not to be a white man. The world has moved on since then, and the genius and unassailable dignity of men like Duke Ellington have had a lot to do with that advance.

12 JANUARY 1963

Duke Ellington died of lung cancer in New York on 24 May 1974, aged seventy-five. More than 12,000 mourners attended his funeral, filling a Manhattan cathedral and the surrounding streets. Ellington's only son Mercer took control of his father's band, keeping the flame alive.

Tony Elliott

CHAPTER 27

TONY ELLIOTT – TIME OUT

"I don't believe you can topple the structure.
All you can do is chip it away."

Forty-five years ago Tony Elliott, a student at Keele University, founded a weekly publication. He had less than £100 in his pocket. The magazine, called Time Out *after Dave Brubeck's iconic jazz LP, listed the cultural events and entertainments in London that week. The magazine, which carried a lot of political news and comment, is today recognised as among the most successful publishing enterprises to be launched in England since the Second World War.*

Tony Elliott is a young, talkative Englishman who has recently become something of a media celebrity as the founder, editor and owner of *Time Out*, the fast-rising listings magazine whose function is explained in its subtitle: 'A Living Guide to London'. *Time Out* is a seventy-page publication which combines a directory of current events in the city with underground news and articles which vigorously question the processes of British justice, the behaviour of British policemen, the army's role in Ulster.

Commercial success may one day curb his idealism and exuberance, but for the present he speaks for a dissident generation, and his magazine reflects their aspirations. He told me:

'I was never a conscious rebel. Like countless other English children my home life was an anaesthetic. By the time I reached sixteen I'd learned nothing about people from my family, and nothing about life from my school.'

Elliott went to Stowe public school, a period in his life he describes as 'appalling, a complete write-off educationally and socially'.

Elliott's father, when he was a young man, enrolled in the London School of Economics but quit after a year. Tony says,

'I think LSE was too left-wing for him and he still regards universities and students as hotbeds of revolution. The atmosphere at home was really dreadful, totally uncreative. My parents were divorced four years ago. I only see my father accidentally now, but there's nothing we can ever actually talk about. My mother is important to me. She's interested in education and sociological things. I think she appreciates *Time Out*'s political line, but she's fifty-three and unlikely to be able to adopt that creed for herself.'

Tony Elliott is an enthusiast. Despite the diatribes in *Time Out* against the police, judges, army and conventional morality, its youthful editor seems to be a man for whom each day appears as a startling event. He has smooth, shoulder-length hair. A broken middle tooth confirms the impression he gives of a mischievous schoolboy in the *Just William* mould.

'It's easy to get the impression at university that we are a vast movement, that things are ripe for revolution. But in the context of the whole nation any radical direction represents only a slim percentage. I have no time for the wishy-washy radicalism of so many people one meets, who sit round talking endlessly about the revolution, but who wouldn't be seen dead actually doing something about it. There is not going to be an overnight coup. I don't believe you can topple the structure. All you can do is chip it away.'

Time Out has a staff of thirty, unusually large for a so-called 'underground' paper. Tony Elliott says his journalists earn between £20 and £30 weekly. His own take-home is £30.

The alternative press, he says, exists to raise issues which the straight press of Fleet Street won't touch.

'The newspapers of Fleet Street belong to the big-money structure. They are part of a society that can never seriously question the establishment and its positions of power. Fleet Street won't consciously seek out the kind of stories we do. It carefully avoids dealing with any subjects that seem to tear at the fabric of society, unless it is forced to.'

Elliott cites the case of the recent brutal police harassment of a coloured vagrant in Leeds as the kind of story that Fleet Street will only touch when it must, or when it is safe to do so – 'but the underground press runs stories like that all the time'.

Fleet Street, he said, was interested in scoops, and dropped stories as soon as it suspected that the public had become bored.

'The scoop mentality doesn't exist in the underground press. We stay with a story. We follow through. The alternative press owns itself, we work for ourselves, we deal with subjects that affect our own lives. Nobody follows an editorial line handed down by the editor or publisher. That's why *Time Out* is full of amazing contradictions.'

Time Out accepts no cigarette advertising. This was a group decision. The magazine lists movies, theatres, rock concerts, political demos. But no strip clubs or nightclubs. 'Places like that are not part of our culture. We don't disapprove. We just don't go.'

Tony Elliott may accept no cigarette revenue, but is himself a smoker.

'I'm a nervous smoker. I'm physically weak in that way. I've got to stop. I don't enjoy smoking pot, so I'm less concerned with the pot issue except in civil liberties terms. There was a time when we all thought pot was groovy and would change the world. Now I do feel more sceptical about it.

Pot can limit energy and creativity in some people, and enhance it in others. It's certainly no panacea. Still, that's no reason to ban it. In any case, I think people have learned now to use pot less indulgently. Nothing is more boring than a lot of people sitting around at a party, stoned out of their skulls. The popular prejudice against pot is based largely on ignorance, like contraception, which once scared the hell out of everybody.'

Elliott sees *Time Out*, which is read by thousands of straight citizens, as bringing the youth counter-culture to the very doorstep of the so-called silent majority. 'A lot of people buy it for the listings, but they get our point of view as well.'

'I see very little of the copy that goes into *Time Out*,' he said.

'I don't write. I don't enjoy the idea of trying to write. I let everybody get on with their own sections. I'm a practical person. I like the producer's role of creating the structure for others to work within, and who do the things I cannot do as well. In any case, I'm a political illiterate. I could not, for example, give you a definition of Marxism. The underground doesn't really exist as a cohesive entity. We all think differently. It's sad that you can't group together all that energy. Maybe it will all come together one day. I believe society will adapt itself to us – but very, very slowly. The important thing is to survive.'

7 MARCH 1972

As its financial fortunes rose ever higher over the years, Time Out *eased up on its political coverage and concentrated on what it viewed as its proper function – an intelligent person's guide to cultural events worldwide. In 2010, faced with falling advertising and circulation revenue, Tony Elliott sold half of* Time Out Group *for around £10 million to the private equity firm Oakley Capital. Recognising the drift of the times, Elliott plans to move more of his publishing activities online. He remains the company's chairman, and owns 50 per cent of the shares. More online-only magazines are envisaged. Tony Elliott also publishes some thirty travel magazines and city guides in ten languages, and claims a worldwide audience exceeding 17 million a year. Tony Elliott was ranked 644th in the* Sunday Times *Rich List.*

Tony Elliott

Jill Esmond with her husband, Laurence Olivier

CHAPTER 28

JILL ESMOND –
THE FIRST MRS LAURENCE OLIVIER

"I always knew he was the much more important person."

Jill Esmond was born on 26 January 1908, the daughter of two stage actors. With her parents constantly touring, Jill spent much of her childhood in boarding schools until she, too, became an actress at fourteen. Later she stud- ied at RADA. In 1928 she met Olivier while both were appearing in John Drinkwater's Bird in the Hand. *When Jill Esmond appeared in the play on Broadway, Olivier crossed the Atlantic to be near her. They were married on 25 July 1930. Their son, Tarquin, was born on 21 August 1936. The Oliviers appeared together in Noël Coward's* Private Lives, *but the marriage was not fated to last. In January 1940 Jill Esmond agreed to divorce Olivier. Some months later Olivier and Vivien Leigh were married in Santa Barbara, California. Katharine Hepburn was one of the witnesses. Jill Esmond stayed in touch with Olivier and it is clear that her devotion was constant and life-long. In a letter to Tarquin she wrote: 'It's funny after all that time how I can still love him so much.'*

Her hair is cropped and turning to silver. Her eyes are the palest blue you ever saw, and I have a feeling that they might weep quite easily. Her voice, taken off guard, has a sort of baritone burr to it – a legacy, no doubt, of a lifetime on the stage. On the telephone she is sometimes mistaken for a man.

Today, matronly and kindly, she tends her neat garden in St John's Wood, north London, longs almost desperately for her roving son, and remembers… Jill Esmond has a good deal to remember. In the climate of curiosity and conjecture that surrounds the private life of Sir Laurence Olivier, it is sometimes forgotten that he was married happily for ten years before Vivien Leigh came on to the scene. Jill Esmond was the girl he married. Today she is almost a forgotten woman.

'Larry and I were both twenty years old when we met in London,' she recalled.

> 'He is six months older than I. When we were courting, I was, I suppose, a bigger name in the theatre than he was, but I was always, always conscious that his potential was enormous. I always knew he was the much more important person…'

As Jill Esmond spoke of the man she divorced twenty years ago, there was no mistaking the quality of tenderness, of adoration, in her manner and in her voice. She has never married again. Her white-painted home in Queen's Grove contains many palpable memories of her life with Olivier. Pictures, ornaments, furnishings – all proclaim and nourish her nostalgia. A water-colour of a woman's head hangs next to a high window. 'Larry gave me that soon after we were married…'

Yet there is no bitterness and, she insists, few regrets.

'I would call myself an unfrustrated happy person,' she told me.

> 'I have wide interests. My life seems very full. I don't spend my time wallowing in forgotten sorrows. Regrets? No more than my normal share. But there are always compensations. That sounds terribly pious, I suppose, but it's true.'

Her blue eyes turn to a framed picture standing on a table. The picture shows a handsome young man in his mid-twenties, with black hair and a brooding expression. This is Tarquin Olivier, the son she bore in the mid-30s. She has raised this boy almost single-handedly in the face of difficulties that might have dented the spirit of a lesser woman. Today Tarquin fills Jill Esmond's life and thoughts. She is wholeheartedly dedicated to her boy.

'At the moment he is somewhere in Burma,' she told me, her eyes still fixed on the photograph. 'He is wandering. Just wandering…'

Burma, the Philippines, Cambodia, Indonesia. For almost two years Tarquin Olivier's restless odyssey has taken him far away from the polite suburban somnolence of Queen's Grove. He will be home in June, and Jill Esmond almost catches her breath with excitement at the prospect of his return.

'I absolutely adore him,' she says softly.

'He writes me such huge, long letters from all those faraway places. He's always moving around. Seeing. Learning. Perhaps he'll be a writer. Or perhaps he'll interest himself in the economics of underdeveloped countries. That sort of thing. He's that sort of boy. As a small child, Tarquin almost died of meningitis. It was touch and go. He was bright as a button one night, paralysed the next morning. It happened two days before my divorce from Larry became final. Just two days. I was alone. Larry was in America. It was a black week. I shall never forget it. I was in a play that closed that week. I was divorced. And my son almost died. The play was called *Judgement Day*. Ominous, don't you think?'

Jill Esmond shuddered just a little.

She remembered happier days. 'When we knew I was going to have a baby, Larry said, "He will be a son and his name will be Tarquin," and Tarquin it was.'

Divorced, she took her ailing son to California during the war. 'Pennies were scarce,' she said, 'very scarce. Things were difficult. But I always wanted my son to be friendly, to love his father.'

'All the time Tarquin was growing up,' she recalled, 'he had a picture in his bedroom of Larry in his Fleet Air Arm uniform.'

'He was brought up to be proud of his father. It wasn't as though there had been a divorce in the family at all. I made it seem as though we were just another family separated by the war. That helped a lot. It is so very hard to bring up a child without a father in the house. I had to fight with myself to prevent being over-possessive. I had to fight like mad. That is always the danger. After the war I brought Tarquin back to England. He was eight years old and met his father, you might say, for the first time. They became great friends. And they still are. In fact, we all are. I still see Larry often when he is in England, and we correspond regularly. I had a letter just this week from Detroit. Look.'

And Jill Esmond showed me a bulky envelope addressed in Olivier's concise handwriting to 'Miss Jill Esmond'.

It was obviously difficult for Jill Esmond to be on equally friendly terms with Vivien Leigh after the divorce. But she managed it, and the two women remain on friendly terms to this day.

'I had a drink with Vivien just a few weeks ago,' she said.

'Vivien has been very, very good with Tarquin. You see, I wanted Tarquin to go on seeing his father, so what was the point in bitterness? It would have only made things so difficult all round.'

Jill Esmond dipped her hand into a cigarette box and brought out a tipped cigarette. 'It's an Olivier,' she said, lighting it. 'Larry insists I smoke the family cigarette!'

The talk returned again and again to the far-roaming Tarquin. 'I have been getting his room ready for his return,' said Jill Esmond. 'He wants it orange. Such a maddening colour to match.' She shook her head in mock exasperation, but it was clear that she was in a delirium of expectation. 'He'll be home so soon, it feels almost like next weekend! I see so many of Larry's qualities reflected in Tarquin. His sensitivity, his love of beauty, his enthusiasm for life, and –' Jill Esmond suddenly restrained herself '– I had better leave it at that.'

No longer active in the theatre ('nobody asks me any more'), Mrs Jill Esmond Olivier ('That's my real name, after all') is a remarkable woman who has retained an almost fanatical devotion to the man she married so long ago. The love of the early innocent years has now been channelled towards the sensitive, music-loving boy who wanders through the Far East searching for answers.

Meanwhile, Sir Laurence has married again and expects another child this year. Again Jill Esmond reveals her kindliness: 'I sent Larry a telegram of congratulations when he married Joan Plowright,' she told me.

'And I had such a charming letter back from Joan. I've never met her. I admire her tremendously as an actress, of course. Yes, I am awfully pleased about Larry and Joan Plowright. Awfully pleased about the whole thing. Really I am. Of course, I wasn't quite so pleased when it happened with Vivien, but there you are. Do you think it strange or remarkable that I should behave this way? Not at all. I want to see Larry happy. I have Larry's happiness at heart. What's the point of being a dog in the manger? Regrets are worthless. They don't hurt anybody except yourself.'

'And after all,' and Jill Esmond looked at me directly and smiled, 'it is twenty years later, isn't it?'

30 APRIL 1961

Jill Esmond died at the age of eighty-two on 28 July 1990, in Wandsworth, London. She never remarried.

Adam Faith

CHAPTER 29

ADAM FAITH – BOY WONDER

"Without these kids, I'm nothing, nowhere."

Before the Beatles there was Adam Faith, the working-class boy from Acton, London, third of five children of a coach driver and an office cleaner. A handsome lad, a little on the short side, fair-haired and firm-jawed, he was not much of a singer, but he recorded a few bouncy ditties which caught the national fancy and won him an instant kind of celebrity, especially with young girls. He started out singing with a skiffle group called The Worried Men who appeared at the 2i's Coffee Bar in Soho, working with bandleader-arranger John Barry, who later went on to become one of the top film composers of the age. Adam Faith's first hit, 'What Do You Want', appeared in 1959. Adam was just twenty and still living with his parents in Acton.

Adam Faith. The name sounds like the title of a new religious programme on television. It is actually the nom de plume of an undernourished London youth with an acne problem and a vast and growing congregation of juvenile girls who worship him as a living god.

Adam Faith. One short year ago the name meant nothing. And the lad who was to wear it like a banner was working anonymously in the cutting rooms of the Elstree film studios. The name on his sparse pay packet was T. (for Terence) Nelhams.

Today that same boy, not yet twenty, drives a fast £3,000 American car and fills music halls up and down the country with shrieking, cash-paying customers. He has also had to resort to adopting weird personal disguises designed to prevent physical assaults upon his person.

Along the way he has developed a recurring stabbing pain in the pit of his stomach and a short temper that can snap like rotten rope at moments of stress. Such are the alarming rewards of rock 'n' roll idolhood.

I joined the wonder-boy in a first-class train compartment at King's Cross station, ready for the six-hour shunt up to Newcastle where he is topping the bill at the Empire. Conversation at first is intermittent, melancholy. He talks in short, hoarse sentences.

'Adam Faith,' he says. 'I thought up the name myself. I like it. It's got character.' He huddles morosely in his train seat – a diminutive figure, smaller than you would expect – and stares out at the passing ugliness of trackside London. His mood is detached, disenchanted. He has just been to a London cinema to see a special showing of his first released film, *Never Let Go*, with Peter Sellers and Richard Todd.

You would think he would be pleased and excited. Everything is happening for him. But he is offhand and cagey. It is the mention of books that sets him on fire for the first time.

'Huxley,' he says. 'Huxley, mate. *Brave New World*. I love that. Fantastic! Has Huxley written anything new recently? I want to know.'

Adam Faith left school at fifteen. Now he seeks to improve himself. 'Everything at school was a big drag.'

His mood is suddenly excited and bouncy. We go to the dining car for lunch. Over beef, potatoes and lemonade (he doesn't touch liquor) he keeps up a steady jet of talk.

'I never feel inferior or inadequate. It's not what you know that matters, it's what you do. I try to understand what people are talking about. I buy books all the time. I got so many books indoors, I can't read them all. They're piling up. I can't get through big books like *Peyton Place*. They take too long, and I'm in a hurry.'

He recommends a book titled *I Am Legend*. 'What's it about? I'll tell you, mate. It's about these vampires ravaging and mutilating everybody on earth after an atomic explosion. Fantastic!'

Adam Faith's defences are down. The talk goes on, mile after mile. There was a time, he says, when he toyed with the idea of being a racing driver. He's fascinated by violence, pain and speed. 'I'm dying to see a bullfight,' he says. 'I'd give anything to go to Spain and go to a bullfight with Ernest Hemingway. That man really is someone, isn't he?'

Like James Dean, Adam Faith loves fast cars. He has just bought a Ford Galaxy. 'She can really move. I've had the needle off the clock … and the clock stops at 120 miles per hour.

'Why do I do it? I don't know. I suppose it's the risk of death that's the kick. This is one of the biggest problems in life – to try and explain why and what I do things for…'

At six o'clock we reach Newcastle. The boy idol clamps a black beret on his thatch of blond hair and takes refuge behind a pair of outsize dark glasses.

We take a taxi to the theatre. Faith begins to get nervy and restless. A clutch of teenage girls has gathered at the stage door, like alley cats waiting for a fish bone.

'I got the pain again,' says Faith, pressing his stomach. He looks suddenly tense and sallow. The cab driver drives past the stage door. Adam Faith blows his top in a sudden electrifying moment of fury. 'Stop now!' he shouts, loud and angry, thumping his knee with a rolled umbrella.

The taxi stops dead. Faith leaps out of the vehicle, signs a dozen autographs without a smile and hurries to a dressing room strewn with fan letters and autograph albums. He switches on the TV set in his dressing room, glumly watching a Western. He brightens up when the guns begin to fire. 'I love a cowboy movie to have a good pub brawl,' he says with relish. 'Get him, boy!'

A pale young girl, stunned by the privilege, is now ushered into the dressing room. Adam Faith signs her book and she retires, transfixed with awe.

'Nice kid,' Faith says. 'Not flash like some of the others.' Adam Faith has a keen interest in girls. But, oddly enough, his sudden fame has cut down the field considerably. 'Can't take them anywhere,' he complains. 'I get mobbed. Still, I go out with as many as I can. Fantastic.'

His brother, Dennis, hurries into the dressing room. Adam enquires: 'How's the audience?'

'They'll do their nut,' predicts Dennis.

Adam beams. 'I like it,' he tells me, 'when I have a lot of girls in the front rows going bleedin' mad!' He proposes to stay a bachelor for a long time. 'The kids like me to be erratic. To move around. To be alive. If I married and settled down, they'd look for something new. Look at this.' He picks up a handful of trinkets – bracelets, beads and crucifixes. 'You wonder how many weeks they saved up for this stuff. They throw it on the stage for me. Without these kids, I'm nothing, nowhere.'

He washes his face and neck, pulls on his stage uniform – drainpipe trousers, blue leather jacket.

We walk together to the wings of the stage. It is 7.52 p.m. Adam steps into the spotlight. Shrieks and screams cascade down on to his bobbing golden head. Bedlam.

Adam sings in a kind of adenoidal murmur, which depends on microphone amplification for its effect. The act lasts exactly twenty-one minutes, then the curtains close abruptly.

The girls, exhausted and uplifted by their devotions, file out into the twilight. Adam Faith returns to his dressing room, lights a cigarette, flops down into a chair and picks up a paperback novel. Silently he starts to read these words:

> 'It was a pleasure to burn. It was a pleasure to see things eaten, to see things blackened and changed with the brass nozzle in his fists, with this great python spitting its venomous kerosene upon the world, the blood pounded in his head…'

Adam Faith lays the book on his lap. 'Fantastic!' he says.

2 JUNE 1960

Adam Faith (born 23 June 1940), recorded seven albums and thirty-five singles. In the mid-60s the Beatles more or less swept boy wonders like Faith aside. Always a canny operator, Faith became a useful stage and TV actor (he played an ex-con in Budgie, *a TV series written by Keith Waterhouse). Adam Faith married dancer Jackie Irving in 1967; they had one daughter, Katya. In the '90s he appeared successfully in the TV sitcom* Love Hurts *opposite Zoe Wanamaker. Faith also appeared in several stage roles. In the '80s Faith emerged as a financial advisor, but was declared bankrupt in 2001 owing (it was said) £32 million. He had a series of heart problems and died of a heart attack on 8 March 2003, following a stage appearance in a play (*Love and Marriage*) at Stoke-on-Trent. He was sixty-two.*

Adam Faith

Peter Finch at home, 1962

CHAPTER 30

PETER FINCH –
THE MAN WHO WALKED EVERYWHERE

◇◇

"I find it very amusing, really – all this buzz about my comeback."

Frederick George Peter Ingle-Finch (a surname famous among professional explorers) was born in South Kensington, London on 28 September 1916 and moved to Australia when he was ten. He became an actor, and was spotted by Laurence Olivier who was touring Australia with his wife Vivien Leigh. Olivier invited Finch to join his company in London. Young Peter jumped at the chance. He also jumped at Vivien Leigh, with whom he embarked on an extended affair. As an actor Finch won five BAFTA awards and two Oscar nominations for Sunday Bloody Sunday *(1971) and* Network *(1976). For his role as a crazed broadcaster in* Network *Finch was awarded a posthumous Oscar. Finch was the biological son of Scottish Major Jock Campbell. His mother was Alicia Ingle-Finch.*

At the age of sixty life is beginning again for Peter Finch, ex-Australian roustabout who was a bright light in British films a decade ago. After years of nomadic living in Italy, Switzerland and Jamaica, where he became a farmer, the restless Finch is suddenly being hailed as one of the new big stars in the Hollywood sky.

The cause of the excitement is a film called *Network*, not yet released anywhere, in which Finch's performance as an American newscaster who goes mad on live TV is being talked of as an Oscar-worthy tour de force. *Network*, written by Paddy Chayefsky (*Marty*, etc.), is a powerful assault on US television's brain-rotting concentration on trash and violence, and its frantic efforts to keep ahead of the ratings rat race. Its story is stark. Sacked when his popularity begins to wane, newscaster Howard Beale (Finch) announces his intention to commit suicide on air. As he begins to crack up, his broadcasts become ever more outrageous and his ratings begin to soar again. Beale becomes known as the 'mad prophet' of TV, ranting against the conformity of American life and the way television stupefies the mindless masses. When the crazed newscaster's novelty has spent itself, Finch is shot dead on live TV – demonstrating how a sterile culture silences its Messiahs.

Also starring in the explosive *Network* are William Holden and Faye Dunaway, giving the most venomous performance of her career. Watch for her among the Oscar contenders early next year.

When I met Peter Finch in a Hollywood coffee shop on Sunset Boulevard last week he was taking his sudden re-emergence as a superstar very calmly indeed. Sipping a polite cup of tea ('coffee gives me the jitters,' he said), Finch shrugged off his renewed eminence: 'I find it very amusing, really, all this buzz about my comeback. In my own mind, I've been there all the time. It's a little ironical to be discovered at sixty. It's nice, but I could have used it at eighteen.'

Finch is still slim and light-footed. His hair is silver-grey but it's all there. He looks good for years to come. Sensing a new upswing in his career, he has put his 250-year-old Jamaican farmhouse up for sale, and has bought a new Hollywood home off Benedict Canyon. He plans a settled life with his Jamaican wife Eletha and his two children – Christopher, fourteen, by a previous marriage, and Diana, six.

A private and scholarly man, Peter Finch spurns Hollywood high life, and must be the only man in this car-obsessed city who can't even drive. 'I belong to no Hollywood set,' he said.

'In this town where everybody drives I have become a great walker. Walking gives me thinking time. I meet a lot of gardeners that way. A lot of my buddies are gardeners. I read a lot, paint a bit. At home we are very much a family who just can't wait to come together in the evenings. We entertain ourselves. We are absorbed in ourselves. Reality doesn't exist in Los Angeles. People are cushioned from reality by distance and all the lush vegetation.'

'There was a time,' Finch recalls, 'when the first thing I did after a day's filming was to disappear into a pub.'

'I didn't drink to escape anything. I enjoyed drinking because it was a way of unwinding the tension, loosening the wheels. I had a reputation as a roistering hell-raiser. Now my biggest joy is just going home at night. I've always been a lucky man. I've never had any dread periods of unhappiness in my life. I have an insatiable curiosity. I am currently reading Chekhov passionately. Life isn't long enough to satisfy one's curiosity. Vivien Leigh was like that, too – a jackdaw of knowledge. My grandfather in Australia became interested in grafting trees when he was eighty-eight. It was a totally new endeavour for him. He taught me to be inquisitive. I don't despise money. But as long as I have enough for one roof over our heads and to pay my dreary alimony, I see no further use for it. I see people chasing money and losing their way in a plastic vacuum. Instead of merely supporting life, money becomes the life force itself. Perfectly normal people become monster-like in the pursuit of the buck. And that's what *Network* is really about. It's a very funny film … but also a punch in the stomach.'

When I met him, Peter Finch had just completed another film, playing Prime Minister Yitzhak Rabin in the first major Hollywood film about the daring Israeli raid on Entebbe earlier this year. 'Every studio in town,' said Finch with some vigour, 'wanted to make the Entebbe film.'

'Producers all over town were squabbling like fishwives to get in first. They were stooping to any dirty method to knock out their rivals. The competition was obscene, it was terrifying. It was almost as if the heroism of those amazing Israelis was being sullied, made dirty. It was a very emotional film to play in. All of us – Charles Bronson, Martin Balsam, and the rest – were very much moved just to be in it.'

Finch drank more tea, said he may come back to London one day to play in the new National Theatre. He missed and loved London. Meanwhile, the new home of this forceful and happy man was here in Los Angeles.

We said goodbye. Eletha and the children were waiting for him at home. I drove home along Sunset Boulevard. Peter Finch walked.

9 NOVEMBER 1976

Some weeks later, on 15 January 1977, scanning the London morning papers over a cup of coffee in my Knightsbridge flat, I was shocked to read the front-page stories of the death in Los Angeles of Peter Finch following a heart attack. While I was absorbing this unwelcome news I heard the morning post clattering through my letter-box (in those days the first post was delivered at about 8 a.m.). When I finally got round to opening my mail, I started with an envelope postmarked Los Angeles. It contained a card from Peter Finch telling me that he had enjoyed, and approved of, my account of our meeting in LA, and thanking me for it.

Theodore Thomson Flynn

CHAPTER 31

THEODORE THOMSON FLYNN – ERROL'S DAD

◇◇◇◇◇◇◇◇◇◇◇◇◇◇◇◇◇◇◇◇

"Errol was always a naughty boy."

Theodore Thomson Flynn, father of roustabout movie star Errol Flynn, was born on 11 October 1883, in Coraki, New South Wales, Australia. He started his academic career as a science schoolmaster. Between 1931 and 1948 he was the head of the Zoology Department at Queen's University, Belfast, Northern Ireland. During the war he was Chief Casualty Officer of the city. In 1909 he married Lily Young, said to be a descendant of one of the Bounty mutineers.

In a cramped, pantry-sized laboratory somewhere deep within the domain of the University of London in drab Gower Street, I came across Professor Theodore Thomson Flynn, Doctor of Science, peering down a microscope. He was tall (6 feet 3 inches), grey and gaunt and quiet-spoken. Few of his students guessed that the Prof. was the father of the famous Hollywood bad boy Errol Flynn.

'I have been studying a slice of an early Australian marsupial just before birth,' he said. 'Look down there.' I squinted through the eyepiece of the microscope at a series of dull pink blotches, the colour of stale blood.

'Let's go and have a drink,' said Professor Flynn, reaching for his hat. We went to a bar at neighbouring Euston station. Professor Flynn drank Guinness with his hat on.

'Errol was always a naughty boy,' he told me.

'At school he was dreadfully, impossibly lazy. Such a pity, because he has a very sharp intelligence. He was always good-looking. He inherited that from his mother. All the girls fell for him, I'm afraid. He was quite a handful, not a manageable child. Yet I never beat him. Funny thing, though, he was always in fear and dread of me if he thought he had displeased me.

The family came to Britain from Australia. I took up a position in Belfast as Professor of Zoology. Errol joined me there after a spell as a tea planter in New Guinea. He was very keen to get into the films. I thought it was a stupid ambition. I told him his chances were pretty thin, but he was always a determined boy. He joined the Northampton Repertory Company and managed to wangle a film test with Warner Brothers. I don't know how the devil he did it. He went into that picture, *Captain Blood*, and suddenly he was famous.

We are very proud of our boy. We like watching him on the films. I've seen them all except *Don Juan*. I know that people, comedians and so on, are always making jokes about Errol and his affairs. It doesn't bother me a bit when I hear the cracks, but I think it bothers his mother. Never mind, that is the price of fame. As far as I am concerned he has been a generous and liberal man.

Yes, old Errol's all right. He has paid off all his wives and he has looked after his children. He's straight. It's chaps like Errol who contribute a devil of a lot, in a very serious age, to the fun of the world.'

10 FEBRUARY 1958

Professor Flynn outlived his famous son by nine years. Errol died in Vancouver, Canada on 14 October 1959, age fifty, a victim of riotous living. His father, the quiet Professor Flynn, died in a nursing home in Liss, Hampshire, on 23 October 1968, aged eighty-five. His wife had died exactly a year earlier.

Theodore Thomson Flynn and Errol Flynn

Christopher Fry

CHAPTER 32

CHRISTOPHER FRY – HOLLYWOOD TAKES ON THE BIBLE

"The Bible was once part of the lives of ordinary men and women."

In the years following the Second World War no dramatist writing in English was lauded as widely as Christopher Fry, a fortyish, Bristol-born ex-schoolmaster, who over one single decade wrote a string of plays in free verse, shimmering with undertones of religion and mysticism. They included, notably, A Phoenix Too Frequent *(1946),* The Lady's Not for Burning *(1949),* Venus Observed *(1950) and* The Dark Is Light Enough *(1954), not to mention a number of profitable translations of French plays by Jean Giraudoux and Jean Anouilh. In drab austerity Britain the intelligentsia exulted in the emergence of one of its own, believing wrongly that the West End stage had at last discovered poetry and would never be the same again. During the war Fry served with the Pioneer Corps as an air raid warden in the Blitz, complaining only that he could not fight rooftop fires since he had no head for heights. His friend T. S. Eliot advised him drily, 'You must specialise in basements.' By the time I met Fry his star had faded, and he occupied himself mainly writing movie scripts, especially high-minded biblical epics like* Ben Hur *(for which he received no credit).*

Whichever way you look at it, it must be the most monumental task he has undertaken in his lifetime. To take the Bible from cover to cover and put it on the movie screen is an undertaking so consuming that any man who does it must have a motive bigger than money, bigger than professional ambition. That man is Christopher Fry. Normally he tends to see the cinema as something of a waste of his time. What drives him now to devote, quite possibly, years of his life to re-writing the entire Holy Bible for the silver screen?

Mr Fry and I went to lunch in London yesterday to talk it over. We lunched at a French restaurant in Jermyn Street. At the table on our left sat

Mr Peter Dimmock, sports supremo of BBC Television. On our right sat two jaunty and hungry nuns. It struck me that Mr Fry's position between them was, in its symbolism, nicely balanced between commercial enterprise and the austere world of the literary mystic.

Both these arenas are keeping Mr Fry busy this year. At the Haymarket theatre a young cast is currently rehearsing *Judith*, Mr Fry's translation of a French play by Giraudoux. Mr Fry's own historical play *Curtmantle* is headed for this year's Edinburgh Festival before a London opening in October. In London's West End next month a new cinema will open with *Barabbas*, on which Mr Fry worked as a scriptwriter. It will be the curtain-raiser to Mr Fry's cover-to-cover translation of the Bible, which will be produced, he told me, in three distinct parts, with a proposed accumulated running time of over ten hours. The trilogy would cost a sum of money that is presently unmentionable and uncountable. Produced by Italian Dino de Laurentiis, it would be the king of Biblical films, a colossus dwarfing all previous religious epics in scope and ambition.

Over lunch Mr Fry talked with modesty about his super Bible film. He talked haltingly, shrugging the whole thing off.

> 'The first part will go from the Creation to something possibly around the fall of Jericho. Something like that. The producer doesn't want to produce a spectacular in the Hollywood sense. His whole approach is admirable, I think. If I felt that we were just taking the Bible as a gimmick and making a spectacular out of it I would never have agreed to come into the thing at all. I am sure of that.'

Mr Fry said that it was his plan to engage actors to play multiple parts in the film. 'For instance,' he said, 'I can see one man playing the three parts of Adam and Abraham and Jacob. In that manner you get a feeling of growing, of accumulating.'

Mr Fry acknowledged that his mounting preoccupation with the film was interfering with his serious play-writing work. Why then, I wondered, has he undertaken to script a series of films that will keep him busy for the next three years, perhaps longer?

His reasons are personal and convincing. Mr Fry, a religious man, feels that he may be able to bring the Bible to the attention of millions unaware of its glories and mysteries. I get the feeling that Mr Fry conceives it his duty as a Christian not to neglect this chance.

'I can't help remembering,' Mr Fry said, 'that the Bible was once part of the life of ordinary men and women.'

'The very way they talked came, very often, out of an intimate knowledge of the Bible. That no longer happens. But perhaps, I tell myself, by making it all visual ... by putting it all on to film, one can again make the Bible part of the life of ordinary men and women ... something they are familiar with. That, I believe, would make the job enormously worth doing in our times.'

Before we parted Mr Fry said something to me which illustrates what a rare person he is. We were talking about the fact that, although he has translated many French plays into English, he has been to France only once in his life – on a three-day trip to Paris last year.

'I don't much like travelling,' said Christopher Fry. 'I always get the feeling things are going to come up in my garden, and I'd miss them if I'm away.'

If anyone is going to put the Bible on the screen that's the kind of man to do it.

8 May 1962

It was not to be. Despite the participation of esteemed director John Huston (who also played the role of a heavily bearded Noah), and a bankable cast which included Ava Gardner, Peter O'Toole and George C. Scott, de Laurentiis's The Bible *was roundly derided as a piece of expensive kitsch, a 'portentous creation' proceeding at a 'killingly slow pace'. More surprisingly, one reviewer complained that 'the script has little religious sense'. American critic Rex Reed observed sharply that 'at a time when religion needs all the help it can get, John Huston may have set its cause back a couple of thousand years'. Christopher Fry, a much-loved and modest man, lived on near Chichester into advanced old age. He died on 30 June 2005, aged ninety-seven.*

Judy Garland

CHAPTER 33

JUDY GARLAND – THE COMEBACK KID

"Hollywood doesn't trust me anymore.
Nobody in that town does."

A child film star, she lived her life in the raw heat of public curiosity equalled only, in later years, by Marilyn Monroe. (Both died of drug overdoses, probably accidentally administered.) Garland was born Frances Gumm in Grand Rapids, Minnesota, on 10 June 1922, third of three daughters of a vaudeville family. The daughters toured as a child act called the Gumm Sisters. Judy was signed by MGM in 1935 as she was entering her teen years. Four years later she was universally celebrated as the Kansas farm girl Dorothy in The Wizard of Oz. *She was cast against the advice of studio head Louis B. Mayer, who wanted Shirley Temple for the role. Garland's life after Oz was a giddying tale of triumph and fame vexed by recurring personal problems. She married five times, had three children (including Liza Minnelli and Lorna Luft). She developed a professionally damaging reputation for self-destructive unreliability, but the world loved her and followed her adoringly to the end of her days.*

'People think of me as a neurotic kid full of fits and depressions, biting my fingernails to the bone, living under an eternal shadow of illness and collapse.' Judy Garland laughed her breathless, quicksilver laugh. 'Damn it,' she said, 'why am I so maligned? Why do people insist on seeing an aura of tragedy around me always? My life isn't tragic at all. In fact, it's all rather funny!'

She shoved her hand deep into an open handbag on her lap and came up with a single mentholated cigarette, the only kind she smokes. We were lunching at Les Ambassadeurs, a plush hostelry in Park Lane favoured by American show business aristocracy.

Garland was happy, bubbling with good spirits. We talked of many things, including songs and lyrics. 'Listen to this,' she said. And she began to sing, snapping her heavily ringed fingers to the rhythm of the words:

'My old man is gonna wind up in a garbage can. If there's a bottle of gin there, he'll stay in there. My old man!'

Judy's joyous cackle could be heard ten tables away. 'Lord,' she said, wiping her eyes, 'that's such a funny lyric. It's so rare for a song lyric to actually make one laugh aloud. That one does…'

This was a Judy Garland I had not expected to encounter. Her history of psychiatric treatment, fretful pill-taking and a widely rumoured suicide attempt ten years ago had preceded her. Gossiping about Judy Garland and her personal nightmares had been a Hollywood sport for a long time. Arthur Freed, producer of many Judy Garland movies at MGM, says: 'Talent? The greatest. But it's a hysterical talent.' One of her Hollywood psychiatrists said: 'Split personality? For people like Miss Garland, we need a new word. We need a word that means a personality that's split at least five ways.'

When she was about thirteen, Judy Garland was captured by the Hollywood studio system. Within two years she was a major world star growing up before the eyes of millions. She made thirty-five movies in fifteen years, nine of them with Mickey Rooney, some of them the biggest and most beloved musical hits of our time.

She had been appalled, she told me, by her early appearances on the screen. 'I was frightening,' she says. 'A fat little frightening pig with pigtails.'

When Judy reached her mid-twenties troubles on a larger scale began to assail her. She broke the terms of her studio contract. Betty Hutton replaced her in the star part of *Annie Get Your Gun* after a million dollars-worth of celluloid had already been shot. Garland sometimes showed up for work; sometimes she didn't show at all. Often she arrived late and locked herself into her dressing room, weeping. She earned $5,000 a week, later $150,000 a picture. She saved nothing. Nobody knows where the money went, least of all Judy Garland. Her relationship with her ambitious mother, always fragile, worsened into separation and feud. On 20 June 1950, a Hollywood publicity man found Judy nursing a small gash on her neck covered by a quarter-inch bandage. 'She was hysterical,' he reported, 'but far from lethally wounded.' The news spread that she had tried to take her own life.

Over and over again Garland was considered wiped out, written off. Always she bounced back. Always she fretted herself into a new collapse.

And now here she was, sitting in a Mayfair restaurant, eating a healthy meal and talking with unaccustomed calmness and candour about her multiple tribulations. 'Hollywood,' she said, 'doesn't trust me anymore. Nobody in that town does. I don't care if I live to be eighty, they still won't trust me. They remember that I acted badly twenty years ago, and so they still say "look out for Judy Garland!"'

She lit another mentholated cigarette. She practically chain-smoked them throughout the two-hour meal. 'Let's go back to when I was a kid,' she said.

'My life was a combination of absolute chaos and absolute solitude. I'd be alone with my teacher for ten minutes, reciting my French lessons. Then some assistant director comes along and says: "Come on, kid, you're wanted on the set." Five minutes later I'd be making a scene for *The Wizard of Oz* with hundreds of people staring at me. I knew nothing. I learned nothing. I had no companions. It just wasn't normal. I wrote poetry to express my loneliness. Until I had my own children I had that funny kind of loneliness I can't explain. Still, I could bear it all. Some people are born lonely, I guess.'

'It was only later,' she said, 'when I was forced to starve myself that my real anxieties began.'

'When I was fourteen or fifteen, I literally had to stop eating to get my weight down for my films. I kept it up for fifteen or sixteen years. I starved my appetite. I starved my system. I suffered from malnutrition. I began, for the first time in my life, to suffer from moods of depression. I remember how terribly happy I'd been in the old days in vaudeville. I had never known stage fright. It was such fun to go out and sing and hear that applause. It was only when I got into the movies that I began to have these terrible fears. One day one of the bosses at Metro-Goldwyn-Mayer called me and said, "You look like a hunchback. We love you but you're so fat you look like a monster."'

Garland recalls the impact of those words. 'It did terrible things to me just to hear them ... to be described as some kind of monstrosity. At MGM you had to be terribly slim. I was weighed every morning. If I put on 5 pounds they put me on what they called a crash diet.'

Insomnia set in. She swallowed pills to go to sleep. And pills to wake her up. She was scarcely alive; like a machine, she made movie after movie. *Meet Me In St Louis*, *Girl Crazy*, *Babes on Broadway*…

'But I did not rebel,' Judy told me. 'Rebellion came later.'

'I was a docile girl. I did what they told me. When I finally did rebel it became world news. The papers were full of my troubles. Perhaps if I had rebelled when I was a girl, everything would have been better and different. People think I ought to be bitter now. But I'm not. I think that bitterness or trying to get revenge is absolutely deadly. I know people who are like that, and they suffer terribly. I think MGM were right. I think I was right. I was difficult. MGM were difficult. There's no reason to feel bitter.'

Judy Garland finished her steak and ordered a big slice of Camembert cheese. There was no studio chief to stop her eating now, and she ate her fill.

'I became afraid of so many things,' Garland said. 'I was becoming sicker and sicker, just from being afraid. But I'm better now. No pressures. I'm losing all my anxieties. I don't even mind flying now. I used to be terrified of flying. My weight is coming down slowly because I'm relaxed. That's a strange thing, isn't it? Every time I get stage fright it puts weight on me. If I'm under any kind of stress I just seem to grow and grow.'

Judy's husband, Sid Luft, came into the restaurant to join us. 'Hello, darling,' said Judy. She puckered her lips and blew him a kiss across the table.

'I'll just have a smoked salmon sandwich and a cup of tea, thank you,' Mr Luft told the waiter, in an unconvincing English accent. And again Judy's laugh exploded like a firecracker in the quiet restaurant.

She's chubby and pleasant and delighted to be back in London. Tonight at 8 p.m. she goes on to the stage of the London Palladium to sing thirty-three songs. Nine years ago the Palladium audience gave her a three-minute welcoming ovation. The audience will applaud her again tonight. It is only right that they should. I'm happy to report that today there is no sadness and no tragedy to be detected anywhere in the personality of Judy Garland.

'I laugh a lot these days,' she told me. 'At myself, too. Lord, if I couldn't laugh at myself, I don't think I'd be alive…'

28 AUGUST 1960

Judy Garland died in a rented London flat on 22 June 1969. Cause of death was given by the coroner as 'incautious self-overdose of barbiturates'. There was no evidence of suicide. She had just turned forty-seven.

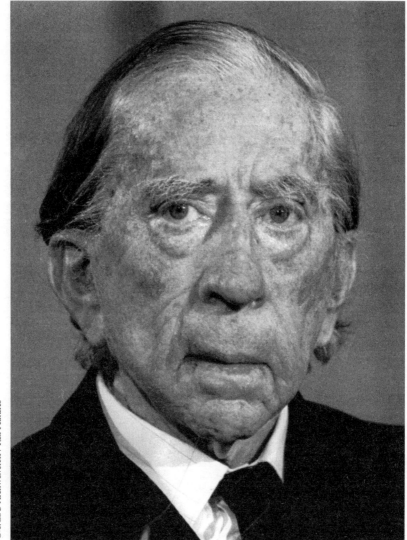

J. Paul Getty

CHAPTER 34

J. PAUL GETTY – MILLIONAIRE MISER

"If you can actually count your money
then you are not a rich man."

It proved unexpectedly easy to arrange a meeting with a man said to be the richest on the planet. It happened this way. One morning, out of the blue, I called the switchboard at the Ritz Hotel in London and asked to be put through to Jean Paul Getty. The next voice I heard was his own. 'Getty here. How can I help you?' After I had explained my business, he said, 'Meet me for tea in the Palm Court downstairs at four.' That was it. No secretaries or personal assistants. Later that day, as I took my leave of him, I expressed wonderment at his readiness to meet an unknown hack from a humble tabloid. He replied, 'Well, you have your job and I have mine.'

He was born on 15 December 1892, parlaying a relatively modest inheritance into one of the great fortunes of the century.

The first thing he said to me was, 'Don't tell anyone where I am living. You must promise me that. They'll all be flooding me with begging letters again…'

Mr Jean Paul Getty spoke in a slow, solemn undertone. We met in a secluded alcove of his London hotel. Sallow and stooped-shouldered, he led me to a settee half hidden in a jungle of potted palms. His manner was that of a family doctor who is about to impart bad news to anxious relatives.

Money, lots of it, is Mr Getty's life and passion. *Fortune* magazine in 1957 named him America's richest citizen. His personal fortune, it is said, equals something in the neighbourhood of £350 million. Some neighbourhood. He owns half of the oil fields in the Middle-East neutral zone between Saudi Arabia and Kuwait. The area, pre-Getty, had been written off as barren, unlikely to produce a worthwhile income. Getty took a gamble and changed all that. He also owns a fleet of supertankers, an airline, a cafeteria chain and the ritzy hotel Pierre in New York.

How much money has Getty got exactly? 'If you can actually count your money,' he told me after a pause, 'then you're not really a rich man.'

Since 1953 Mr Getty has not been able to count his money. He pays £5,000 a day, year in and year out, to King Saud of Saudi Arabia in oil royalties. King Saud of Saudi Arabia enjoys the arrangement. So does Oxford-educated Paul Getty, who told me that he had discussed the deal with the desert monarch in fluent Arabic. Getty also speaks perfect French, German, Spanish, Italian and, of course, English. He is a man who can sound downhearted in six languages.

Getty's mirthlessness may be partially attributed to the fact that he has been married and divorced five times. A brilliant success in international finance, his career as a husband has been an inglorious failure.

Getty explains his dismal marital record:

'After a while a rich man's wife begins to feel useless. At first she enjoys clothes and jewels, but then she begins to feel that it's all a little pointless. She doesn't feel necessary. Servants do all the work for her. Besides, women do not seem to realise that the more money you make, the longer hours you have to work. I work most Saturdays and Sundays. And a woman gets discontented when you cannot spare her a lot of time.'

Mr Getty is a courteous and cultured man who has remained on good terms with all his ex-wives. The most recent Mrs Getty, former showgirl Louise Lynch, described him as 'brilliant, simple and shy'.

Mr Getty is shy about many things. Lifts, for instance. Having been stuck in several, he now distrusts them mightily. 'Especially those alarming French ones.' His voice became even more confidential. 'Some of them look like they haven't been inspected in thirty years.' Mr Getty, despite his sixty-four years, uses the staircase wherever possible.

And aircraft. He owns an airline, but flies reluctantly, and only when the weather is perfect. He would rather travel in an ocean liner, or on one of his own supertankers.

And cars. He dislikes being driven. 'I have some friends I'd just as soon not drive with.'

The richest man on earth also has a reputation for being shy about spending money. When he travels, which is often, he chooses to stay in small, modest hotel suites. He has sometimes complained about the price of breakfasts in Paris hotels. Unlike your average millionaire, Getty does not use the services of a secretary or a personal staff. 'Besides,' he tells me, 'my father always advised me never to discuss money, because you will usually be talking to people who have less than you, and that causes resentment.'

Mr Getty is particularly fretful about the opportunists who assail him with letters (currently running at 3,000 a week) begging for gifts and loans. There is no shortage of grasping hands.

'It does not seem to occur to people who write to me for money that thousands of other people have the same idea. I cannot possibly send money to some unknown person without making the most thorough investigation into their needs. And when you have thousands of letters from dozens of countries in dozens of languages, the mechanics of the thing become quite, quite impossible. Besides, if I helped someone once, the same person may need additional help. It would be an unending process. It does not seem fair to help some worthy cases and to refuse others. And, of course, it is not always those who cry the loudest who are the most needy. Often the most deserving are the very last to ask. They are too proud. In any case, some of their demands are quite startling. Some of them ask me for millions of dollars! Can you believe that? Even governments don't have that sort of money available for distribution. It's all earmarked, you know. The same goes for me, my money is tied up. I am cash-poor...'

Mr Jean Paul Getty looked sadder than ever as he sipped his tea.

24 JUNE 1959

In 1973 Getty's grandson, Paul Getty III, was kidnapped and a ransom of $17 million demanded. When Getty failed to respond, the kidnappers sent a lock of hair and a severed human ear to a London daily newspaper. Getty eventually paid the kidnappers $2.2 million – the maximum that would be tax-deductible. At his death Jean Paul Getty was worth an estimated $1,200 million. Getty died in his English home on 6 June 1976 of heart failure, aged eighty-three. His most quoted remark: 'The meek shall inherit the earth but not its mineral rights.'

Cary Grant

CHAPTER 35

CARY GRANT – LOVE AND MARRIAGE

"When love walks in, most people walk out."

Archibald Alexander Leach (Cary Grant) was born on 18 January 1904 in Bristol, England. His mother suffered for much of her life from severe depression. Cary Grant's unhappy and disrupted childhood was in marked contrast to the impression he gave of unrelenting good cheer. Grant ran away from home when he was thirteen, took various jobs with a travelling sideshow, becoming an accomplished juggler and acrobat. In the late '20s he went to the States to perform with carnival shows, advancing later to stage and movie roles in the early '30s. Paramount Pictures put him under contract in 1932. Grant's career really took off that year when the screen tease Mae West picked him as her leading man in She Done Him Wrong *and* I'm No Angel. *Grant never looked back after that, and by the late '30s enjoyed a global reputation. He had leading roles in* Only Angels Have Wings *and* Gunga Din *(both 1936),* Bringing Up Baby *(1938),* The Philadelphia Story *(1940) and* His Girl Friday *(1940). Some of his best work was seen in Hitchcock thrillers like* Suspicion *(1941),* To Catch A Thief *(1955) and* North By Northwest *(1959). In 1999 he was placed second in the American Film Institute's list of the One Hundred Greatest Film Stars of All Time. Only Bogart beat him to the top spot.*

When I met Cary Grant (by appointment) in a flat in Wigmore Street a few days ago, he said, as we shook hands, 'How do you do? My name is Cary Grant.' An odd thing to say, since I knew very well that he was Cary Grant and, what's more, he knew very well that I knew he was Cary Grant.

Mr Grant was probably reassuring himself that he really was Cary Grant, and nobody else. He once famously said, 'Everybody wants to be Cary Grant – even I want to be Cary Grant.'

He is a complex man, dedicated to the discovery of his inner truths, preoccupied with New Age phraseology and dogma. When speaking, he does not always finish his sentences.

'Let's go somewhere and talk,' he said with that crackling, extrovert geniality that is his trademark.

I proposed Hyde Park. 'Right ho!' he agreed. Minutes later we were heading for the Serpentine in the back seat of his chauffeur-driven Rolls-Bentley.

Cary Grant surveyed London through the car window. And I surveyed Cary Grant. At fifty-six he still seemed indestructibly boyish. Slim-hipped, sports-jacketed, coffee-tanned, practically unlined, Cary Grant in the flesh more than justified the legend of agelessness that clings to his name.

'I find myself returning to this country more and more,' said Grant, who was born when the twentieth century was less than five years old.

'One of the newspapers said this morning that I was going to forsake Hollywood to settle in Britain again. That is not correct. I enjoy the sunshine in California. My friendships are made there. Mind you, I may eventually succumb to the homing instinct, like the salmon. I have no crystal ball. I follow my inclinations.'

A certain confusion now set in as Grant added, 'Everything, you see, is its own opposite. We spend our time getting away from mother, only to return to mother. I try to keep my home inside me, so that I can enjoy it without a specific longing for any one place.'

The chauffeur parked the car and I lit a cigarette. Grant refused one. Not long ago he smoked thirty a day, until hypnotism cured him of the habit.

Cary Grant is like that. Hypnotism, mysticism, yoga, psychological experimentation (he was among the first major figures in Hollywood to try the hallucinatory drug LSD), Eastern philosophy – these have long been the preoccupations of a man whom the world persists in seeing as uncomplicated and easygoing.

Where, I asked him, did he most feel at peace? A long, reflective pause. The chauffeur, faceless and voiceless, stared in front of him.

'I feel most at peace,' said Cary Grant, shifting into hippy mode, 'in the environment of love. Love and peace go hand in hand,' he said.

'A child knows peace in the arms of its mother. But not even the most dedicated mother returns love consistently. There are periods of rejection, you see. And so the child becomes afraid of love and he grows up afraid of love.'

It seemed to me that Grant was talking about himself.

'Eventually you are afraid to give yourself fully to the beautiful blast of love. It
is the most difficult sacrifice in the world. When love walks in, most people
walk out.'

Cary Grant has so far walked out of three marriages – to Virginia Cherrill,
to billionairess Barbara Hutton, to Betsy Drake – because he was unable and
unwilling to give himself over completely to the beautiful blast of love. 'I was
a masochist,' he told me, 'intent on hurting myself. I wouldn't let myself feel
love and because of that I couldn't give it. I fought against happiness. But I
think I have broken the pattern at last…'

It is significant, he says, that all three Mrs Cary Grants have been blondes.
He says that this was hardly accidental. It was a kind of delayed hostility
dating back, in Freudian terms, to infancy. 'Every man's first love is his
mother and every man will always be in love with her. My own mother was
a brunette, so I used to take out and marry blondes.'

Cary Grant claims to have purged this Oedipal complexity from his troubled personality, evidenced by the fact that he is now more frequently seen
in the company of brunettes.

One of the Hyde Park keepers shuffled up to the car. He tapped on the
window.

'Lady asks if she can take yer snap,' said the park-keeper.

'Go ahead,' said Cary Grant.

'Come along then, lady,' said the park-keeper. A pretty blonde came pant-
ing up, juggling an old-fashioned concertina-type camera.

'I don't know how to handle this thing,' she fretted.

'Open the shutter wide and whack away,' said Cary Grant.

'Gentleman says open the shutter wide,' repeated the park-keeper, 'and
whack away.' The blonde took her snap and retreated. Grant returned to his
musings about love and marriage. 'I think if a man finds unity in himself he
can find unity with all people. But especially he must find it with women.'
Grant corrected himself. 'With a woman.'

'Man cannot fulfil himself without a woman. Some men have claimed to do
so. Was the Buddha married? Jesus wasn't … I don't think I was wise enough
to be a father. I have never had the wisdom to impart to a child … I am both
sorry and glad that I haven't had any children.'

Cary Grant now lapsed into a high Himalayan silence. After a while I felt it
was OK to prompt him.

'Sorry because…?'

'Sorry,' he replied, 'because I have very much missed the companionship of children. And glad because I have had no children to whom I can pass on my ignorance. Perhaps if I had had a child, then his very trust would have created a trust in me. Perhaps I ... oh, what's the point in talking about perhaps...?'

The park-keeper returned to the window. 'I laughed when I seen your picture,' he said, clasping his hands behind his back and rocking on his heels like a vicar at a fireside.

'I am glad,' said Cary Grant. 'That was the intent.'

'I seen your picture at the Odeon Leicester Square,' said the park-keeper. 'I laughed when I seen it.' He wandered away.

I lit another cigarette and talked to Cary Grant about his refusal to grow old. It is, he assured me, a conscious denial of the passing years. 'Every man can control what he looks like.' He pointed, with a grin which somehow seemed to be disapproving, at my cigarette. 'The secret is not that I stay particularly young,' he said, 'it is that other people persist in making themselves old. They do it with cigarettes, with liquor, with the wrong food. They poison themselves. My wife taught me to stop smoking, to stop drinking ... Betsy Drake has been a great benefit to my life ... as indeed, I hope I have been to hers. I talked to her only last night in Los Angeles.'

'Yes, we are still married. Am I going back to her? How do you know I haven't already? We are separated and we are living together. We do both. Betsy, you know, was gracious enough to tell me that I was successful as a screen actor because I made it all look so easy. I like to think that is the secret. Like Joe Louis's boxing. It looked so dead easy, didn't it? He cut it down to the essence. Like Hemingway's prose. Like Oscar Hammerstein's lyrics. Like a Picasso sketch. It all looks so simple, so relaxed – all that confidence and command. But it is really the eventual distillation of all experience.'

Dusk was falling. Grant instructed the chauffeur to drive me to my home.

'I am going to Bristol this weekend to see my mother. She is eighty-three now.' Cary Grant thought about this for a moment. 'I am really getting to enjoy my mother's company.'

The ageless boy from Bristol dropped me off at my home, and his car glided away into the evening light.

18 SEPTEMBER 1960

Cary Grant was married two more times after the above interview. His fourth wife was Hollywood actress Diane Cannon, with whom he had a daughter, Jennifer. After retirement he became the public face of the giant perfume company Fabergé. He later toured America with a one-man show called A Conversation with Cary Grant, *in which he responded to audience questions and showed clips from his movies. It was while preparing for one such appearance in the Adler Theatre in Davenport, Iowa, that he suffered a cerebral haemorrhage. He died the same night (29 November 1986) in St Luke's Hospital. Eminent film critic Richard Schickel named Cary Grant 'the best star actor there ever was in the movies'. Doris Day said that he was 'a completely private person, totally reserved, there is no way into him'. Aware that journalists habitually made him seem more articulate and coherent than he was, Cary Grant once observed wittily, 'I improve on misquotation.'*

Charles Hamilton in his middle years

CHAPTER 36

CHARLES HAMILTON – THE MAN WHO INVENTED BILLY BUNTER

"I shall go on writing about boys to the end. A boy can see through humbug quicker than a man."

Charles Hamilton, born in 1876, is estimated to have written 100 million words in his lifetime, the equivalent of 1,200 average novels. He has been recognised in the Guinness Book of Records *as the world's most prolific writer. He wrote almost exclusively for pre-war boys' weekly magazines under a variety of noms-de-plume, spinning out thousands of stories about English schoolboys whose names, particularly that of the grotesque fat boy Billy Bunter, have taken root in modern English mythology. Writing for magazines like* The Gem *and* The Magnet *(both now defunct, victims of wartime paper shortages), Hamilton created dozens of fictional schools and peopled them with an assortment of healthy-minded youngsters who did not smoke or gamble (Hamilton did both). A life-long bachelor, he spoke Latin and Greek, enjoyed a close family relationship with his sister, whose daughter, Una Hamilton Wright, published her own biography of Charles Hamilton in 2006. George Orwell's famous essay, 'Boys' Weeklies', with its central focus on Billy Bunter, is considered one of the more important critical studies of the popular culture of our time.*

Frail and toothless, the man who invented Billy Bunter sat by the fireside of his seaside cottage in Broadstairs, Kent, his small body all but lost somewhere inside the deep folds of his crumpled velvet dressing gown. He wore a black pillbox skullcap and large soft slippers. Physically, there was precious little to him; he was like a thin, pink baby. He sucked at his pipe and told me that he would be eighty-four next birthday, and would I like to hear him sing 'Waltzing Matilda' in Latin? I said I would, and he did. He seemed very pleased.

His real name was Charles Hamilton, but he was more famous as Frank Richards, Owen Conquest, Martin Clifford, Winston Cardew, Hilda Richards and a dozen other aliases. In his prime, at his peak, he sat over an ancient typewriter and tapped out millions of words every year about ageless, good-humoured boys, and very occasionally girls, in English boarding schools. Growing up in a dusty South African town, miles from anywhere, my earliest images of England were derived largely from Charles Hamilton's serial fictions.

Reading magazines like *The Gem* or *The Magnet* in the '30s, I gained the impression that English boarding schools were institutions of unparalleled healthy-mindedness, where upright youngsters whacked cricket balls, ate bumper teas in the glow of cosy firesides and possessed square, honest names like Frank Nugent and Harry Wharton and Bob Cherry. They spoke good conversational English, enlivened by exclamatory cries such as 'oh, my hat!', 'honour bright!' and 'oh, I say!', 'go and eat coke!' 'leave off!' and 'gurgh, yaroo, ooogh, yow-ow-ow', etc.

Foreigners at these schools, whether pupils or teachers, were invariably depicted as comic figures who mangled the language in hilarious ways; they were tolerated but not entirely to be trusted. Exceptions were made in the case of schoolboys who had the good fortune to hail from the British Empire. The Indian boy Hurree Jamset Ram Singh was a decent, well-born English lad with a brown face.

Charles Hamilton's biggest creation, in every sense, was William George Bunter, the contemptible Billy Bunter, a bespectacled mountain of lard, greed and foolishness, a Fat Owl obsessed by cream tarts and tuck-boxes. Bunter has been frequently revived on stage and television screens, his very name a synonym for over-reaching gluttony.

When I met Charles Hamilton in 1958 he was still writing his stories in the same old way on the same old typewriter, now in its twenty-fourth year of service.

Hamilton half-rose from his fireside chair as I was led into his presence. It was a physical effort for the feeble old man. I spent several hours with him in his modest house. Sometimes he appeared to fall asleep. I sat patiently waiting for him to come awake again. The street outside ran down to the sea.

While Miss Edith Hood, his housekeeper for thirty years, fussed around and brought in the afternoon tea, Hamilton talked cheerfully of this and that. He spoke of the modern world, which he did not much like, and his own private world of public schools, which he liked a lot.

'Old Bunter,' he chuckled, 'who'd have thought he'd last so well? Makes me laugh sometimes…' His pipe had gone out but he continued to suck at it. His skin was almost transparent. 'I'm a very old man. I can't have much longer. But it's absurd to worry about death. When death comes it will be like changing trains on a long journey. That's all there is to that.'

After a while he said brightly: 'Look here, I'm thinking of immigrating to Australia!' He sipped his tea, the teacup trembling in his hand. 'After all, I live a quiet, sober and righteous life. Why shouldn't I go on forever? Everything that has happened since 1900 seems like a series of practical jokes, none of them in very good taste. A crisis comes to you every morning with the milk. But life, don't you think, is far too serious to be taken seriously?'

It was all neat, quotable stuff, and the old man knew it. He re-lit his pipe and watched me through the smoke with his pale eyes while I scribbled it all down. Encouraged, he declared, 'Life is a comedy and death is its worst joke.' He seemed glad to have an audience. An open upright piano stood against the wall. Nearly all the books on his shelves were in Latin or Greek.

'I've got a television set upstairs,' he said, 'but I don't watch it much, except for old Bunter, of course. Always watch old Bunter … and Richard Dimbleby.'

He reached for a bell and pressed it twice. 'We'll have some more tea. They say authors become like the characters they write about. I am a little like Bunter. I enjoy puddings and sweets.'

He lapsed into another silence that lasted about two long minutes. It was a late, sunny afternoon. Hamilton said suddenly, 'He's a hearty old fellow, Dimbleby, isn't he?'

Miss Hood came in with fresh tea. When she had gone I asked the old man to tell me more about Billy Bunter. Had he been an invention?

'Oh, no,' said Charles Hamilton. 'Every one of them is real. All the boys. Old Wharton, and Cherry, and Nugent, all of them real, all of them based on real people. All dead now – all dead. One drawback to living forever is that the other people drop off. At my age you outlive everybody. I have to keep going. Everybody thinks I have lots of money but it's not true. I am still writing Billy Bunter stories, you know. There's no sign of him petering out. No, I never married. Not that I remember. But I have always had a family on the typewriter. All those boys at Greyfriars, they really exist for me. When I write about the chaps I am one of them. I shall go on writing about boys until the end. A boy can see through humbug quicker than a man. I think a lot about God and the life to come. I have written a book on religion but nobody wants it. All they want is old Bunter. They won't let me be serious. Nothing ever really changes. And boys least of all… '

Dusk began to descend on Broadstairs. Miss Hood came in to turn on the lights and to add a coal or two to the fire. I left Charles Hamilton, who had lapsed into another long silence, sitting, perhaps dozing, by his hearth. As I rose to leave he reached out suddenly to shake my hand. 'Goodbye,' he said quietly, 'goodbye, my boy, goodbye…'

18 DECEMBER 1958

A year or so later, in November 1961, Charles Hamilton finished his last book and posted it to his publishers. He died a month later, on Christmas Eve.

Tony Hancock

CHAPTER 37

TONY HANCOCK – A DISSATISFIED MAN

"I do not believe in giving the public what they want."

English actor/comedian Anthony John (Tony) Hancock was born in Birmingham, the son of an hotelier, on 12 May 1924. He started out as a teenage stand-up comic, and appeared as a troop entertainer during the Second World War. He was destined for greatness. Indeed, Hancock is seen by many as the greatest of all television performers. He almost invariably played the same character, a down-at-heel comedian with aspirations beyond his class or capabilities, living in shared lodgings with Sid James in 23 Railway Cuttings, East Cheam, a shabby area of outer London. After an apprenticeship in radio, Hancock moved to television in a series, Hancock's Half Hour, *written by Ray Galton and Alan Simpson. The show was an overwhelming success, but Hancock, a chronically dissatisfied man, was already beginning to show early signs of erratic behaviour, born of self-doubt, that would finally steer all that bright early promise into a world of darkness…*

Tony Hancock's dressing-room was thick with cigarette smoke, managers, musicians, the hubbub of show talk. Hancock himself, in the middle of it, didn't hear a word. He has the capacity to shut the windows of his mind and pull the blinds down when it suits him. He stood now, hunched in his dressing-gown, staring ferociously at himself in the mirror, his fingers clenching and flicking, his elbows churning the air like chicken wings, his feet pressing down on the carpet like a man testing a pair of new boots.

This was Hancock loosening up before a show. There is a good deal that needs to be loosened, since Tony Hancock is a contender for the title of the most tense and angst-ridden comic in Britain, out-glooming even Sellers and Milligan.

To understand why Hancock, at the peak of his TV successes, has gone back to stomping round the land in twice-nightly vaudeville is a puzzle without easy answers. On the stage or off it, Tony Hancock embodies bewilderment and indecision.

'I am a fool,' he told me. 'I don't function properly. I have a tape recorder that I can't work and a car that I don't drive. I'm no good with my hands. I'm no good with my feet.'

I sat in the dress circle to watch Hancock's 6:30 show. The house was three-quarters full. For fifty minutes Hancock stood at the mike, joking, singing, dancing and impersonating dated or dead former celebrities like the old English actor George Arliss and Captain Bligh of the Bounty that only middle-aged and elderly customers might recognise or recall. Hancock does not invite applause because he is slick. He requires, instead, that the audience recognises its own ineptitude in his clumsiness. It is a bond that links Hancock with his public. He is a subtler act than you might imagine.

Between shows we sat in his dressing-room and talked, among other things, about feet. Hancock is obsessed with feet. His stage patter is rich in references to shoes and toes and boots. He launched into a familiar rant:

'My feet have been put on all wrong! They don't join the ankle right. At times I can feel 'em flapping like a penguin's flippers. When I cross the lounge of a posh hotel I become so conscious of my feet that they seem to live a separate existence. They just come along with me. Man's shape is ridiculous. That is the mainspring of my humour. Feet are simply a focal point. When I think of bicycle clips I could die with laughter.'

The second house was packed. The Liverpool audience clapped and cheered. They laughed heartily at all the feet jokes.

By midnight we were back in Hancock's hotel room and he was starting to unwind – normally, he told me, a two-hour process. A vodka in his hand, shoeless Hancock listened to soft jazz and talked about the dissatisfactions of his professional life.

'What I'm after on this provincial tour,' he said, 'is to build a new kind of identity in a sort of Las Vegas format – you know, a whole show, girls and singers and all, built around one man.'

'That's the future trend. Music hall began in the pubs. It may well end up in the nightclubs. I'm eliminating a lot of purely British slang and local references. I want an act I can take anywhere in the English-speaking world and have them all understand me.

I can't stand still. If I stand still I go mad … stagnant … dead. What I did with Sid James on TV I had an affection for. But it was a parcel and I've put the parcel away. The world moves on. I have this restlessness inside me that I cannot calm. I want to try new things all the time. If I fail, that's my bad luck.

New things. New paths. I do not believe in giving the public what they want. You must take the people with you. I've never been satisfied with anything I've done for more than thirty-six hours. The trouble with pinnacles is that when you reach one you always see another. That's the story of my life.'

It was after 2 a.m. Hancock rubbed his palms into his panda eyes, yawning. 'I know one thing absolutely,' he said, 'I'm never going to reach a point where I can say: "That's it." No matter how far you go, there is more, there is more, there is always more.'

29 OCTOBER 1962

At the height of his success, Hancock began to resent the public perception that he was no more than half of a double act with Sid James. Eventually, in a bid to prove himself capable of standing on his own, Hancock contrived to get rid of Sid James, his writers and all those who once were part of his support system. This would finally include two unhappy wives: Cicely and Freddie. Hancock became a heavy drinker in the grip of an inconsolable melancholy. He died by his own hand in Sydney, Australia on 24 June 1968, while making a thirteen-part television series called Hancock Down Under. *He was forty-four. A suicide note read, in part, 'things just seem to go too wrong too many times'.*

Noel Harrison

CHAPTER 38

NOEL HARRISON – ESCAPING A FAMOUS FATHER

"Being the son of Rex Harrison destroyed my
confidence in myself."

*Noel Harrison, son of the great Rex, was born on 29 January 1934. He was twice
a member of the British Winter Olympics Ski Team in the '50s. At twenty he
became a professional musician, singing and playing the guitar in restaurants
and smart London clubs. He tried his luck in America where he had a chart hit
with Aznavour's 'A Young Girl'. He later had another disc success with Michel
Legrand's 'Windmills Of Your Mind'. He appeared in the US TV series* The
Girl From U.N.C.L.E., *opposite Stephanie Powers. Harrison toured with the
Beach Boys and appeared on the Johnny Carson TV chat show. He had several
false starts in America. One of them is described in the following article written
in the mid-60s.*

Less than four weeks ago Noel Harrison – son of Rex – was a
relatively obscure entertainer who played the guitar and sang
songs for London's deb set at private parties and small Mayfair clubs.
At thirty-one he was scratching out a living, going nowhere fast. He
hated what he was doing, disliked intensely the debutantes and young
Guards officers who made up the audience – 'the stupidest people in the
world when they are gathered together'.

That situation has changed with barely credible swiftness. Suddenly
Noel Harrison is a man with a new and astonishing faith in himself. He
has received more offers than he can reasonably accommodate. He told me
yesterday: 'I have just lived through the most marvellous month of my life.'

What changed Noel Harrison's life was his just-completed smash engage-
ment at a New York club called The Living Room. New York took to the
unknown Londoner with warmth and affection. The critics adored him. In

the hot glow of American approval Noel Harrison cast off his old timidity and now claims to have grown up overnight as an entertainer and as a person.

Back home yesterday with his wife and four children, agog with plans for his future, Noel Harrison said: 'I don't mind telling you that I had reached the end of my tether in London. If I had failed in New York I guess I would have thrown everything up, admitted I was no damn good, and opened a restaurant or something.'

He arrived in Manhattan determined to make good or quit. Only his wife Sara, who stayed at home with a new baby, shared his knowledge that this was no ordinary club date.

'New York scared me stiff. I flopped there in 1960. This time I got there four days early, walking the streets, riding the subway, getting the pace of the town.'

Harrison opened before a packed crowd of critics and professional show folk, Broadway sophisticates, probably the most jaded audience in the world. 'I did well. It felt good.'

Just how good he didn't know until the next day when he bought the New York morning papers at a street kiosk in Greenwich Village. 'I opened the papers in the middle of Sixth Avenue, my hands trembling something terrible.'

The first headline to hit his eye was the *New York World-Telegram*'s 'Rex Harrison's Son Returns to N.Y. in Triumph!' The enthusiasm was unanimous. The *New York Times* notice read like a love letter: 'Assurance, ease and finesse glowed through everything he did.'

After that everything came up roses for Noel Harrison. He appeared twice on TV, was offered the lead in a new US production of the musical *Irma La Douce*, and has had a new single rushed into release. Night after night the big names in town crowded into The Living Room to hear him. New York loves a winner.

But the real triumph was a psychological one, which began in London six months ago when he decided to stop running away from the crushing fact that he was Rex Harrison's son.

'This affected my mind always, and my work. It destroyed my confidence in myself. I had always thought that people would never take me seriously if they knew Rex Harrison was my father. I desperately wanted an identity that did not include him. Now I don't care. I am Rex Harrison's son, and always will be, and that's that. Why fight it? I shall use all the advantages of my father's name to open doors, to get work, knowing that what finally counts is what I can do as an entertainer. Once I stand up to perform I'm on my own. It doesn't matter whose son you are if you're no good.'

This dramatic revision of his attitude towards himself and his father did not, he says, come easily. 'I took a long look at myself. I opened the lid on myself and removed a lot of snakes I found slithering under the lid. I read a lot of Freud.'

It is fair to add that Noel has always remained on the best of terms with his father. 'We see a lot of each other. We are really very close.'

Noel Harrison returns to New York in six weeks' time for a cluster of personal appearances and TV shows. The money is good. 'A month or so ago, I found it difficult to scratch fifty quid together.'

In his Fulham home yesterday Noel bounced his new baby, Harriet, on his knee. 'It is all beginning to happen at last,' he said, 'and man, it is wild.'

3 MAY 1965

Seven years after this interview Harrison opted for a spartan life, living in a self-built (no electricity) wooden shack in Nova Scotia, Canada. He toured American cities in revivals of Camelot, The Sound of Music *and* My Fair Lady, *in which he reprised his father's iconic role as Professor Henry Higgins. From the late '90s Noel Harrison lived in Devon, England, where he died in October 2013. He married three times and had five children.*

Rex Harrison

CHAPTER 39

REX HARRISON – ESCAPING THE LIGHTNING

"Women aren't what they were."

When he became a professional actor at eighteen, Reginald Carey Harrison (born in Lancashire on 5 March 1908) officially changed his name to Rex. His breakthrough role on the West End stage, in Terence Rattigan's French Without Tears *(1937), established Harrison's unique style (clipped, urbane, throwaway) and reputation. By the late '30s he was an actor much in demand, until the Second World War interrupted his rise. He attained the rank of Flight Lieutenant in the Royal Air Force. Between stage roles he became an accomplished and celebrated film actor, notably starring in* Major Barbara *(1941),* Blithe Spirit *(1941),* Anna and the King of Siam *(1946),* The Ghost and Mrs Muir *(1947),* Cleopatra *(1963) and* The Agony and the Ecstasy *(1965), but he was best known leading the cast in Lerner and Loewe's epochal Broadway musical* My Fair Lady, *a role he repeated with great success in London and on film, opposite Audrey Hepburn.*

A lightning strike has scarred and almost certainly killed a pine tree in Rex Harrison's garden in Bognor Regis. It happened during a night storm two weeks ago. 'My God,' says Rex, who was asleep only 25 yards away from the tree when the lightning struck, 'it went off like a bloody great bomb. The flash, you know, goes right through your eyeballs even if you're asleep. Damned odd, that.'

Sitting in the sunny garden, tieless and sockless, dressed for summer, a glass of iced grapefruit in his hand, murmuring things like 'Damned odd, that,' he squints into the sunlight. He is staying in Bognor while appearing in nearby Chichester in *Monsieur Perrichon's Travels*, a French farce which opened to mixed reviews earlier this week. He says he is unworried by the negative reception the play has received.

'The only way to conduct oneself in this very precarious profession is not to lose your head when you have a triumph, nor to become depressed when you meet failure. And that really applies to the way I try to live my life … One learns nothing from good times. It's only when things turn rotten that one tries to reassess the way life is lived. The extraordinary thing is that some of my biggest successes have come by coincidence, by fluke, by mere chance. It sounds ridiculous, but I only agreed to appear in *My Fair Lady* because I needed to leave London and live in New York for personal reasons I'm not prepared to go into. Lots of chums thought I was out of my mind to do a musical of *Pygmalion*, but I wanted to get away and that clinched it. Just shows you…'

The runaway success of his singing Professor Higgins has been one of the peaks of his lifetime. 'Terribly exciting it was to see that queue of people camping out in sleeping bags outside the theatre, waiting to book tickets. A marvellous time, but it didn't inflate my ego. I just thought I was bloody lucky.'

Rex Harrison is in reflective mode. He expresses his feelings with hesitancy and caution. 'It's so difficult to keep your balance as you live your life … It's not easy to keep one's humour and stay reasonably on top of the game … it's largely a question of luck, anyway.'

Now sixty-eight, he insists that life has not soured him. Still, he admits sadly, you've got to agree that the world is a less nice place than it was. And women aren't what they were.

'I like,' he says 'being with people I like.'

'I'm not a great goer-outer. Never was a great party man. Women have undoubtedly changed, and not for the better. They now want total independence, yet they still want to be taken care of, don't they, in one way or another? The Women's Lib movement is responsible for so much male unhappiness, and female unhappiness.'

He hesitates for a moment.

'Well, maybe one should temper that remark. I think women are in a state of confusion. It's a great generalisation, but women today are not content to be a companion, or a mistress, or a wife to a man. They insist on careers and outside interests – a great pity, I think, for the general happiness of the human race. I don't find that career women are particularly happy. Do you? They are taking on a man's role, responsibilities and pressures which they're not really built to withstand. Soon they'll be dying sooner than we do. Usually men die first!'

This idea seemed to amuse Rex Harrison and he chortled into his glass of grapefruit juice.

The British actors he admires tend, like himself, to be reclusive, private beings. He names Alec Guinness, Ralph Richardson and Paul Scofield.

Like most good actors I have met, Rex Harrison is generous in his admiration of his peers. 'Introverts,' he says, 'make better actors than the eager ones who can't wait to get onto that stage. The quieter, more private actor has to wrench those energies out of himself. Acting is an enforced discipline for me, since I'm not a particularly disciplined person in private life. I always feel better after a performance than I have all day. You've exercised yourself mentally and physically, and hopefully entertained a lot of people.'

Beyond Mr Harrison's garden lies the flat, grey sea of Bognor. The tall pine that suffered the lightning strike still stands, but its days are numbered. Briefly, Rex Harrison considered what might have happened if the lightning had struck 25 yards to the right.

'I'm not ready for that yet. It's been a good life so far, quite an adventurous life. I am very anxious to go on living and see what happens next. I am not ready for the lightning at all. Bugger the lightning.'

5 AUGUST 1976

Rex Harrison was knighted in 1989 and worked steadily until his death from pancreatic cancer in New York on 2 June 1990, aged eighty-two. He married six times; his wives included actresses Lilli Palmer, Kay Kendall and Rachel Roberts. He had two sons: author Carey and singer/actor Noel. Noël Coward called Rex Harrison 'the best light comedy actor in the world, except for me'.

Sonja Henie during a skating routine for the film *It's a Pleasure*

CHAPTER 40

SONJA HENIE – NORWEGIAN ICE

◇◇◇

"You get cold. Your muscles get stiff."

The diminutive figure of Sonja Henie dominated world figure ice skating in the '30s and '40s. At the pinnacle of her success she was one of the highest-paid stars in Hollywood. Born in the Norwegian city of Kristiania (now Oslo) in 1912, she was also a nationally ranked tennis player, swimmer and horsewoman. Fiercely competitive, she toured the world with her ice revues, which, with her endorsement of commercial products and accumulation of art masterpieces, made her one of the wealthiest women in the world. Henie's professional career and vast business interests were managed by her parents, who accompanied her everywhere. Henie carefully cultivated the image of a smiling, fair-haired, spinning figurine. This façade veiled a less attractive woman.

S he came into the hotel room, one of the richest women in the world, switching on her electric dazzle. 'It sure is cold in London,' she complained, her voice a California whine, as caressing as a steel guitar string. 'It sure is always raining.'

Sonja Henie sat down, her doll-like figure (5 feet 2 inches) smartly packaged in a simple black dress. Distributed about her person were chunks of expensive jewellery glinting like campfires seen from afar. On her finger she wore the weightiest single diamond I have seen outside the Tower of London. Envious acquaintances have described this ring as 'the rock pile', but Miss Henie refers to it briefly as 'quite nice'.

She is self-conscious about her riches, is apt to become belligerent, even unpleasant, when questioned about the current state of her bank balance. It is a wide-open secret, however, that she practically owns her own weight (103 pounds) in diamonds, pearls and other baubles. No other sportsman or woman of her era has earned more money than this shrewd Norwegian icicle.

Sonja Henie crossed her still-shapely legs, rested her intertwined fingers on her knees and opened her eyes round as buttons. She was alert, on the defensive.

She's forty-eight now. Soft pouches have started to form under her eyes; time has begun to notch off the years in pencil-thin wrinkles across her elfin features. Yet, even now, she seemed to shimmer beneath her halo of silk-blonde hair. It needed no effort to recall her as the golden girl of the golden years before the war when, like millions of others, I developed an adolescent crush on Henie in her first Hollywood movie *One In A Million*. How, like a dimpled toy, she flashed across the map of memory, her smile and her skates of the same quicksilver sparkle...

Now here she was, a quarter of a century later, in a London hotel on a rainy afternoon, married to her third millionaire, still childless, castigating British curiosity about her immense wealth.

'I don't wanna talk about my money,' she said, emphasising her displeasure with a series of precise nods of her head. 'Everybody in England is sure obsessed with money. They are more money conscious than the Americans or the French. It's all they ever talk about. They call me one of the richest women in the world. It couldn't be more boring.'

Suddenly embarrassed, Henie quietly covered her ring with her right palm.

How much is Sonja Henie actually worth? She pays close to £250,000 a year to the US government in taxes. Her personal fortune is probably approaching, if it has not already surpassed, £4 million.

Much of this fortune has been earned from her touring ice spectacles, a form of entertainment she pioneered. The rest is made up via the ownership of properties in New York, Los Angeles and Florida. She owns homes in Oslo, Manhattan and Hollywood, a big ranch in southern California, a cluster of skyscrapers in Chicago and a chain of sports stadiums. She also dabbles in lucrative sidelines: autographed skates, dolls, skating outfits, ice-making machines and other merchandise, which account for something like an income of £200,000 a year.

Her business cunning has persuaded her to invest large amounts of money, probably more than a million, in jewellery and paintings. Her private collection of 160 paintings, including Renoirs, Picassos, Gainsboroughs and Van Goghs, will soon depart on a grand tour of European galleries, including London's Tate. It occurred to me to enquire whether admission to her travelling art show would be free to the art-loving public. Henie responded to this heresy with a smile that had no joy in it. 'There will be a charge,' she said.

I recalled that her reputation for thrift was practically unsurpassed among show business folk. Though she has spent lavishly on her ice shows (£100,000 for costumes for a new revue), her personal economies have provided gossip material for years. Seven years ago a member of her travelling troupe went on record with the following sulk: 'In the nearly two years the present company has toured with her she has only given one party for the cast. It lasted half an hour, most of which Sonja spent in her palatial upstairs drawing room, with white calfskin upholstery, where she drank champagne with personal friends.'

She employs more than fifty people to supervise the investment operations of Sonja Henie Inc., of which her brother Leif is vice-president and chief treasurer.

To discover the origins of this tough-minded devotion to wealth and success it is necessary to look back to the Norway of 1918 when Sonja, then six years old, acquired her first pair of skates as a Christmas present. Her first target was simple, but significant: she wanted to skate better than Leif.

Leif pulled Sonja's plaited hair, and mocked her. Within a year she was a far better skater than Leif would ever be, and the pattern of her life was already set in an iron mould. She practised like a demon, threw tantrums in all directions and won the Olympic title three times running. No one will ever equal her amateur record. Inside that diminutive body was a clockwork machine which drove her forward relentlessly from trophy to trophy, triumph to triumph. Her enthusiasm and self-confidence on skates ('A great wave of happiness seems to come over me every time I glide out on the ice,' she told me) was counterbalanced by an awkward, stubborn off-stage personality. She was always deep in business dealings and court litigation.

Her first marriage to millionaire Dan Topping fell apart after six strained years. Her second marriage, to socialite Winthrop Gardiner, was even shorter lived. Gardiner later complained that Sonja had 'refused to live up to her wifely duties'. In their four years of marriage, good-looking Gardiner alleged he'd only spent a fortnight alone with Sonja.

Now the woman they call 'The Iron Butterfly of Broadway' is married for the third time to sixty-year-old Neils Onstad, a Norwegian shipping magnate with silver hair and soft blue eyes. This marriage looks like it is turning out to be a success. For the Henie machine is beginning to slow down. She confessed a yearning for rest and peace at last.

Are the days gone when she toured the world in a whirl of luxury and superhuman egotism? Are the years gone when Sonja's souvenir show programmes featured her own photograph no fewer than twenty-eight times, cutting everybody else in the cast down to a few insignificant pages?

'No,' she told me, 'I'm always planning my next show. Next year I may tour again. I may even bring a show to England.'

She spoke brightly about her latest film, an almost plotless enterprise called *Hello London*, to be released here later this month.

But even Sonja Henie could no longer disguise a certain tiredness in her voice and manner as we talked into the dusk. 'People have so many misconceptions about me,' she said, her voice suddenly flat and toneless.

> 'They call me shrewd, rich, clever. The truth is I'd rather talk about art than skating now. I am really a quiet person. I want what other women want. I'm beginning to grow tired. The arenas are cold … Your time is never your own. You get cold. Your muscles get stiff … No, I don't regret not having had any children. My life has been so completely different. Travelling around with children … well, it would have been impossible.'

Sonja Henie forced a hard bright laugh. 'You can't have everything …' said the most durable ice fairy of them all. 'All I've ever really had is the joy of skating…'

There may be other Sonja Henie films to come, new Sonja Henie ice shows. But I won't forget her last words to me: 'No, I don't want to live it all again. I've had it…'

24 JULY 1960

Sonja Henie's off-stage life appears to have been something of a mess. According to a biography written by her brother Leif, she was obsessed with money and sex, reacting with fury when contradicted and mercilessly ambitious. Worse yet, it seems that she scarcely bothered to disguise her Nazi sympathies, greeting Hitler with a Nazi salute even before the 1936 Olympics. For this action she was heavily criticised by the Norwegian press. Hitler personally invited her to lunch at Berchtesgarten, presenting the fawning Norwegian star with a fulsomely inscribed portrait of himself, which was proudly displayed in the Henie family home.

Henie exploited her close ties with the Nazi leadership, persuading propaganda minister Josef Goebbels to facilitate the German release of Henie's first US movie One In A Million. *Henie significantly neglected to support the Norwegian Resistance Movement, although (no doubt for commercial reasons) she supported the US war effort after Japan's attack on Pearl Harbor in December 1941. After the war many in her homeland did not forgive her wartime sympathies, though Norwegian audiences welcomed her travelling* Holiday on Ice *show in 1953 and 1955.*

Henie drank heavily, contracted leukaemia and died of the disease, aged fifty-seven, during a flight from Paris to Oslo.

Valerie Hobson with her husband John Profumo

CHAPTER 41

VALERIE HOBSON – THE STEADFAST WIFE

✧✧✧✧✧✧✧✧✧✧✧✧✧✧✧✧✧✧✧✧✧✧✧✧✧✧✧✧✧✧

"I believe there can only be one master in the house."

When, in 1958, I described my meeting with the English star actress Valerie Hobson, I wrote the following words about her politician husband: 'Today he is Secretary of State for War, tomorrow – who knows?' Nobody would have guessed then that tomorrow would bring disgrace, lasting notoriety and eventually a kind of renewed respect for a life honourably lived and a marriage steadfastly maintained unto death. Valerie Hobson was undoubtedly a star, but never quite starry enough, always on the edge of universal fame but somehow lacking, as an actress, the human touch that might have based her reputation more securely. Her two most famous screen roles showed off a certain unbending priggishness – as the aloof Edith D'Ascoyne in the best of all Ealing comedies, Kind Hearts and Coronets *(1949), and as the somewhat self-satisfied Estella in David Lean's* Great Expectations *(1946). Valerie Hobson was born on 14 April 1917, daughter of a naval captain in Larne, Northern Ireland. From the start, she said, she had an unquenchable 'hankering for the stage'. Elegant and beautiful, she appeared in some decently made British films like Alexander Korda's* The Drum *(1938), and* The Rocking Horse Winner *(1949), based on a D. H. Lawrence story. In 1939 she married distinguished filmmaker Anthony Havelock-Allan, with whom she had two sons. The marriage was dissolved thirteen years later. She had a further son by her second and final husband, politician John Profumo. The name of Profumo would always carry overtones of the scandal that engulfed him and almost brought down the Tory government when the extent and nature of Profumo's affair with Christine Keeler was uncovered. Profumo famously resigned and devoted his life thereafter to charitable works. His wife remained loyal, supporting him in the social work for which he was awarded a CBE in 1975, a belated act of national forgiveness. But all this, of course, still lay ahead of Valerie Hobson Profumo when I met her for the first and only time in February 1961. What follows is an account of that meeting.*

★

On a spring night in 1955, an excited London audience filled the Theatre Royal, Drury Lane to applaud the last public appearance of Valerie Hobson. 'Shall we dance?' she sang as the King of Siam stepped into her cool, amused embrace to thump about the famous stage in Richard Rodgers's catchy waltz. It was a tearful occasion. Valerie Hobson had been on the British stage and in films for some twenty years – an experienced entertainer who had run the showbiz gamut from chorus girl to West End star of *The King and I*. Now she was leaving the stage forever, abandoning the bright lights to dedicate her energies to the role of wife to the rising parliamentarian John Profumo, whom she married late in 1954. This was, indeed, the last dance.

'I never did finish the run of the show,' she recalled. 'It made me very sad. I was having a baby, you see. Such a strenuous role. Herbert Lom and I covered four miles every performance, did you know that? After that dance, I collapsed. I had had enough. It was time to stop.'

She talked in crisp, short sentences, delivered at shorthand speed. Quick, bright and alert, she can talk briskly on a range of topics. 'My life,' she said, 'is extremely full. Extremely satisfying. That's not a sales line. It's true.'

She sat, her long legs curled up beneath her on a wide settee in the drawing room of her Nash-designed villa in Regent's Park. It is probably the most spacious drawing room in London. Valerie Hobson looked as if she belonged there. Was born to it. Her husband is flourishing at Westminster. Today he is Secretary of State for War. Tomorrow – who knows? His wife has kept pace all the way. Valerie Hobson, housewife, hostess and social asset, is clearly a successful production destined for a long run.

She lit a filtered-tip Gauloise. '*The King and I*,' she said, 'was the happiest show I've ever been in. Largely, I think, because it had so many children. I've always loved children. They like me, and I'm relaxed with people who like me. Children do, and animals don't. I suppose that's because basically I'm afraid of animals and they know it.'

At forty-two Valerie Hobson retains the luminous beauty of her star days. Improbably, what drove her to a life on the stage was a childhood revolt against what she perceived as her own ugliness.

'I was a very plain, wishy-washy child. Large, wistful eyes, a real gumdrop. Awful. My sister was exquisite while I was a pasty-faced mouse. Everybody called me "Monkey". I felt it all most terribly. I wanted to be a glamorous princess, and I decided long ago to be a ballet dancer. I was quick. I moved well. I clung to that. It never occurred to me that I wouldn't be a success. Never. Then I got scarlet fever. Funny, hardly anyone seems to get it any more. When I finally got out of bed I was wafer-thin. My bones wouldn't stand up to dancing and I was too tall.

If a child can break her heart, mine broke then. Well, if I couldn't dance, at least I would act. I would learn, I told myself. I must, I must ... I left school at fourteen. I haunted agents' offices. I was a chorus girl, understudy, stage manager, any old thing. The longer you take to get there, I think, the longer you stay and the more satisfying it is while you're there. Nowadays it's all too quick. You're a shop assistant one day, a guitar star the next. Everything is condensed today. We are becoming a *Reader's Digest* nation. Everything is the abridged version, the condensed lesson, the quick, easy way. That's why I'm very strict with my own children. They must read. They're seldom allowed to watch television more than once a week. There is no short way of learning for yourself.'

The door opened and the Profumos' son, David, aged five, popped in, calm and well mannered. He showed his mother a seashell he had painted. 'That's an ashtray for you,' he explained. His mother thanked him and looked at the clock.

'You've got three minutes before you go to beddy-byes,' she said. 'You can have two biscuits and then beetle off.'

The boy gobbled the biscuits. 'That's enough,' said his mother. 'You'll blow up with a bang.'

'Bang!' shouted David. Valerie Hobson kissed him on the head. 'I'll come up and hear your prayers,' she promised. Young David shook my hand solemnly and retired.

Mrs Profumo poured a couple of drinks and sat down again. 'I shall never go back to the stage,' she said.

'There was no conflict between marriage and career. No decision to make. The decision made itself. I believe there can only be one master in the house. If you're going to be happy, physically, and in every way, the man must be dominant. I shall miss the stage emotionally. I deeply loved show business and all the people I worked with. I chose it as a child. But that's over. That's finished. I adore going around with my husband. We've just come back from the Far East. We do a lot of entertaining, both here and at the House of Commons. No, I don't make political speeches. There are many things political wives can do without making speeches.'

She smiled, puffing on her cigarette. 'One learns,' she said, 'to change one's life ... but not oneself.' And Drury Lane seemed a million miles away.

12 FEBRUARY 1961

Valerie Hobson died of a heart attack in London in 1998, aged eighty-one. John Profumo died at the Chelsea and Westminster Hospital, London, on 9 March 2006 following a severe stroke. He was ninety-one years old.

Víctor Jara

CHAPTER 42

JOAN JARA – UNFINISHED SONG

"Silence and screams are the end of my song."

Víctor Jara was literally beaten to a pulp to stop him singing. His name lives on as the embodiment of all that is decent and aspirational in the human spirit. Born into rural poverty in Chile on 28 September 1932, Jara nevertheless secured a proper education and became a distinguished theatre director. With the accession to the presidency of socialist Salvador Allende in 1970, Jara entered more fully into the disciplines of folk song as a proper way to bring hope and pride to his people. He sang songs about the common man and his simple dreams. For this treason he would pay with his life. In London his English wife Joan keeps the flame burning.

Víctor Jara – a dark, happy Chilean, famous in his own country as a theatrical producer and folk singer – was killed two weeks before his thirty-fifth birthday. He was tortured. His hands broken. He was machine-gunned to death.

The circumstances of his terrible end and the passion of his songs have combined to transform Víctor Jara into a growing international legend. He was seen as a new Che Guevara who carried a guitar instead of a gun.

In modern Chile, ruled by a right-wing military junta, it is forbidden to mention Jara's name. Yet everywhere in that distant strip of mountainous land, his music is played in secret. In Europe, too, with each passing year, the myth of Jara grows. Turin recently hosted the first international festival devoted to Jara's songs. A biographical book of Jara songs, published in London, surprised everyone by practically selling out its first printing in under a year. And in a quiet, white-walled mews house in north London, the English wife of the murdered singer lives with her two dark-eyed daughters and the memory of their father's cruel death.

Joan Jara is a self-effacing ex-ballet dancer who went to Chile twenty years ago and joined that country's national ballet. There she met and married Víctor Jara.

'For the rest of my life,' she told me, 'I shall go on where Víctor left off. That has become the keystone of my life.'

The son of a Chilean ploughman, Víctor Jara was stirred from early youth by the injustices of Chile's social and political structure. When Salvador Allende led Chile's new Left-wing government to political power in 1970, Jara quit the theatre to dedicate himself to writing and singing songs in the cause of social change. His credo was simple. 'Whether they are songs of love, of accusation, of laughter, or of struggle, my songs are rooted in the reality of my people, the peasants and the workers of Chile.'

In mines, schools and factories Jara's resonant, unaggressive voice reflected the mood of the new Chile.

On 11 September 1973 Allende was murdered in the right-wing coup led by General Pinochet. Víctor Jara and thousands of others were arrested and herded into the giant sports stadium in Santiago, the Estadio Chile. During the few days of his imprisonment there, Jara continued to sing and play his guitar for the other prisoners, until the guards shattered the bones of his wrists and hands with their rifle butts. 'Play for us now,' they mocked him in his agony.

A few days later grief-stunned Joan Jara identified her husband's bullet-riddled, half-naked corpse in the city's makeshift morgue.

Now, four years later, facing me across a bare table in a room hung with posters of Jara tribute concerts in Italy, Australia and Japan, Joan talked to me of her life. She appears regularly at such rallies and has trained herself to cope with the burgeoning industry of Jara songs, memorial albums and books. It is not a role she chose, or feels equipped to play. She hates public speaking, and still feels intimidated and inept in front of an audience.

'I was just an ordinary little girl, born in Highbury,' she said.

'My father was a rather eccentric antiques dealer who never actually sold anything. We never had any money. I was the last of six children. It was not a happy childhood. I was very shy. I didn't know how to talk to people. When I discovered that I could dance, well, it was nice, because I could say things without talking. I never identified with classical ballet. For me, dancing had to have some meaning, something to say.

   Víctor was twenty-two when I met him in Chile. It wasn't a sudden or an overnight thing. But I gradually became aware of him. Once I displaced three spinal discs and was in traction for months. I thought I would never dance again. Víctor came to see me all the time. He was cheerful and patient and refused to allow me to lose faith in myself as a dancer.'

The Jara children, Manuela, sixteen, and Amanda, twelve, go to the Camden School for Girls.

'They are very proud of Víctor,' says Joan.

'They love him. After he was killed, after I saw his body there in the mortuary, full of machine-gun wounds, with his hand hanging from his wrist, I was too hurt to feel things properly. Now, nearly four years later, I find I can talk to the girls about their father with humour. Víctor was a warm, funny person. As a father he had a deep belief in the power of example. The years have been very hard, but we've turned a corner somehow … we look to the future. They killed Víctor because of his music. But they could not silence his voice because it contains the voices of all those who were tortured and murdered with him. When people have seen closely, as I have, what Fascism really means, it is something that changes your whole life. Víctor's songs are sung around the world, and I know in my heart that the girls and I will return to Chile … one day.'

6 JUNE 1977

True to her word, Joan Jara has spent the rest of her life fostering the memory and example of her legendary husband. She has written a book about him called The Unfinished Song. *She has spoken at hundreds of rallies and commemorative concerts, calling for the pursuit, identification and punishment of the Chilean military who tortured and machine-gunned Víctor Jara, firing thirty-four bullets into his dead body as a final insult to the man they hated.*

Since Chile's return to democracy, the name of the Estadio Chile, the stadium where Víctor was murdered, has been changed to the Estadio Víctor Jara. His last, unfinished song, written on a scrap of paper in the changing room of the Stadium before he was called out to die, and smuggled out of the prison in the shoe of a fellow rebel, ends with the line 'Silence and screams are the end of my song…' Joan Jara has always said, 'They could kill Víctor Jara but they couldn't kill his songs.'

Ingo

CHAPTER 43

INGEMAR JOHANSSON – BIG SWEDE

"When it hit a man ... boom!"

Born 22 September, 1932 in Gothenburg, Sweden, Ingemar Johansson, when I met him, was the heavyweight boxing champion of the world. He won the title by defeating Floyd Patterson.

I had breakfast at the Savoy with Ingemar ('call me Ingo') Johansson, the smug Swedish prizefighter who was reigning heavyweight champion of the world. His face was huge, pretty and pampered, free of bruises and other disfigurements. He was not a widely popular figure. The charges levelled against him were that he was sullen, avaricious and not a load of laughs.

'The man who beats Johansson,' wrote a US sportswriter, 'will not only be world champion, he will be mighty popular, too.'

'Nobody understand me,' Johansson complained. 'Sure I say my sister can beat Brian London [a British heavyweight] but that is not conceit, only truth. These press guys make me some kind of monster.'

He advanced his thumb towards my nose. 'Maybe you tell the truth about Johansson. Most those guys never even meet me.'

Ingo ordered bacon and eggs, washed down with scalding gulps of tea. His blue Scandinavian eyes watched me closely. He has a way of scrutinising you for reactions to what he is saying. 'You meet Johansson. You write down like I say.'

He did not smile. His conversation drifted around, then found a focus in his enormous right fist. Soon he is talking about his fist as if it did not belong to him. This was the fist that had won him the title and made him famous. He regarded his fist with a kind of awe.

'No man can stand up to it. When it hit a man ... boom! It is hard to find words. It is something I call mystic. Sometime I feel it is not me what moves the arm ... It move itself, faster than my brain can tell it. When it happen, I feel good right down my arm. You can believe me. I am good.'

Johansson talked in stumbling, murmured phrases. 'I learn English at home in Gothenburg from movies. I see four, five American movies a week. School bore me, my teachers do not like me, I never done my lessons.'

He did not read much, not even to keep up with press coverage of his professional career. He relied on helpers and hangers-on to tell him what the sportswriters were saying.

He had rebuffed a Hollywood offer to make a movie of his life.

'Some guy write I turn down the movie because I think I can get more money later, but is not true. I turn it down because I am twenty-seven and my life is not finished.

The hardest thing about being champion is keeping the money. I see guys all over America who have only one interest – stealing the money from fighters. I look after my own money. In America boxing is a rough game and there is lots of people I hate, many guys looking to make trouble.

I don't feel sorry for anybody in the ring. When I fight Joe Erskine I hurt him bad. His eyes close up. In the thirteenth round he is bleeding everywhere. But I don't feel sorry for him. What for?'

One of the Savoy waiters brought over a breakfast menu to be autographed. Ingo obliged. 'Is good to be recognised. I like it.'

Some of the more puritan Fleet Street hacks had feigned surprise because Johansson had checked into the Savoy with his girlfriend Birgit Lundgren. 'People lift the eyebrow,' Ingo said, 'because I take Birgit with me everywhere. But in Sweden, you know, is okay. Nobody lift the eyebrow.' He looked at me in an interested kind of way. 'Do you lift the eyebrow?'

'Not me,' I said, fast.

Ingo leaned back in his fragile chair, which creaked beneath his bulk. 'I look calm but I fight to win. I know I am good but I always respect the other guy. Maybe he get in a lucky punch and then is *me* that goes boom!'

As we were leaving the Savoy Grill Room the Hollywood movie actor Henry Fonda was eating his breakfast at a nearby table. 'Hi, champ,' Fonda called out.

The heavyweight champion of the world smiled for the first time that day. 19 June 1960

★

In retirement, Ingo became a marathon runner, participating in international events. Johansson and rival heavyweight Floyd Patterson became good friends and visited each other every year. They remained close until Alzheimer's felled them both. Ingo married and divorced twice, and is survived by five children. Birgit, his second wife, was with Ingo when he died on 30 January 2009.

The Red Dean

CHAPTER 44

HEWLETT JOHNSON – THE RED DEAN

"History will decide who was right.
The future shall be my judge."

The Church of England has produced many controversial figures in its time, but few have proved more infuriating than the Communist fellow traveller Dr Hewlett Johnson, who was the Dean of Canterbury from 1929 to 1963. Known universally as the Red Dean, Hewlett Johnson hero-worshipped and defended Stalin's Russia until his death, turning a blind eye to the gulags, famines and persecutions of the Communist hegemony. He visited Russia several times, met all its leaders, but never saw anything that might shake his faith in a universal Marxist future. He showed superior gifts as an orator, and spoke twice at Madison Square Garden in praise of Stalin. MI5 had him under surveillance for thirty-five years and banned him from addressing British troops during the Second World War. The Archbishop of Canterbury, nominally his superior in the Church of England hierarchy, called him 'blind, unreasonable and stupid'. Hewlett Johnson, son of a wire manufacturer, was born on 25 January 1874, married twice (each time for about thirty years), became a father at sixty-six, and survived all attempts to remove him from his high position in the Church.

The old man offered me a small brown cheroot. 'I love the smell of good Havana tobacco about the place,' he said.

He sank into a scuffed leather armchair, spread his sturdy black-gaitered legs in front of a bubbling oil stove and nibbled on a bread-and-butter sandwich. We were talking about his life. 'It is true, perhaps,' he said, 'that I have sometimes been unwise in my expressions ... that I have been carried away by my tongue. I am not, mark you, sorry for anything I have actually done. But looking back over my life, I now regret some of the things I have said. I have shown my temper too easily. Ideally, one should show one's anger only to God.'

It wasn't, I grant you, much of a confession after a lifetime of overheated controversy. But penitence on any level is not normally a distinguishing mark of the fanatic. And so, even this small regret was a considerable allowance coming from the normally intractable Dr Hewlett Johnson, Dean of Canterbury.

The man who has been called 'a stain and a blot on the Church of England' was eighty-six years old last week. By way of celebrating his birthday he announced that he had absolutely no intention of retiring just yet, thus confounding the prayers of his innumerable enemies who have long hoped that the old man in his dotage might be put out to pasture and silenced forever.

'Look here,' he told me in a confident tone, 'did you know that only the Crown can sack me, on the advice of the Prime Minister? I don't imagine they plan to do anything like that!'

He spoke with the matter-of-factness of a man sure of his position. 'Anyway,' he added, 'I have always lived on the brink, you know … always.'

He fingered an ornate crucifix (made in Russia) dangling from a silver chain against his chest. 'Many's the time I thought I was going to get the push,' he said. 'But here I am still.'

He turned his head towards me, smiling. As he did so, his soft, silver hair, circling his otherwise bald head, took on the appearance of a halo.

Getting hot under the collar about Dr Hewlett Johnson has been a British pastime for more than half a century. Over the long, bloody decades since the Russian Revolution, this tall, unlikely Englishman has consistently defended Communism, praised Stalin, and condemned the stupidity of the West for failing to appreciate the wonders that Moscow offered the world. Dr Hewlett Johnson sees himself as a man placed on earth to spread the Gospel according to Marx and Lenin. He is convinced that God has meant him for this work. What's more, he has found no difficulty in combining a blind faith in Communism with an equally profound belief in Christianity.

'I well know that I am vilified,' he told me.

'I know what the average man thinks of me. I have been shockingly attacked and distorted in the Press. Never mind. History will decide who was right. The future shall be my judge. My published sermons on Christianity and Communism were sold out in seven hours in Moscow … The Chinese just leapt at it … Canterbury has never flourished as it does today.'

Communism, he allowed, has had its faults. But its glories, he insists, far outweigh its tragedies. 'Look for the positive benefits,' he says.

'The Russian invasion of Hungary in 1956 was a blunder. A blot. But there have been dark and tragic blots in the lives of most good things. Stalin made mistakes, but let us not forget we reaped the benefit. Let us not forget that at

Stalingrad the Russians tore the guts out of the German war machine. Even Churchill admitted that. You really should not judge Communism by our own churchgoing habits and our hymn-singing. Communism is doing something. It is following Christ's standards. I was hungry. I was naked. I was starving. What are we doing about that?'

He would love to reach the great British public more directly through television. But the TV companies are reluctant to let the Dean loose on the air. Somewhat plaintively, the Dean grumbled about this.

'Most people who are frightened of me change their minds when they see me and meet me. But the BBC will never let me on, you know, unless I'm in the Cathedral during a service. I do wish the television companies would approach me, though. I'd let them okay my manuscript before I went on the air. I wouldn't spring anything on them. Why, I wouldn't even mention the word Communism. I would simply talk about my travels around the world. But I doubt whether I shall be asked.'

It was growing dark now in Canterbury. Outside the wide uncurtained windows of the Deanery, the ancient cathedral rose up like a mountain of rust-coloured rock.

Down here, next to the oil fire, the Dean knelt down nimbly on the carpet to stroke his Persian cat, Glyn. 'Good old Glyn. He never bites us,' cooed the Dean.

I had heard that he owed his longevity and liveliness to a Rumanian rejuvenation process called H3.

'Yes,' he agreed. 'Quite true. I've never felt healthier.'

'About a year ago I had arthritis in my shoulders and I began to get bad head colds. But ever since I started H3, the arthritis and the colds have gone altogether. Marvellous stuff, H3. Comes in a little phial which you inject. My wife's taking it, too. It means I can go on, you see. There is still so much to do. For instance, I am beginning again to think about these psychic and spirit worlds. Fascinating. I shall make explorations in this field. Perhaps that is my next task, to interpret the psychic link. Meanwhile, there is still the task of explaining Communism to England.'

31 JANUARY 1960

Dr Hewlett Johnson died on 22 October 1966, aged ninety-two.

Boris Karloff

CHAPTER 45

BORIS KARLOFF – A VERY ENGLISH MONSTER

"Horror is a stupid word … a wrong word."

The name of Boris Karloff still suggests the macabre. It is not an English- sounding name. It is a name designed, it would seem, to strike terror. The man who bore it, however, was a gentle soul who wouldn't harm a butterfly. He was born in Peckham, England on 23 November 1887, into a family of distinguished Foreign Office diplomats. His paternal grandmother was the sister of Anna Leonowens, a lady whose life as a governess in the Royal Court of Siam provided the source of the musical The King and I. *Karloff's maternal grandmother was of Indian origin. Karloff was considered the failure of the family because he chose to be an actor. As a young man he went to Hollywood, where he appeared in small roles in dozens of silent films. Between movie jobs he drove trucks and dug ditches. His role as Frankenstein's monster made him a global star. His name and fame appear to be imperishable in the story of modern popular culture.*

Boris Karloff, sunk deep in an easy chair, a well-used pipe in his mouth, was checking the cricket Test scores in the *Daily Telegraph*. Behind his tortoiseshell spectacles his face seemed almost unnaturally tanned, practically coffee-coloured. His hair was abundant and glossy and dramatically white. A silver stubble glittered on his upper lip.

He told me that his real name was William Henry Pratt, acknowledging without hesitation that it 'was not a good name for an actor'. He was the youngest of eight sons. 'I never knew my father; he died when I was a baby. He had been an official with the civil service in India. I was brought up by my brothers, really.'

Karloff wanted to talk about cricket. I wanted him to speak about Frankenstein's monster, daddy of all screen monsters, right down to the steel bolt in his neck. Karloff graciously allowed himself to be diverted. He was soft-spoken, fond of gardens, very English.

Karloff said:

'I played Frankenstein's monster three times in Hollywood films. Then I refused to play him anymore. He had exhausted his possibilities; he was going downhill, becoming a clown. That monster is my best friend. Until I played him I had been an unknown, unsuccessful actor for twenty years. My fan letters from young people invariably expressed compassion for the monster. I played him as a poor, helpless, inarticulate thing, a victim. Young people understand that. The *Frankenstein* films are called horror films, but horror is a stupid word … a wrong word, with a connotation of revulsion. Shock is a good word. The folklore of all nations is full of it; it's a deep-rooted human thing. There's nothing more shocking than *Mother Goose*. Talk about cruel and savage. A Frog He Would A-Wooing Go. By golly, a cat kills a mouse and a rat, and a frog is eaten by a duck, and whatnot. As for Grimms' fairy tales, well, for heaven's sake! Children enjoy shock films. It's all pretence and they know it. It gives them relief and release. Most people enjoy thinking there's something behind the door when there isn't.'

Karloff was a remote family name on his mother's side. 'I did not think Pratt a terribly good stage name. The name Karloff has been a very fortunate name for me, a very lucky name.'

Then he began talking about cricket, telling me that he always tried to plan his acting year so that he could be in England during all the international test matches. He was one of the British colony of expatriate actors who introduced cricket to Hollywood in 1920.

'It was old Aubrey Smith who really got the game going over there,' said Karloff. 'Basil Rathbone played sometimes. So did Clive Brook. Ronald Colman did not play but we used to knock him over for a subscription. The game will never take on in America. It's quite foreign to their temperament.'

Karloff had recently turned seventy; he seemed to think it was quite an age. 'Fun is fun,' he said, 'but you don't want to get to the point where you become a nuisance to yourself and everyone else. Our vices are our virtues run to seed, they say. That can also be true of living too long.'

30 JUNE 1958

Boris Karloff went on living for eleven more years. He married six times and fathered one child, a daughter by his fifth wife. Though Karloff only made three Frankenstein *movies, the monster he created soon became a catchphrase and an industry, living on in comic books, paperbacks, TV series and comic Hollywood spin-offs. Karloff made other films, sometimes playing exotic foreigners. He lived out his last years in the Hampshire village of Bramshott. After a long battle with emphysema and pneumonia he died in the Edward VII Hospital in Midhurst, Surrey, on 2 February 1969. He was eighty-one.*

Gene Kelly on the movie poster for *An American in Paris*

CHAPTER 46

GENE KELLY – WAITING FOR
THE KIDS TO COME HOME

"Even when I started my career in Hollywood,
I was already over-age and past my prime at thirty-four."

*Eugene Curran (Gene) Kelly was born in Pittsburgh on 23 August 1912. He revealed
an early interest in dance, unusual in Catholic-Irish society, and often was forced into
fistfights in order to prove his manliness. He pushed himself hard as a dancing pupil
and got his first break in a Cole Porter Broadway revue called* Leave It to Me *(1938).
A year later Kelly choreographed Billy Rose's* Diamond Horseshoe *and particularly
noticed a member of the cast, Betsy Blair, whom he would marry two years later. The
role that brought Kelly lasting fame was as the eponymous nightclub singer* Pal Joey
*(1940), in which his character was described as a 'half-pint imitation' in Lorenz
Hart's lyric of* Bewitched, Bothered and Bewildered. *As a result of his success in* Pal
Joey, *Gene Kelly was called to Hollywood and never looked back, enjoying a long
and adventurous career as a dancer-choreographer-actor-director. In these capacities
his shows include a string of MGM super musicals, notably* On the Town *(1949),*
American in Paris *(1951) and* Singin' in the Rain *(1952). Kelly directed the Barbra
Streisand film* Hello, Dolly! *(1969). The film fared only moderately at the box office.*

G ene Kelly sits in the sunny living room of the Beverly Hills farmhouse
that has been his home for thirty years. He is sixty-four years old, a
stocky, sensible man who knows that his dancing days are over. He does not
resent the disappearance of the physical agility that made him, next to Fred
Astaire, the best-known male dancer of our time.

'Every dancer knows in his heart that the older you become the worse you
get,' he tells me in that light, husky, familiar voice.

'I have recognised throughout my career that the day would surely dawn
when I wouldn't be able to jump six feet into the air. I have known other

dancers who refused to face that fact, and who were psychologically very hurt when the collapse of their capacities stared them in the face. In London the other day a crowd of young dancers from the Royal Ballet came to see me. It was a very nice thing to be treated as an eminence grise … as an elder states-man of the dance. Little by little my physical powers have waned. As a movie actor I'm just too old to get the girl. But intellectually I'm better equipped now to handle these things.'

Nobody in the business would write him off as a has-been. As a director and non-dancing actor his career remains in healthy shape. He has just finished shooting *Viva Knievel*, in which he co-stars with the daredevil motorcyclist Evel Knievel. Now Kelly is about to play the role of Oscar Hammerstein II in a two-hour TV tribute to ace songwriter Richard Rodgers.

'In the Knievel picture,' said Gene Kelly, 'I play a middle-aged ex-motor-cycle jumper who's out of it now and has taken to drink.'

He spoke warmly of his high-risk co-star. 'Knievel,' Kelly said, 'is a marvellous guy – someone I don't quite understand, a folk hero to American youth today, just like Charles Lindbergh and baseball star Babe Ruth used to be in my own youth.'

'As a family man myself I've asked myself why a man like Evel takes such enor-mous risks, but I find no answers. He's completely unafraid and all broken up, you know. I have seen him in various stages of undress. His body is a mass of scars, like a bullfighter. What I do understand about Knievel is the compulsion to test yourself … to see just how much further and faster you can go than you went last time. I never knew a good dancer who didn't try to make his body do a little more each time out. There's a streak of masochism in all dancers and athletes. We push ourselves to the limit. We hurt ourselves continually. Those who won't do it wind up having very short careers.'

Outside the open back doors of his living room the sun shone hard on the still surface of the inevitable Hollywood pool. Gene Kelly has lived in this cosy, rambling house in North Rodeo Drive since he came to Los Angeles – 'twenty pounds overweight and strong as an ox' – in 1946.

The Kelly home, once an isolated farmhouse, has long ago been swallowed by the creeping suburbia of Beverly Hills. In all that time Kelly has never moved, and must be the only Hollywood star who has never changed his telephone number.

From time to time Kelly glanced out of the back door. He was waiting, he said, for his two children – Tim, fourteen, and Bridget, twelve – to come home from school. Since the death of his dancer wife Jeanne Coyne four years ago, of leukaemia, Gene Kelly's two young children have become the centre of his life. He also has a married daughter, Kerry, by his first wife Betsy Blair. Kerry lives in London and works as a child psychologist.

'I was always a late starter,' said Gene Kelly.

'Even when I started my career in Hollywood I was already over-age and past my prime at thirty-four. My first boy was born when I was fifty. I try never to be away from my children for more than a few days at a time. I won't have them going through the trauma of an absentee father. I am not taking any bows for this. On the contrary, I love it. Having young children keeps me playing ball in the backyard.'

'The public,' he said, 'don't know me at all.'

'My life is a quest for privacy, but I know I can never have it except in the quiet seclusion of this home. Luckily, as a male actor in Hollywood, I can go on working a while yet. Women don't fare so well out here. As soon as their wrinkles begin to show they tend to get pushed aside.

I am a happy man. My life is a little rounder, a little easier, a little less tense. Both my kids are very bright and can go into many different things. And it's nice to be able to have a beer without bothering about how much weight I put on. Dancers who are worth their salt should be overjoyed that they've had a good life in the world of dance. We are brighter than most people give us credit for...'

From the backyard came a sudden clamour of barking from the Kelly dogs: Bambi, a Scotch Collie, and Ginger, one of a new breed out here called a Cockapoo, a mixture of Cocker Spaniel and Poodle.

The voices of children sounded brisk and bright in the quiet afternoon. 'There's a bunch of my hoodlums out there now,' said Gene Kelly.

He got up to greet the children he loves. Later that evening, he would attend a parents' meeting at their school.

'At the school,' he said, 'nobody says "there goes Gene Kelly, famous dancer". There I'm just another parent. It's all taken for granted. I like it that way. I might just as well be an insurance salesman.'

13 OCTOBER 1976

Gene Kelly died in his sleep in his Rodeo Drive house on 2 February 1996, following a stroke. He was cremated on the same day, having left instructions that there was to be no funeral or services of any kind. He had long before abandoned his Roman Catholic faith as too supportive of fascist regimes (e.g. General Franco's Spain). He was a man of progressive political opinions and supported the Irish Republican Army.

Sean Kenny

CHAPTER 47

SEAN KENNY – REBEL WITH A CAUSE

"My battle is with the whole bloody claptrap of gilt clichés.
This is the reason I'm in the theatre."

Sean Kenny was a stocky Irish maverick with a Hamlet haircut who set out to change the world. Six months before I met him he was a relatively unknown stage designer with paint on his fingers. Overnight, it seemed, his stage sets decorated no fewer than five West End productions including the new musical hit Oliver!. *His designs were brave and daring, challenging all conventions. Kenny was a breath of fresh air, a new voice in the theatre. Our meeting took place in a Piccadilly pub.*

You would look in vain into his pale-green eyes for any reflection of this sudden, dizzying success. Sean Kenny is gratified to have a widening audience, but otherwise remains wholly unaffected by acclaim. He wholeheartedly detests the chi-chi of West End theatre, utterly rejects the cocktail party chumminess of its established stars and producers. He possesses but one second-hand suit ('It was given to me by someone') and practically lives in a pair of baggy trousers and a rumpled black sweater.

Kenny, at twenty-nine, is a missionary. He wants to see the theatre torn down brick by brick and rebuilt as a human adventure.

'It is not enough to build good sets,' he says in a soft Dublin brogue.

'The hell with that. We've got to get rid of the whole idea of the theatre as it is now. We must kill that damn great stage and with it the idea of an audience sitting in one room and the actors performing in another. That's what it is, really. The audience look through a knot-hole at a kind of dream lullaby world being enacted in an old-fashioned Victorian birdcage we call a stage.'

Kenny sips at his refilled glass. 'The physical shape of the theatre is the enemy … This plaster frame with its curlicues, its cupids, its angels with flutes, its darkness, its chocolate boxes and its tea cups. My battle is against the whole bloody claptrap of gilt clichés. This is the reason I am in the theatre.' The barman interrupts our conversation, wipes his nose on his sleeve and bellows, 'Time gentlemen, please.' Mr Kenny and I, expelled by the barbarian curfew, cross Piccadilly in the March sunshine to subside on the green grass of St James's Park.

In the hard light of early afternoon Mr Kenny looks even paler and blonder than before. Like a leprechaun on the point of becoming invisible. He lights a cigarette and tugs at the grass. He's restless and eager. A man in search of a private vision. The quest has taken him to some faraway places.

He grew up in Dublin, one of nine children of a builder. He always wanted to be an architect. He worshipped at the shrine of Frank Lloyd Wright, the white-maned American genius of modern architecture. Eight years ago Kenny climbed aboard a 30 ft shrimping boat with two friends, and in this frail craft crossed the Atlantic on a pilgrimage to meet his idol.

Sean Kenny joined Frank Lloyd Wright's community of students in Wisconsin and Arizona. 'It was magic,' he recalls.

'The most significant, elevated time of my life. We worked together, lived together. It was like joining a monastery. But our religion was architecture. There was no conventional authority. Wright didn't care if we got drunk every night, or broke windows, or jumped up and down, or shouted in the street. The only thing he asked was that you loved architecture. We learned that building had to do with people, with their lives, their cries, their joys. And when it was all over, well, dammit, I couldn't just return to Dublin and start working in an office.

I heard about a disused gold mine called the Lost Dutchman, south of Phoenix, Arizona, in the Superstition Mountains. So I began prospecting for gold. That's how I found this village of Apache Indians. I lived with them for seven months, in shacks made of clapboard and Coca Cola signs. I urged the Apaches to build with stone. They told me they were not allowed explosives. Well, I managed to get some dynamite with my prospector's licence. I blasted a mountainside for them. They began building with stone for the first time in their lives. Marvellous, dignified people, those Apaches. The only other people who came near them for dignity are the fishermen of western Ireland. Big, white-bearded men I remember as a child … men who stood higher than the cliffs…'

The ever-restless Kenny trekked west to Hollywood in 1953, dodged the American draft by signing on as a sailor on a 200ft schooner bound for the south seas on a natural history undersea expedition.

All the time Kenny's interest was with people – 'what they wanted to say, how they wanted to live'. He got to know the Polynesians as he had got to know the Apaches and, before them, the giant seafarers of Arran.

But the long honeymoon was ending. 'It was time I came back to Dublin to rebuild Ireland,' Kenny said with a self-mocking smile.

Disillusionment came fast. The Irish refused to entertain off-beat designs. They wanted safe, sure houses, like everyone else. Kenny refused to compromise. And he starved.

Only one client commissioned a house from him. Kenny moved to the actual building site, lived in a little shack, hired the masons and carpenters himself. Eventually he built the only house he is proud to have designed.

'It's on the river Foyle,' he told me, 'in Londonderry, just across from Donegal. People who came to look at it either smiled or sneered. The house belonged to where it stood,' says Kenny – and this is his architectural credo – 'it belonged to the man it was built for. It was right for the land. It grew out of the land. So I guess it will be all right for all time.'

While the house was being built, a beautiful blonde Irish girl named Jan would come to observe Kenny's progress. 'She was the only one who didn't sneer,' Kenny recalls fondly. 'I married her.'

Otherwise, Ireland for Sean Kenny was a failure. Disgusted by the short-sightedness of his compatriots, he went to Canada with his bride, took a soul-destroying job as an architect's assistant working on the new Queen Elizabeth Hotel in Montreal. 'It was sheer prostitution. But prostitution with good pay.'

Eventually, for the first time in his life, Kenny came to England. He worked on the mass production of houses for Harlow New Town. ('Horrible, sterile, rabbit warrens, street after street of them, plonked straight down on green fields. Nothing belonged at all, not even the people when eventually they came to live there.')

Next came a short sterile flirtation as a designer with BBC Television.

'My first job was to design a background for a gal who sang a song about love. Then I had to arrange three chairs for a discussion about life. Everything became strange and unreal, everything became reduced to something 18 inches by 2 feet. No matter how big you thought, it always came out small. It was like looking at the sky through a pinprick in a blind. All you can really see is the pinprick.'

So Sean Kenny turned, at last, to the theatre. And found glory.

Today this stocky Irish rebel lives quietly in a pseudo-Georgian house in Holland Park, avoiding crowds. ('I hate crowds … I never know when they are suddenly going to try selling me toothpaste, or soap powder, or war.') Kenny is the father of three boys: Maclear, who is five; Shane, one year younger; and Mark, six months old.

For the time being, Sean Kenny has come to rest. He has seen a lot, and learned a lot. He is ready for the world. But is the world ready for Sean Kenny?

19 MARCH 1960

Sean Kenny later married model Judy Huxtable who left him to marry Peter Cook. Kenny lived with actress Judy Geeson until his sudden death on 11 June 1973 from a heart attack and brain haemorrhage at the age of forty-three. Kenny's dream of buildings that would stand like 'steel fingers in the sky, rooted deep in deserts' precisely foreshadowed the construction of oil-rich mega-cities like Dubai in the United Arab Emirates half a century later.

Sean Kenny

Osbert Lancaster

CHAPTER 48

OSBERT LANCASTER –
FLEET STREET'S LAST CELEBRITY

"We tend to romanticise the age just beyond
the reach of our own memories."

When I worked for the Daily Express *in Fleet Street in the '60s and '70s, I had
the good luck to occupy a desk adjoining that of the great cartoonist Osbert
Lancaster. Thus I saw him practically every day. He was always friendly to me,
as he was to everybody. From his waste-paper basket I once retrieved about half
a dozen of his unfinished, rejected cartoons. I took them home and framed them.
Osbert was the most colourful and exotic figure on the paper, and I consider it an
honour to have shared the time of day with him.*

*Sir Osbert Lancaster CBE was born on 4 August 1908, raised in upper-
middle-class Notting Hill. His father, a businessman, was killed at the Battle
of the Somme in 1916. Osbert read English at Oxford and planned a legal
career but, after failing his bar exams, he entered instead the Slade School of
Art. As a young man he joined his Oxford chum John Betjeman on the staff
of the* Architectural Review. *Together they derided contemporary building
design, reserving particular scorn for featureless office blocks and pretentious
suburban dwellings (Osbert invented the phrase 'stockbroker Tudor'). At the
same time Osbert revealed superior gifts as an illustrator, stage designer and
author. He wrote many books, usually about architecture, always illustrated
by himself. In 1939 he published his first 'pocket cartoon', a single-column
drawing with a topical twist, for the* Daily Express. *All in all, he would
draw some 10,000 front-page cartoons over the next forty years, gently satiris-
ing the English upper crust, typically represented by the fictional figures Lord
(Willy) and Lady (Maudie) Littlehampton.*

At first glance, the celebrated pocket cartoonist of the *Daily Express* might
strike one as an Edwardian dandy, a clubbable toff, an extravagantly

moustachioed old fogey yearning for the more genteel England of his long-cherished youth.

There may be a hint of truth in these allegations, but the real truth about Osbert Lancaster – the last genuine celebrity in Fleet Street – defies simple definition. His celebrated nostalgia, for example, is a myth that crumbles at first touch.

'In point of fact,' he told me, 'many of the more publicised survivors of the Edwardian era I personally remember may fairly be described as rude, intolerant and insensitive.'

He regards the Victorian era, since he did not experience it, with a more forgiving eye. 'By and large,' he said, 'people always tend to romanticise the age just beyond the reach of their own memories.'

Osbert Lancaster has large blue eyes which tend to become suddenly very round and unblinking at the moment when he translates a private realisation into the actual currency of language. Thus, round-eyed, he disposed of nostalgia by saying:

> 'One may think occasionally how enjoyable it might have been to be alive in the eighteenth century, but then one considers what it must have been like to have all your teeth pulled out without an anaesthetic. Nostalgia may be emotionally conditioned, but never intellectually endorsed.'

Mr Lancaster has two homes – a Victorian Italianate pile at Henley-on-Thames, with 3 acres of garden, and what he calls a 'characterless little modern flat' in Chelsea, which he acquired when he realised how much time was wasted making the daily trek from Henley to Fleet Street.

He said: 'When one has passed beyond the age of fifty, one can no longer afford to waste three hours of every day just moving oneself from one place to another.'

Osbert Lancaster's daily cartoons, featuring upper-crust creatures like Willy and Maudie Littlehampton, have etched themselves into the mythology of our times. The cartoons are always drawn late on the day before publication.

Osbert Lancaster generally arrives at the black glass *Daily Express* building in Fleet Street at about 4 p.m. and goes directly to his desk in the general features department, a noisy and exposed part of the office where he sits, puffing Turkish cigarettes, surrounded by telephones, typewriters and the general hubbub of a newspaper giving birth to itself.

Not for Osbert Lancaster the quiet calm of a private office. He wants to be in the thick of it day after day, exchanging small talk and political gossip with journalists, secretaries and tea-girls. 'My mind works better in this kind of atmosphere. Sitting in some remote office upstairs, I would only cut myself off from some casual source of inspiration that might blow up during the afternoon.'

Most of his drawings depict the same small cast of characters talking to each other, but Osbert Lancaster refuses to prepare a batch of ready-made cartoons to which only topical captions need be added as required.

So, day-by-day, Maudie Littlehampton and others of the Lancastrian issue are drawn afresh. The characters change with the years as Lancaster himself has changed. Maudie is no longer the unlined beauty she was. The years have left their mark on that perky, bony face. Maudie remains, however, as acute and politically literate as ever. About Maudie Littlehampton, Osbert Lancaster declines to be specific. Many ladies have claimed, with a thrill of self-recognition, to be the prototype. Osbert Lancaster is too polite to rebut these claimants entirely. He tells them that Maudie is a 'composite' of several ladies of his acquaintance; they go away satisfied.

Osbert Lancaster, of course, is more than a cartoonist, and Maudie remains his most direct spokesman. 'That is why,' he explains, 'though she is a figure of upper-class fun, Maudie must never be made too silly. One wants to keep her as a mouthpiece for what one hopes are worthwhile observations on the times we live in.'

Mr Lancaster's own wife (first wife was Karen Elizabeth Harris) is quite unlike Maudie. She takes no interest in politics whatsoever, he says, and 'doesn't really notice' what is going on in London's parliamentary and social milieu.

An expert on architecture and Mediterranean cultures, a first-rate designer for the theatre and opera stage, Osbert Lancaster with his imperturbable manner, his extravagant moustache ('it was a compensation for something or other, but don't ask me what'), remains, uniquely, an outstanding Englishman of our day.

4 MAY 1964

Osbert Lancaster was married twice, fathered a son and a daughter. His second wife was the Fleet Street journalist Anne Scott-James. Knighted in 1975, Sir Osbert died in Chelsea of natural causes on 27 July 1986. His obituaries remembered him fondly as 'witty and civilised ... with a profound understanding of the vagaries of human nature'.

Alan Jay Lerner

CHAPTER 49

ALAN JAY LERNER –
LYRICIST SUPREME

"Even when we recorded the original cast album two weeks after the opening night, I did not believe that *My Fair Lady* had any hits in it."

Alan Jay Lerner was born on 31 August 1918 in New York City, and married eight times. One of his wives reportedly said, 'Marriage is Alan's way of saying goodbye.' He was educated at Bedales, England, and Choate, Connecticut, where he was a classmate of John F. Kennedy. He was blinded in his left eye during a boxing match at Harvard. In the mid-40s he teamed up with Viennese-born composer Frederick (Fritz) Loewe. Their first hit was Brigadoon *(1947), a Scottish fantasy. Bigger things were to follow.*

Tea at Claridge's with Alan Jay Lerner, who wrote the lyrics for *My Fair Lady*, *Gigi* and *Paint Your Wagon. My Fair Lady* would have been enough to secure his immortality. It is a musical without a flaw. It has a glory about it, like *Oklahoma!*, but not many others.

Lerner was a small, dapper, nervous man who wore spectacles and bit his fingernails, though not while I was with him.

'I find nowadays that I need about three weeks to finish the lyrics of a song. The older you get the slower you become. Simple songs take longest. "Wouldn't It Be Loverly?" took six weeks. The success of *My Fair Lady* was a surprise. Even two weeks after the opening night I did not believe the show had any hits in it.'

In his later years Lerner lived in London. Married to his eighth and last wife, a slim English singer-actress named Liz Robertson, Lerner seemed content and his fingernails were allowed to grow.

One night at about 1 a.m., after day-long rehearsals for the musical *Les Misérables*, I was sitting with Trevor Nunn in a restaurant in Covent Garden. We were working on Eponine's big song 'On My Own', an important moment in the show. I had been chipping away at the lyric for months, with little usable result. The problems were largely technical, having to do with certain cadences in French popular music which had no ready equivalents in the English language.

Our table was a mess of abandoned lyrics and empty coffee cups. Alan Jay Lerner and his wife Liz stopped on their way out. Lerner eyed the detritus of songwriting activity. 'Isn't it true,' I asked the great man, 'that there's always one lyric in every show that's an absolute bugger to finish?'

Lerner raised both hands, snapped open all ten fingers. Then he held up two fingers only. 'Twelve,' he said. There were no easy songs for him.

Cameron Mackintosh had invited Lerner to provide the lyrics for the British production of *Les Misérables*. Lerner felt unable to write about 'these kinds of people', i.e. beggars and revolutionaries and so on. So the job was offered to me instead.

28 April 1958

Lerner was considering writing the lyrics for Andrew Lloyd Webber's Phantom of the Opera *when he began to suffer memory loss, the beginnings of a brain tumour. He died in New York of lung cancer on 14 June 1986, aged sixty-seven.*

My Fair Lady composer Frederick Loewe and lyricist Alan Jay Lerner

Frank Loesser

CHAPTER 50

FRANK LOESSER –
THE MAN
WHO WROTE *GUYS AND DOLLS*

"Ulcers are for people who are afraid."

Frank Loesser (pronounced Lesser) was one of the rare handful of total songwriters who created both the words and the music for their musical shows, a list that includes in Loesser's own case such distinguished titles as Where's Charley?, How To Succeed In Business Without Really Trying, Hans Christian Andersen, *and his masterwork,* Guys and Dolls. *He was born in New York on 29 June 1910 into a cultured German-Jewish family. His father was a classical piano teacher who despised show-tunes. By his early twenties Loesser was playing piano in a New York nightclub where he met (and later married) singer Lynn Garland (an unpopular lady, it would seem, who was famously described by a Hollywood wag as 'the evil of the two Loessers'). With new bride Lynn at his side, Loesser moved to Hollywood in 1936 to write music for the movies, e.g. 'Two Sleepy People' and Marlene Dietrich's 'See What The Boys In The Back Room Will Have'. After the war Loesser moved back to Manhattan and began writing the hits that would make him one of Broadway's most distinguished names. He divorced Lynn after twenty-one years of marriage (and two daughters) to wed another singer, Jo Sullivan, who had played the lead in his semi-operatic musical* The Most Happy Fella. *Frank Loesser was known for his quick wit and irascible nature. It is said that he once impulsively punched a leading lady in the jaw because she wasn't singing his lyrics properly. He quickly apologised.*

A nervous genius named Frank Loesser ('I get songs in my head like other people get colds') flew into London yesterday. Mr Loesser, who, unusually, writes both words and music for all his songs and shows, is a short, dark, alert, lemur-eyed New Yorker of fifty-two with permanent disenchantment etched upon his face and an unfailing capacity to turn out the sort of songs that seem to grow old without ever losing the bloom of youth.

Lighting up cigarettes in a chain of puffs and sparks, Loesser told me in a voice as gritty as gravel, 'I've written maybe two thousand songs and one thousand of them have been published.' Among them are such winners as 'Baby It's Cold Outside', 'Two Sleepy People', 'Spring Will Be A Little Late This Year' and 'On a Slow Boat to China'. Songs pour out of Loesser like water out of a fireman's hose. The impact of such compulsive creativity upon his physical capacities is enormous. He can sleep only four hours at a stretch.

> 'I sleep twice a day, sometimes three times. I'm affable for an hour or two, then irritable for a stretch. I'm glad to see friends, then I treat 'em like they're poison. My friends put up with me. If I'm not up at six in the morning I scold myself all day. But I've never had an ulcer in my life. Ulcers are for people who are afraid. I am constantly dissatisfied, but never harassed. I consider myself inept and inadequate, but never oppressed. Ulcers are an employee's disease.'

Loesser writes songs anywhere and everywhere – in buses, taxis, trains.

> 'I invent songs in my mind's ear, if there is such a phrase. I hear my songs, while I write them, beautifully and perfectly accompanied by a hundred-piece string orchestra. They never sound so good in a theatre. I idealise my songs while I compose them, in the same way as you idealise a beautiful girl. When you're in love you see girls in Technicolor. I sing my songs to myself before I send them out into the world. To myself I sound like Caruso…'

He lit another cigarette ('I smoke maybe seventy a day, never smoke 'em all, always leave 'em long') and explained his creative process. 'My mind is always working; the motor is always idling. If a rhyme occurs to me, or a title, it sticks to me like glue. My mind is triggered to receive such things. I'm on that wavelength. That is my purpose.'

I asked him what song he would have liked to have written.

'"Chopsticks",' said Mr Loesser. '"Chopsticks." No matter what you do to it, no matter what variation you thrust upon it, it always remains "Chopsticks". It is a brilliant, primitive musical invention. It will never be lost. "Chopsticks" will never die.'

11 DECEMBER 1962

Frank Loesser's last musical, Pleasures and Palaces *(1965), folded during its out-of-town tryout. He died in New York City of lung cancer in 1969, at the age of fifty-nine.*

Anita Loos

CHAPTER 51

ANITA LOOS –
GENTLEMEN PREFER BLONDES

"I think the kept girl has disappeared from modern society."

Although a single book made her rich and famous, Anita Loos (born on 26 April 1888) was always more than a one-trick pony. Her career as one of Hollywood's most enduring screenwriters spanned the glory years of the movie industry, beginning when she wrote captions for D. W. Griffith's silent epic Intolerance *(1916) and the subtitles for a series of movies which established Douglas Fairbanks Sr as a star. In partnership with writer-director John Emerson (whom she would marry in 1929), Anita Loos was prolific and untiring. Her marriage to Emerson was unhappy. He was neurotic, manipulative and spent time in psychiatric hospitals. Yet she could never quite shake him off and remained married to him until his death in 1956. Her celebrated novel* Gentlemen Prefer Blondes *was based, it is said, on American writer H. L. Mencken's infatuation for a dumb blonde. Excerpt: 'Kissing your hand may make you feel very, very good, but a diamond and sapphire bracelet lasts forever.' This line later inspired the famous song title 'Diamonds Are a Girl's Best Friend' (1949) and the de Beers sales slogan 'A Diamond Is Forever' (1948).*

A diminutive Californian woman named Anita Loos was the first person who ever said that 'Gentlemen prefer blondes'. That simple three-word phrase is now in the *Oxford Dictionary of Quotations*, and Miss Loos is in the black, having lived comfortably on the proceeds of that observation for more than forty years.

Miss Loos – I was mildly surprised to discover that she is a brunette – and I drank tomato juice in Park Lane soon after her arrival in town from Paris yesterday. She is now nearing a trim and lively seventy, but with her small, volatile face framed in all manner of bangs and bobs she still managed to conjure up the era of flappers, racoon coats and the Jazz Age.

Miss Loos wrote *Gentlemen Prefer Blondes* as a series of *Harper's Bazaar* sketches in the mid-20s. They concerned a blonde, gold-digging native of Little Rock, Arkansas, named Lorelei Lee. Lorelei's amorous adventures have over the years been turned into a movie, a musical and a best-selling novel in thirteen languages. Next month Miss Dora Bryan comes to the Prince's Theatre in London in a British version of the Broadway musical based on the book.

'Lorelei,' says Anita Loos, 'just can't be killed – thank heaven.'

It would be a mistake to think of little Miss Loos (4 feet 11 inches, 6 stone 8 pounds) as an ageing flapper who still dreams of a world of shrill trumpets and bootleg gin.

'During the '20s,' she says, 'I was merely an onlooker. Always on the sidelines, never a participant. I was married to a man who was a chronic invalid. You didn't find me charging all over the place doing the Charleston. I have no particular nostalgia for the '20s. On the contrary, it seems to me to have been a very silly period.'

Still actively writing plays and scripts, Miss Loos starts her working day at the infamous hour of 4 a.m.

> 'I do it for the quiet. Come ten o'clock and the phone starts ringing and I can't work in all that excitement. My father, who was a writer too, always started to work at midnight. I can remember, as a child, getting ready for school and seeing the light still burning in my father's room.'

Anita Loos sees the world today as no longer capable of producing flappers. 'Flappers,' she says, 'were created by the prosperity of the times.'

> 'Back then, you had a lot of men with a lot of time and money. All the Loreleis I know today – pretty girls, photographers' models, and such – are working very hard. Many of them in fact are supporting their husbands. I think the kept girl has practically disappeared from modern society.'

Childless herself, and widowed, she told me that she has found enchanting compensation in her patronage of a three-year-old coloured girl who lives with her, travels everywhere with her, and who last week, in a Paris fashion salon, sat on the lap of designer Balenciaga, who was clearly entranced by the dark-skinned little moppet, who is already something of a Manhattan celebrity, and answers to the name of Miss Moore.

Says Anita Loos:

'Miss Moore is one of seven Harlem children whose apartment building burned down. I looked after the child while her home was rebuilt. Later, when I told her mother I couldn't bear to part with her, she replied, "Miss Loos, I've got six more at home and they're all drivin' me crazy. You just keep her!" I've had Miss Moore with me ever since. By the way, she can't pronounce the L of my surname, so she calls me Misuse.'

Misuse sipped her tomato juice and laughed a warm laugh of pleasure.

Her affection for coloured people is no affectation. When Governor Orville Faubus denied black schoolchildren access to the schools of Little Rock in 1958, Anita Loos cut loose with a withering letter to Faubus in which she observed: 'I chose Little Rock as the birthplace of my ignoramus heroine of *Gentlemen Prefer Blondes* because I wanted her to come from the lowest possible stratum of intelligence…'

It is doubtful whether Governor Faubus ever replied.

30 JULY 1962

Following John Emerson's death in 1956, Anita Loos remained socially active, a tireless participant at Manhattan smart set gatherings. 'Diamonds Are A Girl's Best Friend' was played at her memorial service in New York by the song's composer, Jule Styne. Anita Loos died on 18 August 1981, aged ninety-three.

Shirley MacLaine

CHAPTER 52

SHIRLEY MACLAINE – A HARD-WORKING WOMAN

"Black Power. Flower Power. Nothing really worked."

She was born Shirley MacLean Beaty on 24 April 1934 in Richmond, Virginia, daughter of a psychology professor and a drama teacher. She began ballet lessons in order to strengthen her weak ankles but soon grew too tall to continue as a dancer. She was an understudy in the original Broadway production of the musical The Pajama Game *in which she was spotted by Hollywood producer Hal B. Wallis. In 1956 the renamed Shirley MacLaine appeared in the improbable role of an Indian lady of high caste in Mike Todd's film* Around the World in Eighty Days. *She made a big impact in Billy Wilder's* The Apartment *in 1960. Other significant roles included* Can-Can *(1960),* Irma La Douce *(1963),* Sweet Charity *(1969),* Two Mules For Sister Sara *(1970),* Turning Point *(1977),* Terms of Endearment *(Best Actress Oscar 1983),* Steel Magnolias *(1989) and* Postcards from the Edge *(1990). MacLaine is also known as an author with a special interest in themes relating to spiritual belief and reincarnation.*

Shirley MacLaine woke up yesterday morning to ecstatic press notices for her London Palladium opening the night before. By 8 a.m. she was fixing a light bulb that had fused in her Park Lane apartment. The magnitude of her conquest, the drama of the occasion, seemed to pass her by. When I met her a couple of hours later she seemed outwardly unaffected by her triumphant impact on London. She did, however, betray an uneasiness about having to do it again tonight and every night for a two-week Palladium run.

'I suppose I could be enjoying this success more than I am,' she said. 'But no performer ever does. I'm not in this to enjoy it. I'm in it to bring the enjoyment to others. That takes work. On stage I'm constantly concerned whether they're getting it. I guess that's why I always play underdogs.'

Basic to her nature is a small-town American puritan devotion to such unfashionable notions as self-discipline and the demands of the will.

'Of course I'm happy about the reviews today ... but I'm not one of those types who can ever sit back and float. I was born, you know, with ankles that were almost deformed, too weak to support my weight. My mother sent me to ballet class as therapy. I fell in love at once with the discipline of ballet, its rigorous requirements ... I realised immediately, even that young, that I was being challenged to produce my best potential, a feeling that has stayed with me all my life.'

Fortyish Shirley MacLaine wore a mud-brown sweater and everyday slacks. She had run out of make-up. 'Go down to the chemist and get me some,' she instructed one of her household.

She talked about her life as a political activist, world traveller, author, scorning the idea that entertainers need be nothing but glamorous ciphers.

'You can't be a good professional and just be a sort of show business turnip. If you really sat down with Liza Minnelli, and Bob Dylan, and John Lennon, and Frank Sinatra – the real greats – you'd find an amazing complexity of social attitudes that colour all their work and that make them stars. I don't think that there's such a thing as a great performer who has nothing to say.'

In the US presidential elections of 1972 she worked tirelessly for George McGovern, an experience that ended in a lamented Nixon landslide. This year's US poll she views with a more jaundiced eye.

'None of the candidates are saying anything that's getting through to me. Nobody's got it clear, so I've kinda tuned out. I'm not disillusioned with politics, exactly, but people are beginning to work things out for themselves, rather than listen to some high-falutin' leader who never delivers what he promises. All those movements in the Sixties ... Black Power. Flower Power. Nothing really worked. People are listening to themselves, and that's good.'

She was certain that the stories about John F. Kennedy's sexual escapades were engineered news leaks designed to discredit brother Teddy as a presidential nominee in 1976.

'I wasn't kidding the other day when I said that I'd rather have a president who screws a woman than one who screws the country.' She paused to light a cigarette. 'There's something wrong with a country that needs heroes.' Longer pause. 'The people are the heroes.'

Her well-publicised trip to China awakened her to the fuller possibilities in herself. 'A trip to China today is like a trip into your own interior. When anything adverse happens to me,' she said, 'when anything knocks the breath out of me, my tendency is immediately to turn that to an advantage. That's what makes me an optimist. Maybe that's why people respond to me, because things are kind of bleak these days. That song I do in my act, "It's Not Where You Start It's Where You Finish" … I really love that number. I really believe that stuff.'

4 FEBRUARY 1976

From 1954 to 1982 MacLaine was married to businessman Steve Parker, with whom she had a daughter, Sachi. Shirley MacLaine is the elder sister of actor Warren Beatty.

Matthew Manning

CHAPTER 53

MATTHEW MANNING – PSYCHIC BOY

"I have bent spoons and stopped clocks – but that's just show business."

Matthew Manning, born on 17 August 1955, is one of Britain's best-known psychics. In the wake of sensational spoon-bender Uri Geller, Matthew Manning, still a schoolboy, emerged in the '60s when his respectable home in Cambridge (his father was a well-established architect) was apparently 'attacked' by a poltergeist. It is not unusual for poltergeist activity to attach itself to a pre-adolescent living in the affected house. Matthew also discovered that he had a gift for unconscious, automatic writing in languages he could not understand, and for psychic drawing in the styles of famous artists long deceased. He wrote a book called The Link, *which sold a million copies in sixteen languages.*

The day that changed Matthew Manning's life was 18 February 1967. Early that winter morning, just after 7 a.m., a Cambridge architect who was the father of three young children, came downstairs and found his Georgian silver tankard lying on the living-room floor. Nobody in the household could explain how the prize antique had fallen from its shelf.

Four days later it happened again, and went on happening. The tankard incident was the first of a three-month chain of events that interrupted the well-ordered calm of the Manning household. Ornaments, chairs and pictures were routinely dislodged and moved around the house. Vases of fresh flowers were discovered yards away from where they had been placed, with not one drop of water spilled.

Matthew's father suspected a poltergeist and called in Dr George Owen, Fellow of Trinity College, Cambridge, and known as a poltergeist investigator. The door of the living room was sealed with wax, cotton threads suspended across it, while Mr Manning and Dr Owen kept watch from outside. Nothing was seen to move. Yet when they entered the sealed room, seconds later, it had again been 'attacked'.

Dr Owen concluded that the force, whatever it was, resided in Matthew. The boy was just eleven. Architect Manning drew precise blueprint plans tracing the movement of objects. He was relieved to note that 'outwardly my family is taking the matter light-heartedly'.

After three months the disturbances ceased. The family moved to an eighteenth-century house in the village of Linton, near Cambridge. Matthew was sent to Oakham, a public school. The poltergeist matter was more or less forgotten.

Then, some four years later, beginning on Easter Sunday 1971, an even more violent and inexplicable series of events shook the domestic balance of the Manning home.

Matthew declares that, on that night, his bed began to vibrate, then rose a few inches from the floor and pitched itself, together with its frightened young occupant, towards the centre of the room. He rushed downstairs to his parents, who were saying goodbye to some party guests at the front door. When Mr and Mrs Manning and their son tried to re-enter the living room they found a heavy settee blocking the door.

The entire Manning family now began to witness a succession of disorders. Armchairs were strewn across rooms, tables piled on each other, brooms balanced miraculously on the banisters. The house was in chaos almost every morning. Mrs Manning, thoroughly alarmed, began to spend part of her days wandering around the village shops rather than face alone the noises and thuds in the house. The disturbances pursued Matthew to Oakham School, where the matron, as well as nineteen boys who shared his dormitory, observed unexplained scenes like the movements of heavy bunk beds. Table knives were seen to ricochet off the walls of the dormitory. Though nobody was ever hurt, parents of other pupils became worried. The headmaster, Brigadier Buchanan, twice requested the Mannings to remove Matthew from the school, but relented each time.

Never able to draw, Matthew now discovered that he could produce – with no conscious effort – pictures in the style of Picasso, Aubrey Beardsley, Albrecht Dürer, Beatrix Potter and other artists. These poured from Matthew's pen in their hundreds, together with letters, messages and medical diagnoses in near perfect Latin, Saxon, French and some forms of Arabic script. Matthew now discovered that, when he was engaged in these 'automatic' activities, the poltergeist became quiet. Matthew had found a way, he told me, of controlling forces that had previously controlled him.

Today, nine years after that first experience with the tankard, he is a quiet, elegant youth, with long, shining hair and a neat beard. He has written his first book, *The Link*, and has resolved to devote his life to the investigation of his paranormal gifts.

He was always a shy child, his parents recall, with 'an almost fanatic desire to tell the truth'. In the couple of hours I spent with him, he was careful in conversation, gentle in manner. Matthew Manning is today a calm young man of twenty, who had been consistently described as honest and candid by his headmaster, teachers and some independent scientists, including Nobel Prize winner in Physics Professor Brian Josephson, who has observed and tested Matthew's powers.

'I don't know whether it's a gift or an affliction,' Matthew told me.

'The question I keep asking is: why me? I try not to let it affect me. I could make a lot of money giving sittings and medical diagnoses. But I refuse to make money out of this. I will never perform. Basically I am very much a loner. I don't have all that many friends. People always want to talk about me. It gets very boring. I have bent spoons and stopped clocks, and all that. But that's just show business. Uri Geller did a lot of good, but also a lot of damage. I don't want to be looked at. Psychics cannot perform at the drop of a hat. Basically it's like owning a battery. You use it up and have to wait for it to recharge; it's exhausting! These powers are not mine to abuse. I don't know why I have them. If I can put them to use to help other people I will have achieved something.'

19 February 1976

Matthew Manning continues to devote his life to being an author, lecturer and healer.

Psychic Matthew Manning drew this picture in the style of Aubrey Beardsley while in a trance-like state

Marcel Marceau

CHAPTER 54

MARCEL MARCEAU – THE POETRY OF SILENCE

"We were Napoleon and Charlie Chaplin.
Chaplin was my god."

Marcel Marceau, son of a kosher butcher, was born on 22 March 1923 in Strasbourg, France. When the Germans moved in the family fled to Limoges. In 1944 his father was captured and sent to Auschwitz, where he was killed by the Nazis. His mother, Anne Werzberg, survived. Marcel Marceau, who adopted his name as a tribute to a hero of the French Revolution, joined the French Resistance, escorting groups of children to safety. He started to mime to keep the children amused and silent during dangerous border crossings. Later he worked as a liaison officer for General Patton's army. He became the world's best-known – indeed only – practitioner of the silent art. He married three times.

He has been one of the dominating figures of world theatre for three decades. In all that time he has never spoken a word on stage. Marcel Marceau, the unrivalled French mime, is back in London for a four-week season at Sadler's Wells where nightly, before a hushed audience, this lithe poet of silence creates the illusion of a solid world.

Offstage, Marceau is an intense but friendly man with sombre, restless eyes, a thick, greying tangle of hair the texture of fine steel wool, and a fluent command of English. He enlivens his conversation with quick-change facial expressions and sudden flurries of his fingers. His knuckles fly to his cheeks as he explains that his identification with his mute character is complete and intense: 'When I pretend to pull off the mask that has become fixed to my face, that moment is for me a wonderful physical release … a birth, a deliverance.'

Every time he goes on stage he has to somehow re-create that intensity. He cannot, like a seasoned actor, depend on technique and a good memory for lines. No wonder Marcel Marceau has no rivals, only disciples.

'I must perform every night,' he said, 'as if it's the first time. When I can no longer do that it will show, and I will quit.' His hands fly apart, quitting.

At fifty-one Marceau has kicked a lifelong cigarette habit and now seems trim and ageless. 'I am more serene than I was ten years ago. I am also more disillusioned. I am not the idealist I was at twenty. My eyes have become cold.'

What has not changed, he told me, is his faith in the goodness and mystery of ordinary people. On stage, his lifelong striving has been to share with his followers a wordless moment of truth. 'I want the man in the audience to feel his own inner experiences through me. He must dream with me … When I pretend to be on a tightrope I have heard a woman shout out: "Ah! Don't fall!"' Said Marceau: 'A single moment in a theatre can stay with someone the rest of his years. It is that moment I try to catch … the essence of life.'

As a nine-year-old boy he formed his first street theatre, inventing stories to be read out by his friends, while he illustrated them soundlessly. 'We were the wind. We were the rain. We were flowers, and fishes, and trees. We were Napoleon and Charlie Chaplin. Chaplin was my god.'

Marceau raised two sons and divorced. He paints in his spare time, has held several one-man exhibitions. He recently completed writing and illustrating a book about his milk-faced clown Bip.

'I'll tell you something,' said Marceau, 'we are saved by the idea that we are eternal. Otherwise life is an absurdity. Man is a continuity. The artist must see all, feel all. I am a witness of our age.'

For an instant his pale eyes opened wide, staring dead ahead.

22 AUGUST 1975

Marceau died on 22 September 2007 at a racetrack in Cahors, France. He is buried at Pierre Lachaise cemetery in Paris.

Marcel Marceau

Groucho Marx

CHAPTER 55

GROUCHO MARX – MELANCHOLY FUNNY MAN

◇◇◇

"Don't give my regards to the Queen."

*Actor-comedian Julius Henry ('Groucho') Marx learned to make people laugh as one of the three Marx Brothers, a knockabout music hall act which became universally famous in a series of Hollywood comedies in the '30s (*Duck Soup, A Day At The Circus, A Day At The Races, A Night At The Opera*). Born in New York on 2 October 1890, Groucho cultivated a distinctive appearance – painted-on moustache and eyebrows, cigar, a loping stoop-shouldered gait and thick-rimmed glasses, which he didn't need. Groucho was always assigned the largest role in the act, purveying an irresistible flow of insults, wisecracks and word play ('I'd horsewhip you … if I had a horse'). Brother Chico played the piano and spoke his lines with a supposedly Italian accent. Harp-playing brother Harpo was a grinning mute, having no lines to speak at all. Two other brothers, Zeppo and Gummo, dropped out of the act and did not appear in any of the classic MGM movies. After the act broke up, Groucho went on to a successful solo career as a TV game host (*You Bet Your Life*). His three marriages ended in divorce. A self-educated man, he maintained a long correspondence with the English poet T. S. Eliot. Groucho once said, 'I believe television is very educational. Every time anyone switches on a TV set I go into another room and read a book.'*

Groucho Marx, last of the famous Brothers, met me without a smile and said in a dry, old man's whisper: 'What's on your mind?' He is eighty-six, and looks every day of it – a small, thin, grey figure who walks in small, child-like steps. The sign outside his Beverly Hills driveway says simply: 'Please Keep Out.'

Conversation was slow and painful, interrupted by long morose silences from Groucho. He sometimes seemed past caring. He said he remembered England fondly but didn't much like the idea of the royal family.

'I think they ought to be abolished,' he said. 'Why should they live off the people? London is broke. I am against all monarchies. They've got a great racket. I'm in the wrong family.'

'You're hardly in the wrong family,' I said. 'The Marx Brothers are better known around the world than the Windsors. And probably more widely beloved…'

Groucho appeared to think about that for a while. Then he said, 'And funnier!' The only time he made me smile.

He talked about his friend the poet T. S. Eliot and how he, Groucho, made a joke at Eliot's memorial service. 'I made them laugh,' Groucho said. 'I was the only one who did.'

After thirty minutes of desultory, awkward conversation Groucho suddenly repeated, word for word, his story about T. S. Eliot's memorial service. He said again, 'I was the only one who made them laugh.' Then he got up slowly. A red heart, hung from a gold necklace, rested against his thin chest. 'Got enough?' he said.

'Goodbye.'

Groucho's handshake was limp and cool. 'Don't give my regards to the Queen,' he said, and walked slowly to his bedroom at the back of the house.

8 NOVEMBER 1976

Groucho died in Los Angeles on 19 August 1977, three days after the death of Elvis Presley. For his own tombstone epitaph Groucho suggested 'Excuse me if I don't stand up' (his suggestion was not followed up). My meeting with Groucho was arranged by Erin Fleming, the advisor-companion of his late years. The story Groucho told at the T. S. Eliot memorial service concerned an English nobleman about to be publicly hanged. As he mounted the rickety scaffold the doomed man said anxiously, 'I don't think this damn thing is safe!'

Chico, Harpo, Groucho – the Marx Brothers

Rod McKuen

CHAPTER 56

ROD MCKUEN – IN SEARCH OF HIS FATHER

"I've offered one hundred thousand dollars to anyone who can look at five babies in their cribs and pick out the 'illegitimate' one."

In terms of book sales, at least, Rod McKuen may claim to be the most successful poet living today. He has written thirty or so books of poetry, which sold in the millions – some say sixty-five million. Nevertheless, it is fair to say that serious poets do not take McKuen seriously. He was born Rodney Marvin McKuen in Oakland, California on 29 April 1933. He ran away from home and an alcoholic stepfather when he was no more than a boy, took on a series of manly jobs and wound up reciting his homemade verse alongside beat poets Jack Kerouac and Allen Ginsberg in San Francisco in the late '50s, though he was never seen as part of the inner circle of the counter-culture. He had, however, his champions too. W. H. Auden described McKuen's poems as 'love letters to the world … I am happy that many of them came to me and found me out'. McKuen was particularly successful as an adapter of foreign songs. His translation of Belgian composer/singer Jacques Brel's 'Ne Me Quitte Pas' (McKuen's title: 'If You Go Away') remains a world bestseller.

'Everyone's noticed,' said Rod McKuen, 'that I have become a different person, a calmer human being.'

> 'I go about my life with more confidence and power. My lyrics are better. There's a freedom about my life I never thought I would experience. I finally know who I am. I never knew before. I might have dropped from the planet Mars. I always thought I would die young. I used to say: Ten more years and I'll be dead. Now I want to live forever. They will have to drag me out now. I have no desire to go.'

There was no denying Rod McKuen's sense of renewed life. It happened to him, he says, on Friday, 13 February this year when McKuen's life-long search for the father he never knew finally came to an end.

Born out of wedlock in a Salvation Army hostel forty-three lonely years ago, McKuen distilled his feelings of deprivation into 1,500 songs and a series of slim volumes of sentimental, soul-driven poetry.

His ignorance of his father's identity was the spark that propelled the McKuen machine. His life has been one long identity crisis ever since he escaped from home and knocked around as a lumberjack, shoe salesman, ranch hand and navvy.

In the mid-60s he leapt from obscurity with one hit song, 'Stanyan Street'. He has never looked back, except in search for his father.

He took to the stage, padding about on plimsolled feet, singing his own songs in a gravelly voice that vibrated sympathetically in the bosoms of millions.

Highbrow critics of poetry have almost invariably found McKuen's stuff embarrassing and naïve, dismissing him as a purveyor of 'second-hand emotional clichés and easy generalities'. American novelist Nora Ephron called his poems 'superficial, platitudinous and frequently silly'.

As his star ascended, the problem of the identity of his biological father obsessed him more and more. He was diagnosed as a clinical depressive. Last year a detective agency was commissioned to join in the hunt. Advertisements were placed in newspapers in the San Francisco Bay area. Hundreds of cranks and claimants applied for the post, eager to get their share of the McKuen inheritance.

When the search finally ended six months ago, Rod McKuen discovered that his father has been dead for fifteen years.

When I talked to McKuen in London yesterday, he would not be drawn any further on this subject. He had been infuriated, he said, by the red tape and bureaucratic stonewalling that had frustrated his enquiries. He assured me that he would devote the rest of his life lobbying to alter the laws governing parental identification for those born out of wedlock.

He has told the whole story in a new book: *Finding My Father – One Man's Search For Identity*.

McKuen has always had a social conscience. He employs twenty-six people, he told me, to run his charities and lobbying activities, which include a scholarship fund called Animal Concern, endowment funds providing for the education of veterans (McKuen served in the Korean War), and a department bluntly known as Bastard.

The object of Bastard is, perversely, to abolish the very word itself, which McKuen hates as much as he hates the word 'illegitimate'.

'The English language is the only one that uses the word "illegitimate", with its connotations of crooked dealing, to describe a child born out of wedlock. I've offered $100,000 to anyone who can look at five babies in their cribs and pick out the "illegitimate" one. Equally, the word "bastard" should be saved to describe a certain kind of politician. I don't see why a baby should be saddled with it before he can even crawl across the floor.'

When McKuen isn't writing poems, or singing them, he busies himself writing and conducting symphonies, operas, orchestral works and film scores (*The Prime of Miss Jean Brodie*, which won him an Oscar nomination).

'Am I happy? You bet. More than that … I'm delirious.'

15 SEPTEMBER 1976

Long retired from public performance, Rod McKuen now lives in southern California with his brother and his record collection, one of the largest in private hands in America.

Henry Miller

CHAPTER 57

HENRY MILLER – MAN OF THE TROPICS

"It has turned out badly. What has come out of it is pure crap."

Henry Miller was almost certainly the most notorious literary figure of the '30s. His books – notably Tropic of Cancer, Tropic of Capricorn *and* Sexus *– challenged all known conventions, combining elements of erotica, social protest and confessional autobiography, and were routinely banned in America. Typical expressions of outrage include the Pennsylvania Supreme Court's description of* Tropic of Cancer *as 'a pit of putrefaction, a slimy gathering of all that is rotten in the debris of human depravity'. On the other hand, Samuel Beckett hailed* Tropic of Cancer *as 'a momentous event in the history of modern writing'. And George Orwell named Miller as 'the only imaginative prose writer of the slightest value who has appeared among the English-speaking races for some years past'. Henry Valentine Miller was born in the German quarter of New York City on 26 December 1891. He spent the '30s in Paris, associating with leading figures of the Surrealist movement, quitting the French capital only when war threatened in 1939. In 1940 Miller settled in the wooded California coast near Big Sur, moving in his later years to a trim, suburban home in Pacific Palisades, where I met him in late 1976.*

The first thing that catches your eye as you walk up the well-swept garden path to Henry Miller's unexpectedly suburban house at 444 Ocampo Drive, Pacific Palisades, California, is the following typewritten notice pinned on his front door:

'When a man has reached old age and has fulfilled his mission, he has the right to confront the idea of death in peace. He has no need of other men. He knows them already and has seen enough of them. What he needs is peace. It is not seemly to seek out such a man, plague him with chatter, and make him suffer banalities. One should pass by the door of his house as if no one lived there.'

'It's a quote from an ancient Chinese sage,' explained Henry Miller when, by appointment and despite the discouraging notice on the door, I entered his home to plague him with chatter. We had met by chance the previous night when, enjoying a lone sushi meal in a Japanese restaurant on Sunset Boulevard, I was hailed by a friend, film director Jim Frawley, who had just walked in with a small group, which included Henry Miller.

Invited to join the party, I took a seat on Miller's immediate left where, such being his state of physical frailty, I had access to his one good ear, but had to contend with his one blind eye. Whenever Henry Miller spoke to me he had to swing 90 degrees to his left so that our eyes could meet. He was a rheumy old man and his mouth hung open in a kind of permanent lop-sided grin, the after-effects of a stroke. He was friendly and courteous and easy to be with.

Emboldened by his charm, I suggested (into his good ear) a more extended interview; he quickly agreed, and so here I was next day in his house a few miles outside Los Angeles, a few hundred yards from the sea. 'Henry can give you forty-five minutes,' warned his loyal Finnish secretary, but actually we talked – or rather, Henry Miller did – for a couple of hours.

Miller was eighty-four years old. His mind was lively. He had lived a long and in some ways notorious life and had survived to become an eminence of international literature. Paris, where he spent most of the '30s – scrounging, talking and writing with unstoppable energy – had been the turning point in his life. In Paris he discovered to his delight that it was no disgrace to be poor. The photographer Brassaï commented: 'In Europe poverty is purely a matter of bad luck. In the United States it is a sign of moral defect, a badge of shame that society cannot condone.'

Miller agreed. 'I have walked the streets in many countries of the world,' he wrote in *The Tropic of Capricorn*, 'but nowhere have I felt so degraded and humiliated as in America.'

Before the war, his books had established the Brooklyn-born writer as a free-living sacred monster. Published in Paris by the Olympia Press, the books were smuggled out of France in their thousands.

Miller had never quite outlived that notoriety. Almost forgotten is the respectful attention he received from distinguished contemporaries with his first book. T. S. Eliot and Lawrence Durrell hastened to welcome *Tropic of Cancer*, Durrell adding that he had found it 'a messy and unnerving book that defied all the canons of good taste and literary convention'.

Brassaï, who was close to Miller in his Paris days, wrote a revealing memoir about their years together, which spoke of the 'savage, primitive exuberance of Miller's prose'. He described his friend as 'this wonderful, crazy American … brimming with energy, frothing with wit'.

Miller, I discovered within a few minutes, was less than gratified by the performance of the literary liberation movement he had helped to unleash. 'It has turned out badly,' he told me. 'What has come out of it is pure crap. I don't regret writing those books; but I see the damage I have done as well.'

It was mid-afternoon. Miller had just finished reading the pile of letters that arrived daily at his house. 'Because of my name and reputation, I have the biggest mail you ever saw. I read everything that comes in unless it is blatantly crazy, vituperative or dull. Students keep showing up at my door, most of them writing projects and theses about me. I am the busiest goddam man you ever met. Going blind is a terrible handicap for me.'

We sat near a full-sized ping-pong table which he can no longer use because of his faltering balance. He occasionally raised a handkerchief to wipe his watery good eye. 'Goddam thing is packing up on me.'

But mostly he was in good humour and full of talk. Here follows a sampling of Henry Miller's conversation:
Growing Old:

> 'The older and wiser I get, the sadder I become. I have no homosexual tenden-cies but I try more and more to respond to the world in a feminine, intuitive way. I have discovered serenity.'

Intellect:

> 'People of intellect have never given me the impression of being happy. I believe more and more that ignorance really is bliss. I don't interest myself in the great questions like "Is there a God?" and so on. I am not interested in righting the wrongs of the world.'

The British:

> 'The only real gentleman I met in my life was an English banker. But in general I don't like the English and they have never liked me. We simply don't hit it off. When I was younger I was sent back to France from Newhaven because I didn't have enough money. It was done in a particu-larly slimy and pompous way. I love the Irish and adore the Welsh. I've been to Scotland and did not find the Scots mean or inhospitable. But the English … no.'

Jesus Christ:

'Jesus has never appealed to me, though I don't deny his greatness. I can't take his meekness and humourlessness. They say Jesus smiled but I simply don't believe it. Jesus was a man of sorrow. He was Jewish to the hundredth degree. I think Jews really cultivate their misery. I see that element in them. Thankfully, they can also laugh at themselves. I like Jews and have been befriended by them all my life, but I remain aware of their faults.'

The Future: 'The West is doomed. There is no hope for us. We are destined to fail by our own mistakes, not from an attack by an outside enemy.'

Leadership: 'No leaders worth a damn are arising in our society. Nor should we listen to them if they did suddenly appear.'

Happiness:

'I am not a squeamish complainer. One can still live a full rich life while the world crumbles about you, provided you don't meddle in politics. Everywhere you look, life is terrible. Despite all, my motto is a line from a song in a musical comedy I saw when I was seventeen – "always merry and bright". I like that line. Always merry and bright. Lawrence Durrell, who used to know me in Paris, nicknamed me the Happy Rock.'

Heroes: 'Alexander the Great, Napoleon, St Francis...'

Japanese:

'I love going to Japanese restaurants. I love Japanese women. It would seem to me that the Japanese woman was put on this earth to introduce a note of beauty and joy in a world which men from the beginning of time have tried to make ugly and unlivable.'

Ping-pong:

'I used to spend hours and hours a day playing ping-pong while the phonograph played music by Bach and Scriabin. But I can't stand up now without the danger of falling down. God, how I miss ping-pong. I miss it more than... [Miller paused to search for the right word, and found it] ...sin.'

Writing: 'I write only one or two hours a day. The secret is never to write yourself out each day. Never exhaust the reservoir.'

Memory:

'I remember the first ten years of my life with great vividness, even the names of the
boys I used to run around with – Johnnie Paul, James Reardon, Jimmy Dunne …
and I can remember what I did last week, last month and last year. But the great
central part of my life, the years in Paris, Greece and California, seem a blank. I can
recall them with an effort but the memories don't come unbidden.'

Temper: 'I can get very over-heated. But I'm not an angry old man.'
Eventually Henry Miller rose and courteously bade me farewell, request-
ing that I should convey his feelings of admiration to the Irish writer Edna
O'Brien, whom he said he had never met. He shook my hand, then transferred his grip to a wheeled walking frame, which he leaned on when he
moved about the house. He did not strike me, despite the notice on his door,
as a man confronting the idea of death. At eighty-four Henry Miller was still
alive and well and living fruitfully in California.

8 NOVEMBER 1976

*In 1978 Henry Miller wrote to me (and others) unusually soliciting our support
for his unsuccessful bid to be awarded the Nobel Prize for Literature. I responded
positively, citing his travel book* The Colossus of Maroussi, *an account of his
time in Greece as the guest of his friend Lawrence Durrell. Henry Miller died on
7 June 1980 of circulatory complications in his Pacific Palisades home. He was in
his ninetieth year. His ashes were scattered off the coast in Big Sur.*

henry miller 444 ocampo drive – pacific palisades california 90171   8/23/78

Dear friend, *Herbert Kretzmer*

   In my attempt to obtain the Nobel Prize for Literature
this coming year I hope to enlist your support. All I ask
is for you to write a few succinct lines to:

   Nobel Committee of the Swedish Academy
   Borshuset
   11129 Stockholm
   Sweden

Please note that the Committee urgently requests that the
name of the proposed candidate not be publicized.

                              Sincerely,
                              Henry Miller
                              Henry Miller

"WHEN LOVE COMES TO THE FORE WOMAN WILL BE THE QUEEN OF THE UNIVERSE." Eliphas Levi

Max Miller

CHAPTER 58

MAX MILLER – THE CHEEKY CHAPPIE

"The whole thing has become too quick ... too easy."

Brighton-born Thomas Henry Sargent (born 21 November 1894) was a cocky working-class lad who became, many would say, Britain's most popular music hall comic star of the '30s, '40s and '50s. Adopting the professional title of Max Miller, the Cheeky Chappie, he was invariably dressed in a gaudy, floral plus-fours suit and a jaunty hat one size too small for him. Max was a classic song-and-dance man who specialised in risqué songs, some of which he wrote, and near-the-knuckle patter, which got him banned more than once by BBC Radio. A puritan at heart, and despite his salacious tales of philandering travelling sales-men, he stayed married to the same wife for forty years and never swore on stage, preferring the double-entendre and the device of the unspoken last line, leaving the audience to complete the rhyme or saucy tale.

When playwright John Osborne created the character of the music hall comedian Archie Rice in his play *The Entertainer*, it was widely and wrongly supposed that Archie was a portrait of Max Miller, the grinning, vulgar-tongued solo act much admired by Osborne and millions more of his generation. As a boy in the '30s I was addicted to a children's comic magazine called *Film Fun* in whose flimsy pages Max Miller loomed large, an exotic creature, sharp as a bookie.

When I met Miller in London, he was sixty-three and waiting in his dressing room to take part in a television show. His TV appearances were rare; he belonged to an older school and regarded the medium with distrust.

On first glance, his head seemed altogether too small for his large, muscular body. He was chirpy and flushed, smoking a cigar, a regular barrow boy.

When I paid him some ice-breaking compliment about his apparent state of rude health, he was off and running.

'I'm strong. Oh yes, I'm a strong boy, all right. Every morning you'll see me on me bike riding between Brighton Pier and Black Rock. Two hours, up and down, in me big sweater. I'm good for another twenty years, so they tell me. I look forty-four on the stage, marvellous, isn't it? I'm a freak. Put that in your paper. Put in Max Miller's a freak. And for why? Because he's cheatin' nature. That's a good one. Put it in.'

He giggled hoarsely and flicked a speck of cigar ash off the lapel of his dapper brown suit.

'The kids these days with their guitars,' he complained, 'they're turning the theatre game inside out. Silly, isn't it?'

'We've lost the nice people. The nice people don't come to the music halls no more. I see it everywhere I go. It's all these performing kids now, fifteen, sixteen, most of them. Ridiculous, isn't it? Did you see that piece in the paper, where it said Terry Deene can't even play the guitar. Now, take me. I play the guitar. Took me a lifetime to study, boy, a lifetime … They're breaking all the rules, they come late to rehearsals, they go on late, they don't care. It can't be right, now, can it? Me, I began at three pounds five shillings a week for old Jack Sheppard. Three shows a day including Sunday, on the lawns at Brighton. That's what these new boys don't have, see? – the ex-pee-rience! Then I went up to six pound a week. Then up to nine. It was hard goin' but we learned the game, boy. Biggest salary I ever got was at Coventry. They paid me a thousand and twenty-five pounds a week. Lovely! The whole thing has become too quick, too easy. I never thought to see the day when a boy goes into a music shop, records his own voice, sends the disc to the BBC and gets his own television series. No, son, I never thought to see that day. Television kills comedians. They do their act and forty million people see it. They're washed up. One … two years and they're kaput. So why be jealous about them? After forty years up there why worry about them?'

His voice was dry and crackly, like firewood. I said: 'How do you relax, Max?'

'Now, that's a title for a song,' he said. 'Yes, I'll write it … How Do You Relax, Max? Put in your paper you gave Max Miller an idea for a song. Got that? Put it in.'

He puffed at a cigar. He smoked four a day.

'I live comfortable, that's what money's for. They say to me "Max, what are you looking for?" I always say, I'm looking for a girl who doesn't smoke, doesn't drink and doesn't whatchacallit … make love. Why I'm looking for her I don't know!'

Max Miller appeared to choke with laughter, shaking all over but holding his cigar up carefully so that the ash did not drop on him. 'Marvellous gag,' he said. 'Put that in. Why I'm looking for her I don't know. Boy oh boy, what a gag.'

He was still flushed and laughing when he was called to rehearsals. He turned at the door. 'How do you relax, Max? Yes, that's a song all right. What an idea! Marvellous, isn't it?' And he was gone.

14 FEBRUARY 1958

Max Miller died on 7 May 1963 in his home, aged sixty-nine.

Spike Milligan

CHAPTER 59

SPIKE MILLIGAN – AN ANGRY MAN

"I am basically the unfunniest person on earth."

Terence Alan Patrick Sean ('Spike') Milligan was born into a military family in India on 16 April 1918. He is rightly regarded as the innovative genius who changed the nature of British comedy, particularly with his BBC radio series The Goon Show, *in which he starred with Peter Sellers and the Welsh tenor Harry Secombe. Milligan was also a poet (*Silly Verse for Kids*), novelist (*Puckoon*), actor and playwright. He wrote in the surreal tradition of Edward Lear and Lewis Carroll. John Cleese called him 'the Great God to us all'. Milligan served with the Royal Artillery in the Second World War, and was wounded in the Battle of Monte Cassino. He suffered from the effects of shell shock ever afterwards. Recurrent bouts of manic depression hospitalised him several times during his troubled lifetime. ('I cannot stand being awake. The pain is too much…') Milligan was also an accomplished jazz trumpeter. He married three times.*

Spike Milligan enters his Notting Hill office in a chunky green jersey and a foul temper. He is against everything and everybody. Yesterday's stubble peppers his chin, lending him the appearance of an Embankment tramp. To nobody in particular Milligan announces: 'I hate the human race.' He says it with such vehemence that there is no doubting that he does.

He sits down at his desk to start the day's work. There is not much work, it appears. 'I am unemployed,' says Milligan. 'Nobody wants me. Television doesn't want me. The BBC doesn't want me. I have become little more than a nuisance to the cowards and idiots who run the BBC. To hell with them!'

Milligan's detestation of the BBC has become fused into his maverick personality. It is just one of the destructive obsessions that devour the man. Milligan sees himself as a man persistently harassed and harried by giant, unseen bureaucracies – gas boards, electricity showrooms, employment agencies, Government Ministries. Everywhere there are faceless men persecuting him. Even a burning electric light bulb symbolises to Milligan these invisible curbs on his liberty. 'Somewhere some idiot in a bowler hat is totting up the amps. It's costing us money to bloody well sit here and breathe...'

Milligan is venerated as a comic genius. But he insists: 'I am basically the unfunniest person in the world...'

He sees himself as a compassionate Roman Catholic, but his capacity for hate is practically boundless. The basis of his humour has always been ridicule, essentially mirthless. In his youth he thought of becoming a priest. Today he seeks to follow in the bare footsteps of Gandhi. 'I would not detest the human race did I not love them so much,' he told me.

But the hate remains, warping his days. He worries himself sick about Russian dogs shot into space and emaciated children starving in African famines. He can be witheringly scornful of people who do not share his anger and his pity. 'When they crucified that dog in space, I couldn't sleep for nights,' he says.

Milligan imagines himself increasingly unemployable but his sense of martyrdom has no real basis in fact. In any terms other than his own, Spike Milligan is remarkably successful. Last year, for instance, he starred in two MGM films: *Invasion Quartet* and *Postman's Knock*. He issued a long-playing record called *Milligan Preserved* and a book, *A Dustbin of Milligan*, which became a bestseller.

His tenure as radio compère of *Children's Choice* (a BBC appointment, as it happens) was a runaway triumph.

Milligan appeared in the Mermaid Theatre production of *Treasure Island*. He also found time to make two short films, write a comic novel about Irish partition called *Puckoon*, and a play about a man suffering from the delusion that he was a bed-sitting room.

Despite all the evidence of a busy and successful professional life, Milligan insists on viewing 1961 as a disastrous year, which saw him tottering on the brink of bankruptcy. 'I'm living on the cash I've saved. There is nothing to say about me except: send money.'

In the few hours I was with him he behaved like a man on the run, fighting back. He dictated a letter addressed to an employment agency, ending it crossly: 'Until you have adjusted your fees, don't bother me.' Then he picked up the telephone and issued curt instructions to his housekeeper: 'Mrs Beveridge, I want you to measure the children [Milligan has three, was divorced last year]. I never know what size to order when I buy their clothes.

Measure their arms, feet, chest, legs, everything.' Milligan put the phone down without any goodbyes.

Up came the phone again. He called the electricity board and became stiff and white-faced over some real or imaginary mistake the electricians had made in his home.

Milligan looked at me, breathing hard. 'I'd like to drop a bomb on the whole world. I mean it. I can't be funny anymore. Standing on the gallows is no place for laughter.'

He picked up the phone again. 'Mrs Beveridge, I've just realised that the kids may be playing with the electric clock in the airing cupboard on the landing. See that they don't.' Down banged the phone.

Milligan said:

'Listen. I placed a picture of a starving coloured kid downstairs in the entrance hall next to a collection box. All these people who come to these offices, carrying Bernard Shaw under one arm and a book of intellectual philosophy under the other, do you know what they put in that box, all of them? Five shillings we collected. Five lousy shillings. Don't tell me about man loving man, mate. I had six hundred Christmas cards from people I've never seen. Two of the cards actually had pictures of Jesus on them. Think of it … two. Marvellous, isn't it?'

Milligan jumped up and silently paced the carpet for a minute. He said:

'The only picture I ever saw that really looked like Jesus was one by Da Vinci which showed him as a dark Jew. The other paintings, the popular ones, always show Jesus as a kind of Robert Taylor [a handsome movie idol of the time] with a wig.'

He barked again through the telephone: 'Mrs Beveridge, take the baby to the clinic. She's underweight. I want a diet. Put it all down on paper.'

The phone went down. Came up again within twenty seconds. 'Mrs Beveridge, you must take the children to the zoo much earlier. They don't have enough time there. One pound for an hour is too expensive.'

Milligan said to me: 'The trouble with having a maid is that you can't walk around your own house naked.'

Thus Spike Milligan's morning sped on. He made more phone calls, shouting angrily at any hint of incompetence or stupidity; throwing the phone down whenever his temper touched explosion point. He is an anarchist whose enemies are everywhere, toeing the line, obeying the rules. He sees the future as a nightmare, bringing up his three children under the shadow of the Bomb he is positive one day must fall.

> 'Make no mistake. This war will come. People forget that the bomb has already been dropped – thousands are still in need of treatment. What is the future of my children? I can tell you, mate. Nothing. Of course I'm a rebel, a revolutionary. What else is there to be? What do you want me to do – dammit – lie down? That's what the world wants. That's what the BBC wants. They would love me to be timorous and quiet, a tame idiot, someone they can swallow whole. Not me. Not yet. What the hell, I'm the last man alive who speaks the truth.'

13 MARCH 1962

I interviewed Spike Milligan several times over the years. Occasionally we wined and dined together. In contrast to the bitterness revealed above, the following piece, published nine years later, shows him in a happier frame of mind. Milligan continued to be a law unto himself for the rest of his days. He called the Prince of Wales a 'little grovelling bastard' on live TV, then sent a fax message to His Royal Highness: 'I suppose a knighthood is out of the question?'

He has passed his fiftieth birthday, but looks a good fifteen years younger when he shaves. He was shaved when I met him last week. He was full of bounce and banter. His pale-blue Irish eyes seemed constantly amused. He whistled in admiration to a blushing girl passing his office window.

He knows too well another darker mood. I remember him not long ago shuffling on to the stage of the Mermaid Theatre in his prophetic play *The Bed-Sitting Room*. Grey-bearded, somehow boneless in a threadbare raincoat, he looked a haunted old man slowly pacing a sick room. At such times, and they occur regularly, Spike Milligan is the companion of a familiar and profound melancholy that unnerves him and crushes his spirit. It is then that he retreats into a private world whose colours and contours he has recently begun to depict in oils. His painting of a dead cornfield at sunset burns with the manic glow of a Van Gogh, a painter with whose outcast personality Spike Milligan feels a special affinity.

'I can only paint,' he said, 'when I feel utterly depressed. I can't pick up a brush when I am all right. Like now.'

Now he talked a lot and laughed a lot and fed broken biscuits to the greedy pigeons who call regularly at his office window.

'This is little Fred, bitten by some dog. It's great to make new friends, isn't it, for a few crumbs?'

Spike in full cry is a fireworks display. Ideas, bizarre and wonderful, burst like crackers out of his restless brain. While I was with him he jotted down half a dozen ideas for future use, including a plan to stage a political argument in the Centre Court at Wimbledon, with a tennis umpire in his high chair calling out the score. Most people will recognise that idea as pure, undiluted Milligan. He and Beachcomber [celebrated humour columnist of the *Daily Express*] stand alone as innovators of the absurd.

These two gifted men recently met for the first time at a BBC lunch and, says Spike, got on like a house afire. Milligan insists that it was Beachcomber who turned him on to humorous writing.

'A lot of my attitudes towards comedy came from reading Beachcomber in the *Daily Express* during the war. He extricated me from a world of dross, made me feel that I had something to offer. After our lunch meeting, Beachcomber took an early leave, saying: "I feel a severe attack of British Railways coming on." I loved meeting him. He did look a happy man.'

So, last week, did Spike Milligan. But those who know him are all too aware that his comic genius is rooted in disgust. A Milligan sketch almost always seeks to ridicule the buffooneries of real men, whose stupidity so outrages Spike that he literally becomes ill.

Recently Spike gave me a slim, hand-printed book of his verse. The following lines appear in his foreword: 'In this book there are some poems which were written in mental agony caused by creatures who are laughingly called human beings. I was once afraid of death; now I welcome it. I personally can't wait to say Goodbye to this world. – January 1969.'

It is precisely that kind of unpredictable despair that discourages would-be employers and sponsors from using his services. Consider the continuing case of Spike Milligan v. *Housewives Choice*, now renamed *Family Choice*, the popular BBC morning radio request programme that each week employs a different, jovial master of ceremonies. Spike's frequent applications to compère the programmes have been consistently declined.

'For six years I've been trying to get on that programme,' Spike said.

'They told me that their compères were always booked a year ahead. I asked them to put me down for next year. Finally they admitted they'd had a meeting and had found me unsuitable for the job. I want to know what kind of talent I need to say: "This record is for Mrs Plinge of 24 Paddington Road, Leeds." I want to know what's wrong with me, what kind of a leper I'm supposed to be. I am married. I have four children. I wash and bathe every day and go to church maybe once in seven Sundays. I am chairman of the Children's Anti-Vivisection Society. I am active in wildlife preservation. It can't be me who is diseased. It's them, the dead, dead, dead people.'

He thought about this for a while and added, 'The world isn't round, mate, it's bent.'

Milligan once considered going into politics, but now sees that ambition as irretrievably outdated.

'I used to think of my friend Michael Foot as a progressive politician. Now he's old hat. People like Michael have enormous integrity, and are probably fighting a damn sight harder than I am, but they are lost in a system that has totally come apart. It is finished; it is over. The hippies today are closer to the Christian idea of love and tolerance than anyone else around. They express a new instinct, a new feeling that is abroad in the world. It was the young who made military might look so silly when they threw flowers at the Russian tanks in the streets of Prague. Why do people still take their children to see the Changing of the Guard? To me it is a big joke – hysterically, sadly funny. I find them very, very lovely, the young people these days. It's the greatest chance the world has ever had. To follow the old paths is to follow yourself back to the start.'

He is busy and productive, not only in his new-found fields of poetry and painting but in his career as an actor as well.

Later this year he will co-star with Eric Sykes in a new TV series by Johnny Speight about a bigoted imperialist (Sykes), who receives a houseguest called O'Brien, only to discover that O'Brien is a Pakistani. 'It sounds a hilarious idea,' he said. 'You can say a lot of things.'

His reverence for life, his love for the young, his worship of children, were poured into a just-published poem whose lines shine with pity. It is called 'Children of Aberfan' (a Welsh coal-mining town where a colliery slag heap collapsed on homes and a school in October 1966, burying 116 children).

And now they will go, wandering
Away from the coal black earth,
The clean white children holy as the Easter Rose.
Away from the brainless, sludge-filled desks,
Away from the imprisoned spring that opened its mouth
  to breathe fresh air
And moved a mountain to find it.
Away they will go – the children,
Wandering – wondering,
More loved
More wanted
Than ever.
I don't burn coal any more.

2 MAY 1969

Spike died in Rye, East Sussex, on 27 February 2002. In a BBC poll in 1999 he
was voted Funniest Person of the Last Thousand Years.

John Mortimer

CHAPTER 60

JOHN MORTIMER –
THE MAN WHO INVENTED HORACE RUMPOLE

◇◇

"Of course, I've known about loneliness all my life."

When John Mortimer died on 16 January 2009, The Guardian *saluted the passing of 'One of the great characters of contemporary British life'. Mortimer lived several lives simultaneously: he was a lawyer of progressive opinions. He was an author and dramatist who wrote movingly of his blind, irascible barrister-father* (A Voyage Round My Father, *a role most notably played on stage by Alec Guinness and Derek Jacobi, and on TV by Laurence Olivier). But Mortimer's most enduring creation will be Horace Rumpole, QC (*Rumpole of The Bailey*) embodied by the harrumphing Australian character actor Leo McKern. John Mortimer was born on 21 April 1923, and educated at Harrow and Brasenose College, Oxford. Unfit for military service because of poor eyesight, he joined the Crown Film Unit where he wrote wartime propaganda documentaries. He was called to the Bar in 1948, aged twenty-five. He was a man of civilised tastes – opera, theatre, summers in Tuscany, which he was the first to call 'Chiantishire'.*

John Mortimer QC rose from his bed today at 5 a.m., went downstairs to the cluttered, comfortable room with the Matisse prints and the houseplants and the glass-topped desk, and got to work.

Mortimer is a one-man phenomenon who combines careers as a successful playwright and an eminent barrister celebrated for taking on unpopular libertarian causes like the *Oz* defence (*Oz* was a satirical magazine at the centre of an obscenity trial in the summer of 1971; what particularly riled the prosecution was a cartoon of Rupert Bear with an erection). Mortimer's new play *Heaven and Hell*, starring Denholm Elliott and Eleanor Bron, opens in Greenwich next week.

Plays and film scripts roll out in an unquenchable flow from the Mortimer factory, which is situated alongside the picturesque canal of London's Little

Venice. Hot from his typewriter currently are six TV plays on Shakespeare's life ('There's so little to go on,' complains Mortimer), a musical with Leslie Bricusse about Sherlock Holmes, and a planned TV series about an Old Bailey hack for one of Mortimer's favourite actors, Leo McKern.

Mortimer, at fifty-three, is beginning to yearn for a less pressurised life. 'My temptation,' he said, 'is to disappear into the country, pull up the draw-bridge, grow vegetables, and never be seen again.'

He has considered cutting down on his legal workload. But a deeply rooted respect for his dead father, whose own career in law was cut short by blindness, keeps John Mortimer in court. 'I feel, in some funny sort of way, that I have to compensate for my father's interrupted life,' said Mortimer.

> 'What's more, I find the law much easier than writing. I get very lonely, writing. Of course, I've known about loneliness all my life, having been born an only child. So getting dressed up in wigs and gowns, and such, and going to the courts is a real relief, and a reassurance that I am part of a society. Both my lives, legal as well as literary, are genuinely frightening. Whether it's a new play or a new Old Bailey case, every time out is the first time. Everything I do is a new test, a new trial. Bank managers don't get judged every week of their lives. But I do. Terrifying or not, it certainly sets the adrenalin flowing. Maybe that's why I like writing shorter plays. I'm too impatient for longer work. I love being able to do it all in one movement, so to speak.'

As the barrister at the centre of the *Oz* trial, Mortimer views the shift in public attitudes since then through disappointed eyes.

> 'At the time of the *Oz* thing in the '60s there was a feeling of a slight lurch forward, but the puritan backlash is now absolute and predominant. Nobody cares about free speech any more. The puritan streak in England is deathly and terribly depressing. Now we've got this awful paternalistic, self-protective society which insists on putting people into seat-belts and Sikhs into crash helmets. The state is becoming our nanny and it's all very sad.'

Nonetheless, Mortimer sees hope in today's increasingly liberated youth. 'I think kids today are a good deal less promiscuous than we were when I was young. They are also less liable to be swayed by colour prejudice, more kindly, and less excited by the issues that so enrage the puritans.'

Mortimer brightened.

'My own life is very happy. I am very happily married [to second wife Penny, still in her twenties, by whom he has a young daughter, Emily], and we have a lovely house that my father built in the Chiltern Hills and where I grew up. That house is my escape, my drug. One day I'll go there and you'll never hear of me again.'

19 MAY 1976

John Mortimer married twice (both wives were named Penny). A biography of John Mortimer, as he grew older, revealed a youthful indiscretion (a lost son) to which Mortimer happily confessed, taking the newcomer to his heart. Mortimer was knighted in 1998 and died on 16 January 2009, aged eighty-five. He was survived by five children, including actress Emily Mortimer.

Arthur Murray with his wife

CHAPTER 61

ARTHUR MURRAY –
TEACHING AMERICA TO DANCE

◇◇

"For Arthur, dead is dead."

Born Moses Teichmann in Austria-Hungary on 4 April 1895, Arthur Murray began teaching dance in Manhattan at the age of seventeen, having been instructed by the popular dance team of Irene and Vernon Castle. Always a shy child, Murray learned to dance in his early teens in a bid to gain social confidence. He would eventually establish a worldwide chain of 3,560 dance studios bearing his name. His pupils included Eleanor Roosevelt, the Duke of Windsor, John D. Rockefeller and heavyweight champion Jack Dempsey.

There was a famous American song by Johnny Mercer called 'Arthur Murray Taught Me Dancing in a Hurry'.

When you actually meet Mr Murray you learn that he does nothing in a hurry. He moves and talks slowly, never smiles, keeps looking down a long, pinched nose as though the world were a bad-smelling egg. He is a chill, impassive, shy introvert who has never shaken off a childhood stammer. He is addicted to three-second pauses.

'I don't think [pause] you ever quite overcome [pause] the disabilities [pause] you are born with. I have never really overcome [pause] my timidity.'

He talked about the chain of dancing studios he has established around the world. Tiresome people, he complained, were always hauling him off to court and claiming that they had been bulldozed into signing on for an expensive course of dancing lessons they could ill afford.

'This sort of hysteria is drummed up by lawyers trying to save clients who can't meet their payments,' he said.

'We wouldn't dream of high-pressurising anyone. A dentist once sued me for
$850. I retaliated with a return suit of $100,000. This is my favourite sum
for lawsuits [pause], a nice, round figure.'

Volatile Mrs Murray now interrupted her husband. 'With Arthur it isn't the
principle, it's the money.' Arthur Murray did not laugh at his wife's quip. It
was hard to tell whether he reacted at all.

Kathryn Murray, eleven years younger than Arthur, offered me another
engaging detail about his thriftiness. 'Arthur cannot bear to throw away razor
blades and uses a sharpening gadget that gives him thirty shaves out of every
blade.'

I looked at Arthur. He was nodding his head slowly up and down like
the Grand Lama in *Lost Horizon*. 'At the same time [pause] I give away 50
per cent of my income [pause] to charities. I have given away more than
5,000 TV sets to old folks' homes [pause] as well as mental and tubercular
hospitals.'

Kathryn, who contributes to the family coffers by writing brisk little
books with titles like *Kathryn Murray's Tips to Teenagers* and *The Best Day
for Every Little Girl*, agreed that her husband was generous 'as well as being
a tightwad'.

The Murrays had recently acquired a weekend home outside New York
where, according to the American wit Lou Parker, 'everything is laid out so
nicely – especially Arthur'.

The Murrays, who were visiting London to check on his dance studios
here, now wanted to look at some paintings. We went to a pokey little gallery
in St James's. Arthur kept his long, lean hands clasped tightly. He did not
like any of the paintings.

Kathryn kept telling me how mean Arthur was.

'He despises extravagance, so that he has even written into his will, in the
very first paragraph, that his funeral is to cost no more than $500. I ask
him, Arthur, what kinda funeral can you get for 500 bucks? He has no
belief in an afterlife. He's not a religious man, though he is the most moral
man I know. So he won't spend any money on fancy funerals. For Arthur,
dead is dead.'

16 August 1961

Arthur Murray died in Hawaii on 3 March 1991, aged ninety-five. Arthur and Kathryn had twin daughters. One of them, Jane, married Dr Henry Heimlich, who developed the Heimlich Manoeuvre, which has saved countless people from choking.

Patricia Neal with her husband Roald Dahl and two of their children

CHAPTER 62

PATRICIA NEAL –
ON THE DAY SHE WON THE OSCAR

"What happened to my baby in New York has taken all the joy
out of that city for me."

*Kentucky-born film and stage star Patricia Neal won a Best Actress Oscar
for her role in* Hud *in 1963. She married the English writer Roald Dahl in
1953; the couple had five children. She lost one child and saw another suffer
severe brain damage. She was born Patsy Louise Neal on 20 January 1926.
Her earliest, and only, ambition was to be an actress. When she was ten she
wrote to Father Christmas telling him 'what I want for Christmas is to study
Dramatics'. In 1949 she appeared in the film* The Fountainhead *opposite her
married co-star Gary Cooper, twenty-five years her senior, with whom she
began a lengthy affair. Director Mike Nichols invited her to play Mrs Robinson
in* The Graduate *(1967). Neal declined the role because she was still recovering from a series of strokes during pregnancy. Her personal life was complex
and tragic.*

Patricia Neal caught the 12.57 p.m. train to London yesterday at Great
Missenden, Buckinghamshire, took a window seat in a second-class
carriage, rested an outsize raffia handbag on her lap and lit her first cigarette.
Nobody recognised her. Nobody guessed that the quiet lady in the corner
was not only a celebrated American film star but one who, a few hours earlier,
had been awarded the Hollywood Oscar as the best actress of the year for
playing Anna, the slatternly housekeeper in *Hud*.

Patricia Neal's day started yesterday at 6 a.m. with a phone call from
Hollywood, from an old friend, French actress Annabella.

'I knew something was up.' Patricia Neal recalled the moment. 'I wasn't
even fully awake, and there was Annabella yelling: "You've won, Pat! You've
won, you've won!"'

Telling me about it, Pat Neal's smile was one of genuine, radiant delight. Although she is an intelligent and choosy actress, married to writer Roald Dahl, she did not attempt to disguise her childlike joy at having, at last, come top of her class.

'Oh, everybody wants the Oscar!' she said as our train clattered and hooted through Chalfont and Chorley Wood towards the city. 'Every actress dreams of it. I've always had fantasies about winning that prize. I've even made up little speeches in my head. What I would say. And I wasn't even there when it happened.'

Patricia Neal is a beautiful woman of thirty-eight, her strongly sculpted face alive and alert, yet touched with the suggestion of grief firmly controlled.

While the Oscars were being awarded Patricia Neal was asleep in her white Georgian farmhouse at Great Missenden with its 6 acres of orchard and its 200 rose bushes. Near her were her husband and her two surviving children. Shattering catastrophe has twice touched the life of the Dahls. In 1960, their youngest son Theo was being wheeled across a Manhattan street when a cab jumped a red light and crashed into the baby's pram. The baby has undergone multiple skull operations but may never fully recover. Two years later their oldest child Olivia came down with measles one afternoon. She was dead within hours.

The 12.57 pulled away from Harrow-on-the-Hill on the final leg of its brief journey to London.

'I am having another baby in six weeks,' said Pat Neal. 'And we'd like another after that. But it's getting awful late for me. I wish now I'd started earlier…'

Patricia Neal spends roughly half her year in the rustic peace of a small Buckinghamshire town, doing all the family shopping and cooking, occasionally opening village fetes and awarding prizes. The other half is spent filming. She seldom goes now to New York. 'What happened to my baby there has taken the joy out of that city for me.'

Her husband seldom accompanies her. She said:

'He's a terribly good writer, but can't bear to be a camp follower. Nor do I want a husband who devoted his life to me. We get along very well. We don't socialise greatly. No London parties, that sort of thing. We don't know all that many people, when you think about it. I suppose this Oscar will mean more money for a while, but I'm not wildly ambitious any more. If I do work I won't want to be ashamed of what I do.'

The newsreel cameras were waiting for the Oscar winner at Marylebone. The stationmaster wore a shiny top hat to greet her.

'Good heavens,' cried the best film actress in the world. 'I feel just like Elizabeth Taylor!'

She said it like a village housewife who had suddenly won the pools.

15 APRIL 1964

Patricia Neal died at home in Martha's Vineyard, Massachusetts on 8 August 2010, aged eighty-four. Her thirty-year marriage to Dahl ended in divorce in 1983, following Dahl's affair with set designer Felicity Crosland. Neal's granddaughter, Sophie Dahl, is a well-known English model and author who is married to English jazzman Jamie Cullum. In her 1988 autobiography, As I Am, *she confessed to having had an abortion during her relationship with Gary Cooper. She wrote: 'If I had only one thing to do over in my life I would have that baby. I cried myself to sleep for thirty years afterwards.' The night before her death from lung cancer Patricia Neal told the family gathered around her bedside: 'I've had a lovely time.'*

Anthony Newley, Joan Collins and daughter Tara

CHAPTER 63

ANTHONY NEWLEY – SEEKING PEACE

"Everything in my body revolts against what I do for a living."

Anthony George Newley was one of the rare English singers who was equally famous in America, where he starred in several of his own Broadway musicals and appeared regularly on TV and in Las Vegas. He was numbered among the last of the black-tie 'saloon singers' like Sammy Davis Jr, Dean Martin and the great Sinatra. He was born on 24 September 1931 in working-class Hackney, east London, to unmarried parents. A wartime evacuee, he was brought up by his mother Grace, to whom he remained loyal and loving to the end of his days. He became an office boy at the Italia Conti Stage School, where he was paid a pittance but was given free drama lessons. He came to the attention of director David Lean who cast Newley as the Artful Dodger in Lean's 1948 hit film Oliver Twist. *In* Idol on Parade *(1959), Newley played the role of a rock 'n' roll star enlisted in National Service. The role awakened him to an aware-ness of his own gifts as a singer and composer, which thereafter dominated his professional career.*

D ressed as the devil, cradling his forked tail in his arms like a docile pet, Anthony Newley took his final bows at the Prince of Wales theatre last Saturday, at the end of the run of his musical *The Good Old Bad Old Days*. You should have been there. The crowd rose to Newley, pounding their palms in a hurricane of applause, urging him to return, clamorous in their admiration for one of the last superstars left in the field.

Only a handful of people in that happy mob were aware that London was seeing Newley performing for the very last time. He has grown into his maturity as an intensely private man, an awakened man, disgusted by the tinsel of showbiz and the humiliations of public performance.

'Everything in my body,' says Newley, 'revolts against what I do for a living.'

'It's almost as though the real me is being told to dance like a mad puppet. A lot of actors must love what they do. They tap their little feet in the wings, dying to get on. But for me the whole day is coloured by the thought that I have to go on stage. It's so bloody depressing. I know it's awful to say things like this. It sounds like a betrayal of the audience who, after all, pay for a certain commodity. But I have never felt contempt for an audience. I wish them no harm. I just don't want to be there, baby. I mean, what am I actually doing out there, frightened, scared, smiling to please…? What's doubly terrifying is that every night is first night. You never get off the hook. I've never thrown a performance in my life. I couldn't. I'm terrified someone's going to stand up in the third row and shout: "It doesn't work! It isn't funny! I can see the joins!" I live in fear of that.

Anyway, just how damn good am I? I guess I'm just about 75 per cent ego and 25 per cent talent, and it's not enough. I wanted to be the best there is, and I know I can't be that. Another thing that worried me a lot is that I started to drink before I went on, had to have a couple of shots. I hate that in performers, the drinking thing. I felt it could happen to me, and then it's over. Booze may make you feel better, but finally it robs you, impairs you. I'm not a drinker. All it did for me was damage my liver.'

Anthony Newley returns to Los Angeles today to be reunited with his family, which now includes a new baby daughter named Shelby. For the next six months he faces a backbreaking schedule of personal engagements, from Las Vegas onwards. He's doing it to pay off US back taxes.

And then?

'Well, then we plan to come back to England next spring and settle down for good. I don't give the English any points for being better than anyone else, but there's sanity in England that's very important. I'd like my kid to be brought up here. I'm drawn south to Cornwall … Devon … somewhere. More and more I feel I want to retire from social contact. It may be a sign of old age, but there are very few people you can love in this world, with all due respect to the rest of them. I don't know what I'll do … go on writing songs, write a book, write an opera, make things with my hands. I want to live quietly and think about things. In my deepest moments I feel I have a calling that I've never touched. I'm bored by late Catholics and all those who scurry to the Church in their middle age. But I want life to become precious again, something special, hoped for. Now, at the age of forty-two, one must do something about these things, even if it means stepping back from the life one has known. I am haunted by the ghost of that thought…'

19 SEPTEMBER 1973

I wrote about Anthony Newley several times. He became a close friend. He never did make it to his imagined Shangri La in Cornwall, or Devon, or anywhere else. He was always on the point of retiring. His mind was ever reaching for unknown opportunities. The following piece catches Newley in characteristic mode – half joyful, half despairing. It was published in 1969, while Newley was still married to Joan Collins.

Earlier this year on the island of Malta, to the dismay of local Church authorities, Anthony Newley made a film. What distressed the clerics was the undressed state of some of the ladies involved in the picture, not to mention all manner of sexual mischief.

In the middle of the fuss, Mr Newley, intense and long-suffering, plodded on manfully with the making of the picture, fighting off migraine attacks and, in every inch of celluloid that rolled through the camera, working out his personal destiny.

Let me explain that the hero, if hero he be, of Mr Newley's self-revealing movie is a poor London boy who becomes a singing and acting celebrity. The boy's mother had been a kind-hearted but unremarkable London drudge, while his footloose, itinerant father hadn't stayed around long enough to sign his name on a wedding certificate. Heironymus Merkin (such is our film hero's name) grows up to be a gifted, sensitive brooder, who writes and sings introspective ballads about clowns, fools and fortune, seeking his truths in the sweaty brightness of showbiz and in the embraces of pretty girls casually acquired, carelessly abandoned.

Along the way Heironymus endures a loveless first marriage and sees his first-born baby die.

Anthony Newley not only acts the central role, but he also conceived, co-wrote, produced and directed it, a challenging combination of functions that, he says, 'nearly wiped me out'. The film, which will be released two months from now, must be among the most personal statements ever committed to film. In one scene Merkin's mother (played by Patricia Hayes) acknowledges humbly: 'It wasn't your fault, son. It was me. I was just a stupid girl.'

'That's verbatim,' said Newley. 'I've heard my own mother say that to me.'

But he is disinclined to emphasise the similarities between himself and the feckless Heironymus Merkin. 'I won't talk about that. I've always talked too much. I'm bored with entertainers telling the world how tough it is to get through the day.'

I met Newley in Paris, a city he loathes. ('I've been lonelier here than anywhere.') He was feeling pretty low.

'Seems to me,' he said, 'having been in the biz for so long, I reached a point about five years ago when I didn't want to work for anyone else ever again. I felt I must be doing my own thing.'

His own thing included two eccentric musicals written with Leslie Bricusse – *Stop the World I Want to Get Off* and *The Roar of the Greasepaint*. The big personal questions, which are Newley's thumbprint, were distilled into soaring ballads like 'What Kind Of Fool Am I?' and 'Who Can I Turn To?'

He said:

'I'm really recreating myself over and over again. I am obsessed by a need to chronicle certain things – the image of a dead child, for instance – that keep returning like a song, a need to drag up the old totems, the old questions. It's kind of pathetic that a man should always be voyaging inwards.'

We taxied over to the Left Bank and found a restaurant where the food was very expensive and very poor.

Tony sat hunched over his dinner plate, toying with the wing of a highly spiced goose, then he pushed it away. Beyond the plate glass window, a grim-visaged man with a spiky thatch of hair walked alone.

'Samuel Beckett,' Newley identified the passer-by. A minute later a young French couple – the girl was about seventeen – stopped on the sidewalk a yard away from us on the other side of the glass. The boy kissed the girl on her nose and eyebrows.

This cheered Tony Newley up considerably and he switched into high gear, talking about the people he loved, reflecting happily on his marriage to Joan Collins.

'Joanie regards life as a kind of Mardi-Gras to which she has been invited and from which she intends to be the last to go home. We have struck the same difficulties most people have in marriage, and sometimes things got pretty bad between us. But her intelligence and strength have kept us together. It's a wonder she keeps her patience with me. She is smarter than the average bear, has more vim and vigour than a Marine sergeant, and is the maypole round which we all dance.'

Newley's mood of elation did not last for long. The making of the Heironymus Merkin film has taken a lot out of him.

'I went into it, took on all those jobs, almost like a man intent on destroying himself. I'm not constructed for that kind of responsibility. I'm not a leader. I have no organising ability. It wasn't even fun. The achievement was negated by exhaustion. Can you imagine having a steel band drawn tight around your head? For fourteen weeks making the picture on Malta, I lived with that kind of tension and pain. At the end of it I had a complete collapse – spots, pimples, apathy, the lot. I nearly finished up on a funny farm. Yet I would do it again. I'm a driven man. I could put myself away for all time.'

This struck him as funny and he shouted with laughter. 'Maybe I should see a shrink. There is no such thing, surely, as a worthwhile work of art created by a man who was emotionally and mentally healthy. Deep down all artists are neurotic cripples, trying to work it all out...'

We walked along the banks of the Seine. Tony went unrecognised among the French.

'I'm not that mad about the Gauls on the whole, I must say,' said Newley.

'It is a singular thing to have been brought up an Englishman. More and more, living in Los Angeles, I have come to love English understatement, English justice, English fair play. In my thirties I find that these are the things that matter. Our whole history is in cricket – eleven men being terribly polite about a bat and a ball. It's utterly charming. I didn't appreciate it until I left the country. Now I find I need that kind of belonging more and more. My son is down for Eton in 1980-something-or-other. No, not Eton ... Harrow. I loathe New York and Broadway with all the power at my disposal. New York is the ugliest city on earth. It makes Birmingham seem like Haiti. We live in Hollywood because the tax situation there is kinder. I am allowed to keep some of my money and I have no guilt about that. It has become chic and popular to put America down, but they are going through a terrible time and I sympathise with them in their country's misery. America has been kind to me and Joanie.'

Newley's maternal grandmother was Jewish. 'I feel almost totally Jewish,' he said. 'Jews seem to get to the heart of things, which I love. I feel warm

and happy with them. When I worked with Bricusse,' he added, 'I venerated his intelligence and his scholarship. It's very Jewish to dig talent in
that way.'

He is haunted by death. 'It makes everything pointless. If I was sixteen, I'd
probably be outside the US Embassy holding a banner. But I'm a glandular
thirty-seven, and I have no politics. Politics are out of date...'

His own basic ideology is centred on the future of man as a hostage to
science. The thought exhilarates him. 'We are all just a mixture of acids, and
we shall one day breed the bad out of ourselves in the laboratory. We are on
the edge of the most fantastic discoveries and in London they're still reviving
The Desert Song...'

An uncharitable wind blew up along the quais and sent the Parisians scurrying home. Newley stood brooding at a crossroads. The title of the picture
he made in Malta is *Can Heironymus Merkin Ever Forget Mercy Humppe and
Find True Happiness?*

Can he?

2 DECEMBER 1968

*Anthony Newley died of renal cancer in the arms of his partner, fashion designer
Gina Fratini, on 14 April 1999 in Jenson Beach, Florida. He was outlived by his
mother, Grace, who died in 2003, aged ninety-nine years old.*

A WONDERFUL DAY LIKE TODAY

BY LESLIE BRICUSSE AND ANTHONY NEWLEY

DAVID MERRICK
IN ASSOCIATION WITH
BERNARD DELFONT
PRESENTS

ANTHONY NEWLEY **CYRIL RITCHARD**

IN THE NEW
LESLIE BRICUSSE-ANTHONY NEWLEY
MUSICAL

THE ROAR OF THE GREASEPAINT
-THE SMELL OF THE CROWD

BOOK, MUSIC & LYRICS BY **LESLIE BRICUSSE** AND **ANTHONY NEWLEY**

WITH **SALLY SMITH** GILBERT PRICE JOYCE JILLSON

PRODUCTION DESIGNED & LIGHTED BY   COSTUMES BY   MUSICAL DIRECTOR   ORCHESTRATIONS BY   VOCAL & DANCE MUSIC ARRANGED BY   MUSICAL NUMBERS STAGED BY
SEAN KENNY   FREDDY WITTOP   HERBERT GROSSMAN   PHILIP J. LANG   PETER HOWARD   GILLIAN LYNNE

DIRECTED BY **ANTHONY NEWLEY**   ORIGINAL CAST ALBUM BY RCA VICTOR

WHO CAN I TURN TO (When Nobody Needs Me) • FEELING GOOD • LOOK AT THAT FACE •
A WONDERFUL DAY LIKE TODAY • THE JOKER • THE BEAUTIFUL LAND • THIS DREAM •
SWEET BEGINNING • MY FIRST LOVE SONG • IT ISN'T ENOUGH • WHERE WOULD YOU BE
WITHOUT ME • THAT'S WHAT IT IS TO BE YOUNG • NOTHING CAN STOP ME NOW • MY WAY
• WITH ALL DUE RESPECT • WHAT A MAN • PUT IT IN THE BOOK • THINGS TO REMEMBER •

TRO MUSICAL COMEDY PRODUCTIONS
The RICHMOND ORGANIZATION

The cover for the sheet music of *The Roar of the Greasepaint*

Beverley Nichols

CHAPTER 64

BEVERLEY NICHOLS – MAD ABOUT CATS

"Even a scruffy alley cat is more elegant
than any woman who ever lived."

He was, not so long ago, one of the most famous men in England. He wrote sixty books over a period of sixty-two years, in addition to thousands of magazine articles, essays, weekly columns, plays and musical compositions. Nothing seems to have been outside the range of his energies. (He ghostwrote the 'autobiography' of opera diva Dame Nellie Melba in 1925.) He had ravishing good looks and appears to have lived a charmed life. However, Beverley Nichols is hardly remembered now, so general has been his eclipse. His legacy, however, does live on, mainly as a writer of gardening books. Rex Whistler illustrated the earliest of these, Down the Garden Path, *which was published in 1932 and has never been out of print. Nichols was educated at Marlborough College and Balliol, Oxford University, where he was president of the Oxford Union and the editor of* Isis.

Mr Beverley Nichols practically leapt over the carpet of his living room to reach his piano stool. His fingers caressed the keyboard like a man stroking a favoured cat.

'Rachmaninoff,' announced Mr Nichols, 'was profoundly F.'

I had called to see Mr Nichols in his olde worlde cottage in Ham Common, Surrey, where the celebrated scribe is comfortably settled with his three adored cats (named Four, Oscar and Five), his piano, his paintings, his marvellous garden … and kindly Gaskin, a gentleman's gentleman of the old school who has been in Beverley Nichols' service for something like thirty-eight years.

'Gaskin,' Beverley Nichols told me fondly, 'is very F indeed.'

Beverley Nichols' repeated references to people being F is part of a game he has just invented to amuse himself. According to Mr Nichols, the world is divided into two basic groups: the Fs and the non-Fs.

'An F,' explained Mr Nichols, 'is a person who is basically Feline by nature. I don't mean catty in the bad sense.'

> 'Being an F is largely a question of sensitivity, of elegance, of intense awareness and, of course, of a deep and passionate independence. It is not a question of fashion. It has none of the vulgar connotations of U and non-U – a squalid phrase for second-rate drawing rooms.'

'Being an F goes far deeper,' he says. 'It has to do with the more profound aspects of human nature. Only a minority will understand it, but in that minority will be numbered the true elite.'

All this may seem, to the average reader, either pompous or twee, or both. Neither charge will bother Mr Beverley Nichols. He has been writing opinionated books for practically half a century, and in that time has been called every kind of name under the sun including 'Public Petunia No. 1'.

For myself, I see in Mr Nichols a cultivated mandarin of fastidious taste, a man appalled and offended by the twentieth century, a man born out his time. Nowhere in his house did I see a radio, a TV set, a record player, or even a visible electric light. All these evidences of modernity may be discovered, no doubt, in upstairs rooms. Downstairs, the world of Beverley Nichols stopped dead somewhere around 1830. His rooms and their furnishings indicate a thorough rejection of modern thought, design and architecture. Even Gaskin appears to have walked fully fashioned out of a Dickens serialisation.

Beverley Nichols, in short, presents an image of a man in full flight from the vulgarity and aggression of our age. At the same time he has had the energy and wisdom to write a great many published words about our world and the people who inhabit it. Nichols knows, and has known, everybody who was anybody.

He has been a celebrity in his own right ever since he wore Oxford bags and wrote the earliest of his (so far) thirty-two books. His first, *Prelude*, was written when Beverley was a mere seventeen. When he was twenty-four, he wrote an autobiographical bestseller called *Twenty-Five*. His comprehensive experience of people gives him as much right to divide the universe into Fs and non-Fs as Nancy Mitford enjoyed when she devised her U and non-U factions. Let Beverley Nichols therefore have his say.

'You can tell Fs,' he told me, 'almost by their vibrations.'

'It is difficult to explain. You must feel it. It has nothing to do with greatness or talent. Sir Thomas Beecham is a real F. He is a cat, you understand, and there is no higher praise. Why, you can almost see Beecham's tail wagging when he conducts an orchestra. On the other hand, Sir Malcolm Sargent, who is a close friend of mine, is decidedly non-F.'

'Royalty,' said Mr Nichols recklessly, 'is not especially F.'

'Prince Philip is most decidedly non-F. The last truly F monarch in Britain was Charles the Second. Some superficial historians might claim a degree of F-ness for Queen Victoria, but this would almost certainly be due to her devotion to Benjamin Disraeli, who was flamboyantly F.'

Burly, stately Gaskin now entered the room to announce that luncheon would be served in five minutes.

'All female crooners are non-F,' Beverley Nichols decided suddenly.

'Lena Horne!' I protested.

'Yes, Lena is F,' Beverley conceded after a short pause. 'And so, come to think of it, is Eartha Kitt.'

'What about Cecil Beaton?'

'You'd think, wouldn't you,' Beverley smiled, 'that Cecil would be an F. I mean, he is so elegant, but I am very much afraid that Cecil is non-F. He's so incredibly tough, you see. Cecil is the real he-man of show business and I don't believe the cats are all that tough. Let's take women as an example,' Nichols continued.

'A real F woman does not mind the competition of cats. She would contrive, somehow, to let a cat complement her beauty. She would bring the cat, as it were, into the impression she made in a drawing-room. But a non-F woman regards cats as outsiders and competitors … like this Miss Henrietta Tiarks who is marrying the Duke of Bedford's son.'

We went into lunch. On the way Mr Nichols told me that his friend, the poet John Betjeman, was profoundly F: 'a charmingly scruffy F … a very elegant alley cat'.

Over lunch, Mr Nichols continued to dismiss and decry Nancy Mitford's U and non-U game. 'Nancy Mitford,' said Beverley, 'is profoundly non-F. Do put that in.'

'Nancy is a charming writer and everything, but her U and non-U game is extremely unkind and offensive. It is also silly and inaccurate. What the hell does it matter if you call a chimneypiece a mantelpiece. It was called a mantel-piece long before Nancy Mitford's family was ever thought of. Yes, her U and non-U game is fundamentally cruel. I believe there is only one basic sin in the world and that is cruelty. I cannot bear it in any form. I despise zoos. In my favourite daydream I imagine I am able to unlock all the cages at the zoo. All the animals rush past me, flooding the highways and byways of northern London. They crash through the windows of respectable parlours and descend on plump families watching television and send their teeth crunching through the fat bottoms of the ladies who for so many years have been insulting them with buns.'

After lunch Beverley Nichols led me into the garden. He pointed out a creeping plant. I said I'd never heard of it and Beverley Nichols called me a barbarian.

'I am learning Greek,' he told me a few moments later. 'How fortunate the Greeks are to be able to look up and see the Acropolis – an eternal symbol. Londoners look up, and what do they see? Daz and Omo [popular washing powders]. Nothing has happened of any value in England since 1830.'

'I am a peaceful person. I have surrounded myself with lovely things because they have an eternal value. But I don't live in an ivory tower. I am very consid-erably involved in a great many things. I am so involved it hurts, actually. I live an extremely comfortable life, of course. Gaskin sees to that. Gaskin is my guide, philosopher and friend. My mother discovered him. One day when I was twenty-two, she told me, "As you don't look like getting married soon, and you need someone to look after you and your home, you might as well have a gentleman's gentleman."'

At that moment Gaskin walked across the sun-speckled lawn cradling Beverley's black cat named Four in his safe arms.

'Gaskin,' said Beverley, 'is wonderful with the cats. I adore cats, obviously. So much less vulgar than humans. So much more dignified than women.

Even a scruffy alley-cat,' said Beverley Nichols 'is more elegant than any woman who ever lived…'

11 SEPTEMBER 1960

Beverley Nichols died on 15 September 1983 and is buried in Glatton, Cambridgeshire.

David Niven

CHAPTER 65

DAVID NIVEN –
AN OFFICER AND A GENTLEMAN

◇◇◇

"I am often thought of as shallow and artificial."

David Niven was that rarity: an English screen actor who was adored by all. Charm was his stock in trade, his signature mode. He set out to charm the world and succeeded in doing so. James David Graham Niven was born in London on 1 March 1910, and died seventy-three years later in Chateau d'Oex, Switzerland. His grandfather was slain in the Battle of Isandlwana (1879) during the Zulu War. A military career was envisioned for young David, too. He did well at the Royal Military College, Sandhurst, graduating in 1930 as a second lieutenant with a promising future in uniform. Since there were no wars to fight, Niven resigned after three years and showed up in Hollywood a year later where he was taken on by Central Casting and registered as 'Anglo-Saxon Type No. 2008'. After a few unimportant roles (he played a Mexican in a Western), a non-speaking role in Mutiny on the Bounty *attracted the eye of Hollywood mogul Sam Goldwyn. By the end of the '30s, Niven was playing important roles in films like* The Dawn Patrol *(1938) and* Wuthering Heights *(1939) alongside Laurence Olivier and Merle Oberon. With the outbreak of the Second World War, Niven returned to England to play his part in the conflict. Niven was always charmingly unforthcoming about his wartime activities, but they must have been significant. He ended the war as a lieutenant colonel. When peace came he reasserted his status in films like* A Matter of Life and Death *(1946), and thereafter a score or more of big movies like* Around the World in Eighty Days *(1956),* Separate Tables, *which won him a Best Actor Oscar in 1958,* The Guns of Navarone *(1961) and* The Pink Panther *(1963). Niven wrote four books, including two light-hearted memoirs:* The Moon's a Balloon *(1971), which sold over five million copies, and* Bring on the Empty Horses *(1975). Both these books retold stories of his Hollywood years, though some were seen as fanciful or extravagantly embellished.*

★

'I was born,' David Niven was telling me yesterday, 'right here in London. Actually, I was supposed to be born in Scotland, but my mother came to London to see the doctor and, what do you know, she had me right there and then!'

He chuckled into his cupped hands and raised one eyebrow. He was instantly lovable, and Niven knew it. He knew it as well as he knows his name. For a man two years short of fifty he looks devilishly lithe and youthful, with just the right dash of rakishness about his manner.

We talked about his adopted hometown of Hollywood, California. 'When I first got there,' said Niven, 'Aubrey Smith and Ronald Colman and old Nigel Bruce were running a sort of English colony out there. Lots of cricket and that sort of thing.'

Niven leaned against the chimneypiece. 'I don't belong to any clique, or any group,' he said.

'I've fought against that. In fact, if you must know, I've got quite a bug about this nationality thing. How marvellous it would be, I always think, if people just forgot that they were Poles or Swedes or Englishmen or Germans – and just became people.'

This plea for universal brotherhood, coming from Hollywood's most recognisable British inhabitant, and a Sandhurst-trained officer to boot, echoed in the room like a treasonous utterance. But then, Niven is a puzzle and a paradox. He is, for example, a modest man who adores bombast and exaggeration in others.

'I wish with all my heart,' Niven told me, 'that I was born a really flamboyant character like Bogart or Sinatra.'

'I honestly think that the rest of us, the whole damn movie business, should go down on our bended knees to the Garbos and the Bogarts and the Sinatras and the Wallace Beerys. Because it is their flamboyance and their glamour that have kept Hollywood going ... that has kept all of us going.'

Niven's modesty strikes me as unfeigned. He has a dread of seeming conceited.

'I was absolutely terrified that my two boys might be embarrassed by their father's activities. I did not want them to become inflated if I was doing terribly well, or deflated if I was making a hash of it. I brought the boys up alone, and I used to ask them "what does your father do?" I trained them to answer: "He's a very, very bad actor, but he absolutely loves doing it."'

'It really worked!' David Niven assured me. 'It's the only intelligent thing I've ever done in my whole life.'

Actually, Niven is a very good actor who has just received the New York Critics Prize for his performance in the film of Terence Rattigan's *Separate Tables*. He is eager, to an almost obsessional degree, to be approved of. At one point in our conversation, he said:

> 'I know exactly what I dislike about myself. I am too busy trying to get every-body to like me. As a result, I am often thought of as shallow and artificial. If I go into a room with fifty people, and forty-nine are smiling at me and just one little man is snarling at me – just one – I'll spend the whole evening with that little man until he smiles at me, until he likes me.'

Niven studied his fingernails for an instant. Then he repeated in a softer voice: 'Artificial – and shallow…'

Many who seek the applause of the crowd have lacked the normal affections of family life as a child. David Niven is no exception. 'When I was six years old, I was packed off to Stowe by my step-father,' he said. 'I didn't want to go. At school I was bullied. I had a bad time…'

Niven looked uncomfortable for the first time. 'My parents wanted me to be a general. I didn't want to be a general.'

Then, suddenly, he smiled and donned his armour again. 'My ambition is simple,' he said brightly. 'My ambition is to never resign. I shall go on acting until I am thrown out or publicly spat at. And who knows?' mused the man who is probably rich enough to buy the English south coast. 'Who knows … one day I may even have enough money to buy a little cottage in Brighton … maybe two.'

12 FEBRUARY 1958

David Niven married twice, fathering two sons by his first wife, Primula Susan Rollo, who was killed tragically in 1946 while playing a party game in Tyrone Power's Hollywood house; she walked into what she believed to be a closed closet and fell down a stone staircase into an unlit cellar, fracturing her skull. Two years later, Niven met and married a Swedish model, Hjördis Tersmeden. It was by all accounts a fiery and unhappy marriage, Hjördis lapsing regularly into alcoholism. In 1980 Niven's own health began to show sign of impaired speech and muscle collapse. The diagnosis was amiotropic lateral sclerosis, a degenerative neurological disease. He died on 29 July 1983. Hjördis showed up drunk at Niven's funeral, having been persuaded to attend by her friend Prince Rainier of Monaco. She died of a stroke in 1997, aged seventy-eight.

Edna O'Brien

CHAPTER 66

EDNA O'BRIEN –
THE RICHNESS OF MEMORY

"I'm a very good judge of friends and a very bad judge of lovers."

Edna O'Brien has written twenty-one works of fiction, three works of non-fiction, and five plays. The only child of a devout Catholic family, she was born on 15 December 1930, in Co. Clare, Ireland. She qualified as a pharmacist at the age of twenty, defied her family to marry a Czech-Irish author, Ernest Gebler, a man twice her age. ('It was,' she said, 'like jumping off a moving bus … I rebelled against the coercive and stifling religion into which I was born … It was very frightening and all pervasive.')

Last week her play, *A Pagan Place*, began rehearsals at the Royal Court and her novel *Night* was published. It's proving a bustling autumn for the picturesque and unstoppable Irish novelist Edna O'Brien. 'I suffer from an excess of energy,' she says in a voice that seems to murmur and mesmerise. 'I love people who go on and on, who don't care if they win or lose, who don't believe the nonsense of success. The things that matter are effort, and continuing. My best guru now is obstinacy.'

Obstinate Miss O'Brien remains one of the most successful writers around, issuing a smallish but regular output of novels, plays and movie scripts. She lives in a big house in a green Chelsea square. She has two tall, dark sons, Sacha and Carlos, at the progressive school Bedales. She finds time to keep up friendships and (she will tell you unasked) to fall in love disastrously.

'I'm a very good judge of friends and a very bad judge of lovers,' she said. 'My instincts are good as long as there's no sexual attraction. Then they become doddery.'

I met Miss O'Brien in a King's Road restaurant a minute's walk from Sloane Square where her play, starring Dave Allen, opens later this month.

The play concerns a group of people in Dublin in 1944, cut off from the rest of the world by war and geography. A young girl deserts them to become a nun, provoking her mother to say: 'We're not her kind of people anymore.'

It's clear that Edna O'Brien sees some mirrored aspect of herself in that child who quits her familiar world for keeps. 'My most worrying thought,' she says, gesturing dismay, 'is that I don't live around my own people. But sometimes a country can eat you up unless you get out from under it. Especially when the land is as old and haunted and powerful as Ireland.'

She looked very Irish when she said that, pale and fragile, her hair auburn. Edna O'Brien favours the kind of clothes that billow and drift, like the apparel of a gypsy teacup reader.

She is devoid of social cunning, a sympathetic listener who is equally likely to bare her own soul. Her enthusiasm is reserved for people who, she feels, do not lie. 'My favourite living woman,' she said, 'is the Greek singer Nana Mouskouri.

'There is no untruth in her voice. My favourite dead woman is Edith Piaf. Her unshakable romanticism! When Piaf croaked out those songs I thought: "That's who I would like to be." Oh I loved her.'

Edna O'Brien talks about her bouts of despair. She is profoundly critical of herself.

'It's so difficult, so painful. One has to unlearn so much – to erase the imprint of the early years of our lives. But unless we break the mould and lose the habit of attachment, no progress is possible. I am convinced of that. To be a writer is the hardest thing of all. One must be ruthless and find oneself a hole, or a tower, where one can write without obstruction or dictation from outside. I can work in London because here I feel myself a stranger and keep myself a stranger. I am a little like the woman in my new novel *Night*. Her name's Mary Hooligan. She lives on the richness of memories and, though she has hit rock bottom, she can still say: "I will see a lit-up pane, burnished, and say to myself: all is not lost, all is not bleak … and I will laugh and I will cry. There is little difference. What more do I want?"'

13 OCTOBER 1972

Edna O'Brien and Ernest Gebler divorced after ten years of marriage. She published her most famous book, The Country Girls, *in 1960, a work that eventually became a trilogy. The explicit depiction of sex caused these books to be banned and even burned in her native Ireland. Other notable books by O'Brien included* A Pagan Place *(1970) and* The Girl with Green Eyes *(1962).*

EN ESTE NUMERO: 15 PAGINAS EN COLORES

LIFE

EN ESPAÑOL

LA AMERICA QUE VIO COLON

EL ENCUENTRO DE IKE Y NIKITA

DOMINGUIN Y ORDOÑEZ MANO A MANO

EL MATADOR
ANTONIO ORDOÑEZ

19 DE OCTUBRE DE 1959

Antonio Ordoñez

CHAPTER 67

ANTONIO ORDOÑEZ – AFTERNOONS OF FEAR

"The bull cannot get me in the hotel."

Ernest Hemingway, who knew a thing or two about bullfighting, insisted that Antonio Ordoñez was 'the greatest torero the world has ever seen'. I saw Antonio Ordoñez at work many times. He was a serious and cynical torero born into a family of toreros. He displayed little joy in the bullring. His style was slow and unflashy. The emotion came out of the slowness. He was the son of a bullfighter. His father was Cayetano, who used the professional name Niño de la Palma (Child of the Palm), owned the oldest bullring in Spain, in Ronda, and was the model for the central Spanish character in Hemingway's breakthrough novel The Sun Also Rises.*

When Ordoñez (Or-don-yeth) was being hailed as the new Christ of the bullring, he told me a revealing thing about bullfighters and fear. With an interpreter at my side I had been talking to the great man about one of the threadbare clichés of popular bullfight fiction. The novels and stories I have read about bullfighting seem routinely to include at least one sequence which depicts the hero resting alone in his hotel room trying to contain his gathering panic as the hour of the fight draws nearer. (Bullfights always take place in the late afternoon.) Ordoñez shrugged. 'Yes, I know,' he said. 'But I am never afraid of the bull in the hotel. Why should I be afraid in the hotel? The bull cannot get me in the hotel.'

Icalled at Ordoñez's apartment by appointment, and was welcomed by a small, smiling man who introduced himself as the private secretary. 'The maestro will be with you presently,' he said in a low voice. 'The maestro is listening on the radio to the football match between Spain and Italy.' I was shown into a study furnished in the serene style of a stockbroker's country home in England. A golden replica of a bull's hoof, a hard-won 1958 trophy, rested on a polished oak table. Next to it was a leather-framed photograph of

Ordoñez holding a woollen jersey in both hands and demonstrating a bull-fighting pass to the Hollywood actor Douglas Fairbanks Jr, who appeared to be amused but no wiser.

The double doors swung open suddenly; Ordoñez walked in smiling, shaking his head in apology, a tall, boyish Spaniard who would one day run to bulk, with a glossy mop of ebony hair and a soft, pampered mouth which tended to hang half-open when he was fighting the bulls.

'Bullfighting,' he told me presently, 'is a drug that I need every day. Bulls pursue my dreams. In my dreams I am among the bulls. I am one of them. In dreams there is no fear.'

Awake, it was different.

> 'All matadors are afraid. The moment the bull enters the ring I become afraid and remain afraid until I have killed him and the mules have dragged him out. This fear can never be conquered. It can, however, be controlled. No man is without fear. At the start of every season I know that I will be hurt. It is foolish to pray not to be hurt. I pray only that my wounds should not be large. My life has not changed at all. The friends of my boyhood are still my friends. They can come and go as they please.'

Ordoñez lit up a Camel cigarette and began to whistle 'Colonel Bogey' through the smoke.

27 MARCH 1960

After his retirement Ordoñez, like many bullfighters, prospered as a breeder of fighting bulls. The ashes of his friend Orson Welles were buried on his Spanish ranch. Antonio Ordoñez died of cancer in 1998.

Antonio Ordoñez

John Osborne

CHAPTER 68

JOHN OSBORNE – LOOKING BACK IN ANGER

"Writing lyrics is like writing bad poetry … it's not easy."

Playwright-actor John Osborne, born on 12 December 1929, achieved instant fame with his play Look Back In Anger, *which he wrote in seventeen days while seated in a deck chair on Morecambe pier where he was appearing in a run-of-the-mill touring comedy* Seagulls over Sorrento. *Produced at the Royal Court in 1956,* Look Back In Anger *received mixed notices, but won the enthusiastic endorsements of London's most important critics –* The Observer's *Kenneth Tynan ('The best young play of its decade') and the* Sunday Times's *Harold Hobson ('a writer of outstanding promise'). The play, it is often said, ushered in a new era of theatrical truth and realism and sounded the death knell of the polite traditions of the English West End theatre as represented by Noël Coward and Terence Rattigan. In the late '50s Osborne, it seemed, was riding high and could do no wrong.*

Mr John Osborne, Britain's original Angry Young Man, has a new musical opening in Bournemouth next week. No British musical since the war has been awaited in the West End with such excited speculation as Osborne's *The World of Paul Slickey*. Will *Slickey* consolidate Osborne's soaring reputation as the most significant playwright to arise in Britain in decades? We will have the answer in a month or so. Meanwhile, Britain is not lacking in prophets poised to gloat if Osborne, this time, encounters failure. He has, after all, sired three major successes in a row. Such an uninterrupted run of hits may prove to be unforgiveable.

'People in this country,' John Osborne was telling me yesterday, 'have this weird national thing about success. They dislike it. They resent it. They like to see somebody fall flat on his face…'

I met John Osborne at lunchtime in a tiny pub in Drury Lane directly opposite the theatre where he is directing *The World of Paul Slickey*. Having downed a non-alcoholic mineral water ('most unusual for him', said a worried barmaid), Osborne opened a cigar box, extracted a pencil-long cheroot and proceeded to light it.

'The popular image of me,' said Osborne, holding his cheroot vertically like a conductor's baton, 'is of someone who snarls and says beastly things all the time.' He tried to chuckle but ended up with a sigh. 'I am not like that. But never mind. It is not important. What is important is what you do and its effect on people…'

Many of my Fleet Street colleagues, when they interview Osborne, tend to list his cars, suits, shoes and other evidence of Osborne's wealth. As though, somehow, nobody that rich had any right to be angry. This sort of thing makes Osborne very tired and very cross. Why, he protests, should a writer wearing suede shoes be any less angry than somebody wearing sandals?

'Does success corrupt?' he echoed my question.

'Success only corrupts the really untalented … the people with nothing to say. It does not spoil the real talents. I mean, look at Graham Greene. Look at the money he's made. But he still works like a dog. What he has to say is still worthwhile.'

A little later on we left the pub and crossed Drury Lane into the theatre. 'We'll talk some more at half-past six,' said Osborne, disappearing into a scrum of secretaries and production assistants. 'All right,' said Osborne taking command, 'let's go…' Six leggy girls romped in from the wings.

The musical has been touted as a satire about Fleet Street gossip column-ists. Not so. Fleet Street is just a peg on which Osborne hangs an arsenal of barbs, darts and arrows. The show is a shrewdly observed assault on practi-cally everything about contemporary Britain which Osborne dislikes, which is practically everything. The range of Osborne's targets certainly includes Fleet Street. But it also includes Sex, Marriage, Religion, Politics, the Theatre, Stately Homes … 'You know,' explains Osborne, 'everything we spell with a Capital Letter.'

At 2.15 p.m. the popular South African crooner Dennis Lotis, as Paul Slickey, the Fleet Street heel, walked onto the stage and performed a song of vaulting cynicism. 'There's wormwood in every family tree…' he sang.

Ten minutes and one adulterous act later a girl with a well-bred voice was saying, 'Mummy was so brave when we gave away India.'

After yet another adulterous incident, the leading lady protests, 'No, Michael, I couldn't marry you. Marriage is quite disgusting. For one thing, it makes intimacy impossible, to say nothing of passion.'

At 6.00 p.m. the rehearsal was over. Osborne gave the cast his notes, telling them how he had liked it, where they had gone wrong. Then he joined me in the stalls. 'It's impossible in this business to do anything interesting without making enemies,' he said. 'Too many people want to be loved. You can't do both.'

Osborne has heartily disliked most British musicals he has seen. He was particularly depressed by shows like Julian Slade's *Salad Days*, referring to them as 'amateur, jolly undergraduate things…' He enjoyed writing *Slickey*. 'Writing lyrics is like writing bad poetry. It's not easy.' Of *Slickey*'s chances of success, he said, 'People never know whether they want something new until they have been told that they like it.'

About the British film industry, he said, 'It is run by illiterates and ignorant layabouts.'

About television, he said, 'Shallow and awful. Even a good play is diminished by it.'

About British stage dancers, 'The girls are easy to find. But it has been a hard to job to find male dancers who looked, at least, like men.'

Finally, about failure: 'If you fail in America, you've had it. At least in Britain you can still be a distinguished failure.' He lit another cheroot and looked very sad.

8 April 1959

Osborne wrote twenty-one stage plays, famously hated his mother, cockney barmaid Nellie Beatrice, was himself five-times married (his last union, with critic Helen Dawson, being his only happy marriage) and died aged sixty-five of diabetic complications on Christmas Eve 1994, deeply in debt. He is buried in a Shropshire churchyard alongside Helen, who died ten years after he did. His last word to her was 'Sorry'. The World of Paul Slickey *folded after only forty-nine performances.*

John Peel

CHAPTER 69

JOHN PEEL – VOICE OF THE UNHEARD

"The kids don't complain."

John Peel was the most influential radio disc jockey of the twentieth century. Born three days before the outbreak of the Second World War, he did more than any to create and guide the musical tastes of his generation. After his sudden death from heart disease in Cusco, Peru, on 25 October 2004, while he was on a working vacation, BBC Radio One cleared all schedules for a day-long tribute to him. The Evening Standard *billboards read 'The Day the Music Died'. Though he showed up fairly regularly on television, Peel's natural medium was late-night radio. As a long-serving (1967–2004) radio host, he discovered and promoted challenging new bands which might never have surfaced without his championship; he loved every track of the music he played. His voice spoke for the unsung and unheard. At his posh public school, which he hated, his housemaster R. H. J. Brooke, nicknamed 'Brooky', presciently noted in an end-of-term class report that 'Perhaps it is possible that John can form some kind of nightmarish career out of his enthusiasm for unlistenable records and his delight in writing long and facetious essays.'*

J ohn Ravenscroft, known nationwide as John Peel the disc jockey, possesses perhaps the most distinctive voice on pop radio and a personal collection of 3,573 long-playing records. And one pair of shoes. The shoes are made of canvas and rubber and cost him 30 shillings. He won't wear leather or eat meat, explaining that since animals don't try to kill him he is willing to return the compliment.

Peel has a calm, contained presence. Unlike the many disc jockeys who feign an affinity with the young but are really trying to ingratiate themselves with their parents, John Peel talks directly to the kids. He plays the music of the hard rebel underground, and despises most of the hit parade tracks that

DJs like Tony Blackburn feature on their own programmes – what Peel calls 'easy listening, right-wing stuff'.

Despite such bolshie sentiments, John Peel is regularly voted top man in various polls. His attitude and personal lifestyle connect him directly to the counter-culture, but he is very much his own man, disdaining the hippy generation for its self-righteousness and its self-proclaimed superiority over the square and the elderly.

He talks in a slightly nasal monotone often imitated by lesser-known DJs. On his radio programmes like *Top Gear* he has raised a wide range of controversial subjects (Biafra, VD, drugs, British foreign policy) which infuriate many listeners, who telephone the BBC to suggest a public hanging. But the kids don't complain.

'A lot of disc jockeys,' he said, 'are just not interested in music. They are not even interested in radio. They are really only interested in becoming famous.'

> 'The BBC thinks of British housewives as a subnormal group, you know, capable only of absorbing infantile chat and instant music. Disc jockeys like Bob Harris and myself get squeezed away at the end of the day, in a kind of two-hour ghetto. Yet 85 per cent of the pop records sold in shops is the hard stuff. Of course we have protested, but when you argue with the BBC only one man is going to win.'

Son of a prosperous cotton broker, John Peel was sent to Shrewsbury School, got called up for national service and served two years as a gunner ('a holiday'). After demob he went to America for eight life-transforming years. As a DJ on a Dallas radio station he came face to face with America's youth culture, and got the message. When President Kennedy was shot Peel passed himself off as a reporter for the Liverpool *Echo*; he can be spotted in newsreel footage of the courtroom arraignment of Lee Harvey Oswald two days before Oswald was gunned down by Jack Ruby.

While in Dallas, in 1965, Peel married his first wife, Shirley Anne Milburn. It was never a happy marriage (Peel referred to it as a 'mutual defence pact'). She was fifteen at the time, a detail she artfully concealed from Peel. The couple divorced in 1973. She later committed suicide. On his return from the States Peel was given the midnight slot on Radio London, an off-shore pirate station specialising in the new sounds emerging from the American underground. He was an immediate hit with like-minded spirits who felt they had at last found a friend in an otherwise straight world.

Soon he was receiving a heavier mailbag than any other broadcaster on the station, a phenomenon which did not go unnoticed by the nabobs of the BBC, who were nervously looking for a way of tuning in to the voices of the young.

'When I joined the BBC they were so alarmed by my appearance and reputation that they had another disc jockey in the studio with me, as a kind of co-pilot in case I had to be whisked out in a hurry. They probably thought I was going to rub heroin into the roots of their hair. One BBC type treated me like a freak until I told him I'd been to Shrewsbury. Immediately his attitude changed and he cried, "Oh how's old Brooky?"'

That story, he says, illustrates the needless mistrust between generations, based on false assumptions. The gulf between British parents and their offspring is a recurring theme of Peel's conversation.

'If we faced it honestly we'd admit that great numbers of children are being born to parents who don't like them very much, and don't really want them. I've seen screaming babies in their prams, blue with cold outside bingo halls, while Mum's inside watching the bouncing ball. Think about it. Think about the crummy home life of your average skinhead. They're the frontline victims, yet people would be happy to see them flogged. Thousands of parents of all classes would never admit to themselves that they resent their children. But the kids themselves know it and go their own way. That's where the so-called youth revolution often starts, though if you told these kids that they were revolutionaries they'd laugh at you. Of course I've met dozens of so-called revolutionaries, mostly in universities, who want to topple the structure, bring it all down. But they're only impressing each other. At any rate, how do you beat the English establishment? They just tolerate you to death, anyway. Absorbing you until you are part of it.'

'I am thirty-two,' he said, 'a displaced person belonging to no generation in particular.'

'I have a small cottage in Stowmarket and live there quietly. I come down to London for my radio shows. People assume I live a helluva life, tea with the Beatles and dropping into the south of France to see how the Rolling Stones are getting along. My friends are mostly unknown men in unknown bands. When people in pop music become successful it seems to destroy them as functioning human beings. Few come out of it undamaged. That's why their first records are usually their best.'

Like most vegetarians, Peel doesn't smoke, and drinks little – an occasional glass of cheap red wine.

'Drinking has been the downfall of my family, the curse of the Ravenscrofts. But we were always too well-off to be called alcoholics. My grandfather actually managed to get champagne on the National Health in the last years of his life. My father died of lung cancer. I can never understand why people smoke. It makes them unattractive, makes them smell. There is nothing worse than kissing a girl who's been smoking. It's like licking the inside of a stove. I've smoked pot, but not anymore. On the radio ship I did some of my programmes stoned. But they were exceptionally bad shows, very untidy, with lots of pauses and giggling. Still, it's a lot better than drinking. Reluctantly, I am for the legalisation and licensing of pot, if only because kids would no longer be exposed to pushers who might try to interest them in something even more destructive. The only drug I allow myself is the Liverpool Football Club. When it comes right down to it, the most emotional moments of my life have been spent at Anfield.'

Peel used to live in Westbourne Grove, London's hippy hinterland, but departed because he always felt vaguely menaced by the city, its weirdoes and its football gangs, and the kind of police he used to meet around North Kensington.

Peel's attitude towards the police is fairly typical of the dissident youth movement.

'I am sure that a lot of policemen are full of good motives, but it's like the army. They're eventually corrupted by the old timers telling them how to cut corners, showing them how to get by. If I were burgled in my cottage in Stowmarket, I'd call the police and probably get a fair deal, but if I were burgled in Westbourne Grove I'd let it go by. I mean that. The policemen may not like my face, or my hair, or whatever. A lot of your readers may not believe this but people do get beaten up by the police in England. Our values are all wrong. A bad schoolteacher who overwhelms children by his presence and demands respect as his due is playing fast and loose with young lives and is much more of a criminal than some guy who nicks a couple of hundred quid. Most people don't seem to care. Most people feel that they are being manipulated by forces they can't see, and don't understand, whose only concern is profit.

Love thy neighbour is the most important principle in life. Yet our society is always telling us to compete with our neighbour, to do better than him. Songs about power and revolution are meaningless. People are not moved by protest, but by little things they can understand. That's what the best songs are about, like feeling "alone in a crowd", which is what most people feel. If straight society, the grey men, tried to understand young people instead of screaming at them, they may find them not so bad. Youth is always resented I suppose, because they are thought to be getting more of it than anyone else. There is no real youth revolution happening in England. There is no underground, rather a way of life. An American came over here recently to join the so-called revolution, but went home disgusted after three months saying that the only thing the English underground seemed to be concerned with was fashion.

That's about it. It's play-acting.'

9 MARCH 1972

John Peel's funeral, on 12 November 2004 in Bury St Edmunds, was attended by over a thousand mourners. He had requested that, in the event of his death, all he wanted on his tombstone besides his name were the words 'Teenage dreams, so hard to beat…' Four years later his wish was granted.

Joan Plowright with her husband, Laurence Olivier

CHAPTER 70

JOAN PLOWRIGHT – THE LAST MRS LAURENCE OLIVIER

"I used to experience great pride and joy when people got up and slammed their seats and left in a huff."

Joan Ann Plowright, Baroness Olivier, was born in Brigg, Lincolnshire, on 28 October 1929. Her father was a journalist and newspaper editor. Joan attended Bristol Old Vic Theatre School. She made her first stage appearance in 1951. Five years later she joined the English Stage Company in The Country Wife; *a year later she took over from Dorothy Tutin when John Osborne's* The Entertainer *transferred from the Royal Court Theatre to the Palace Theatre. Joan Plowright was married first to actor Robert Gage in 1953. In 1961 she married Laurence Olivier, who had been married to Vivien Leigh for twenty years. Joan Plowright has always denied that she was responsible for wrecking Olivier's marriage, even though Vivien Leigh named Joan Plowright in her divorce. The Plowright Theatre in her native Scunthorpe is named in her honour.*

'Everybody, outside the theatre,' said Joan Plowright, 'thinks that actors and actresses are soppy people, and that acting is like having a lovely hobby.'

'The truth is that actors are more tremendously disciplined than most. They go on stage with all kinds of things wrong with them. I was taught very early to leave all my troubles at the stage door – all my aches and pains and domestic upsets. You go into that building a blank page, to express what the author bids you do, not what your own life is about.'

The Oliviers will make one of their rare appearances together on British TV on New Year's Day in Eduardo de Filippo's vociferous Italian drama *Saturday, Sunday, Monday*. In the play, Lord Olivier plays Joan's father, an aged hatter.

Miss Plowright seems to relish playing strong-minded Italian women. As the theatrical year draws to an end, the improbable box office champion of London's West End is yet another slice of Naples family life called *Filumena*, again by de Filippo and again starring Joan Plowright. In this clamorous domestic drama she plays an ex-prostitute who has lived with the same man (Colin Blakely) for twenty-five years and is now determined to marry him to give belated legitimacy to her three grown sons.

Why phlegmatic British audiences should have been overwhelmed, both on tour and in London, by this spaghetti soap opera is a mystery, not least to its star.

'It may be,' Miss Plowright ventured, 'popular theatre, but it's of huge size. It's black comedy. It's cruel.'

Joan Plowright projects in real life, as she does on stage, a blunt, uncluttered honesty, backed by what one suspects are deep reserves of strength and contained emotion.

The Brighton-based Oliviers, when in London, live in a capacious flat high in a skyscraper complex near Victoria station. A clutter of smallish coats in the hallway is a reminder that the Olivier family includes three children, whose ages range from eleven to sixteen.

After years of illness, Lord Olivier is again producing and acting at a rate that might stun a younger and lesser man. He is currently filming Ira Levin's *The Boys from Brazil*. Joan's own schedule includes eight performances a week at the Lyric.

'Acting is a splendid kind of therapy,' she says firmly.

'On stage you can purge yourself of anger and resentment and go home a better person. It saves you taking it out on the family. Larry once told me that he wouldn't have known what else to do if he hadn't become an actor – where else he could have found an outlet for his energy and violent passions.'

In *Filumena*, Joan Plowright has what no English dramatist seems capable of giving her – a big, chunky, female role worthy of her talents. English playwrights, she says, simply cannot write for women. The feminine mind is a closed book to them, and they are confused by the changing role of women in society.

'They don't know about us,' Joan Plowright agrees.

'They are too busy writing about themselves. Our woman playwrights, like Pam Gems, seem to be writing for an audience of women. When I saw her play *Dusa, Fish, Stas, and Vi* all the women loved it but the men were snoring.

It's about four girls sharing a flat. The man sitting next to me dropped his head on my shoulder with boredom…'

From her present eminence Lady Olivier looks back to the days when she was part of the theatre rebellion based at London's Royal Court Theatre under director George Devine.

She says:

'I used to experience great pride and joy when people got up and slammed their seats and left in a huff. I was thrilled when people shouted "Rubbish!" I felt that was what the theatre was for. Maybe it's because I'm getting older, but now I quite like to fill a theatre instead of emptying it! I have come to realise that, if you want to preach and teach, you have to entertain. Our children, especially one of them, show signs of wanting to act. I've told them to go into the theatre only if acting is as necessary to them as breathing. It's such a humiliating profession. About 85 per cent are out of work at any time. You see women going for auditions to directors young enough to be their sons. I admire their guts and bravery. I want to open a lot of doors for my children … to give them an opportunity to know about everything. Later they can choose the door they want to go through. As for Larry and myself there is no thought of retirement. Acting is something we want to do, something we have to do. The adrenalin starts to pump the moment we decide to undertake a role. There does not seem to be an alternative.'

30 December 1977

Joan Plowright was created a DBE (Dame) in the Queen's New Year's Honours in 2004.

Otto Preminger

CHAPTER 71

OTTO PREMINGER – HOLLYWOOD AUTOCRAT

"One man must make the big decision… that man is me."

The life and career of film-maker Otto Preminger, born on 5 December 1905 in Witzniz in Austria-Hungary (now Ukraine), span some of the grand themes of the last century – the fall of imperial Russia, the rise of Nazi Germany, the heyday of Hollywood and Broadway. Preminger, a bald, fiery despot of the old school, saw it all and, in the process, made lasting enemies. His father, Marcus, a legal eminence in the court of Emperor Franz Josef, had been offered even higher office if he would renounce Judaism and convert to Catholicism. Marcus, a principled man, refused the bribe but nevertheless received the appointment. As a bright schoolboy, Otto Preminger became addicted to the theatre and became the protégé of the gifted Viennese director Max Reinhardt. Eventually Peminger's career path led him to Hollywood where he associated with Darryl F. Zanuck and other dominant figures of the movie capital's glory days. When Zanuck fired him, Preminger transferred briefly to Broadway where he acted and directed; he also lectured at the Yale School of Drama. As a screen actor, Preminger appeared, notably, as the Nazi commandant in the PoW movie Stalag 17, *starring William Holden. As a producer/director Preminger enjoyed a string of successes including* Laura, Anatomy of a Murder, Bunny Lake is Missing *and* Carmen Jones. *(Preminger conducted a long romance with its black star Dorothy Dandridge. He also had an extended affair with the stripper Gypsy Rose Lee by whom he had a son.) He married three times but led a free-wheeling life as a libertine.*

An industry named Otto Preminger flew into London yesterday to supervise the openings, here and in Paris, of his political movie *Advise & Consent*.

As ever the man was preceded into town by his reputation as a terrible-tempered autocrat, a Hollywood despot, a studio Prussian whose wrath is so awesome that, it has been said, even a broken leg is preferable to a showdown with him.

The bald, bulky Viennese-born producer settles himself at a desk near a phone in a West End hotel suite.

He insists that his reputation as a movie-land ogre is without truth or foundation. He projects an image of sweetness and light. Gentle Otto.

'Legends,' he beams at me, 'are always worse than the truth. Don't you agree?' He does not wait for a reply.

'I am a happy man. I never complain when my pictures get bad notices and I thank nobody for the good ones. Some of my technicians stay with me for years. It must be clear to anyone that I am not an autocrat.'

The phone rings at his elbow. After a few seconds gentle Otto begins barking into the mouthpiece. 'Never mind all that! The essentials! Just give me the essentials! Is that too much to ask?' Suddenly the phone goes dead. Preminger grunts with impatience. Waiting to be reconnected he turns to me and continues to defend himself against accusations of despotism.

'I don't like too much talk,' he said. 'I am a tremendous enemy of confer-ences. I hate the idea of twelve men meeting in a room, each of them with two points of view so they've got an alibi later. One man must make the big decision. In my case that man is me.'

The telephone is active again. 'Listen,' Preminger speaks into it. 'Never mind all that! Just give me the bad news! I know you're a great man!' There is a short pause. Preminger listens. Then he says: 'I don't really give a damn!'

Ludwig Otto Preminger, fifty-seven, has courted controversy all his life. *The Moon is Blue* (1953) was the first Hollywood film to banter the word 'virgin' about. *Carmen Jones* (1954) translated Bizet into an all-black romp. *The Man with the Golden Arm* (1955) crawled about in a junkie's world of heroin addiction. *Anatomy of a Murder* (1955) went into intimate clinical details about a sex crime.

As a result of these enterprises, Preminger has developed a reputation as a crusader for screen freedom. It is probably more accurate to describe him as a man quick to recognise the box-office potential of controversial themes. This is not to belittle his achievement. He has done more than most to bring the commercial American film to a kind of maturity.

'I make mistakes,' he said, 'who doesn't? Jean Seberg in *Saint Joan* was a mistake. I asked too much of her. She lacked depth and experience. She is doing very well today in France. I feel very good about that.'

Paris comes on the telephone line about the cost of the French premiere of *Advise & Consent*. Preminger speaks into the mouthpiece, 'How much am I prepared to spend? How much is Zanuck spending on *The Longest Day*? You can spend all you need.' Preminger immediately contradicts himself. 'Don't spend as much as Zanuck. That's crazy!' He puts the phone down.

'The real autocrats in Hollywood today,' he says, 'are the stars themselves, demanding this, demanding that. I don't subscribe to that. The way I see it, pictures make the stars, and not the other way around.

'Never mind,' he concluded. 'Every day in this business is a challenge. I love it. It's wonderful. I'm a happy man. People who call me a Prussian are ignorant of geography.'

11 SEPTEMBER 1962

Otto Ludwig Preminger died in New York City in 1986, aged eighty, of cancer while in the grip of Alzheimer's disease. His ashes are interred at Woodlawn cemetery, in the Bronx. The late English actress Anna Massey described Otto Preminger as the 'cruellest and most unpleasant director I have ever worked with'.

Cliff Richard

CHAPTER 72

CLIFF RICHARD – UNWISE WORDS

◇◇

"The coloured servants out there don't really mind. They get their food
and their board, so why should they mind?"

*Before the Beatles there was Cliff Richard – a teenage pop singing idol whose
fame and well-judged career have endured over seven decades. Committed
Christian, national treasure, all-round good guy, he has been sustained by the
affections of the British (he never quite made it into the American big time)
by his sheer likeability and his choice of good material well sung. In 1963 he
returned to London from a South African tour. I was one of a covey of Fleet
Street reporters (future TV presenter Barry Norman was another) who met
Cliff Richard at Heathrow. He was only twenty-two, little more than a boy,
so I suppose he could be forgiven for the comments he delivered at the airport
concerning the racial divide he had observed in South Africa.*

If Cliff Richard wants to do himself a favour he might resolve in future
to open his mouth in public only to sing – and not, for Heaven's sake,
to talk.

Mr Richard has been talking in London this week about the tragic and
perilous racial situation in South Africa, a republic from which he and his
Shadows have just returned after a pop-singing tour. He returns, this much-
adored voyager, from a land where the rivers run with tears and sometimes
with blood – a land which sustains itself in comfort and privilege by keeping
the greater part of its population, because of skin colour, in a voteless state
of serfdom.

That Mr Richard saw little evidence of this is not surprising, since he
admits to spending most of his non-working hours sunning himself in
spacious gardens beside the swimming pools of celebrity-conscious social-
ites. Yet, on this very limited basis, Cliff Richard has pronounced on the
present plight of South Africa's native population.

'This coloured thing,' he said with a self-confidence hardly supported by his years, 'doesn't really show. You don't really notice it at all! The coloured servants out there don't really mind. They get their food and their board, so why should they mind? Gosh, you get coloured servants all over the world, they don't mind it at all!'

I expressed to Mr Richard a certain wonderment that his experiences should have been so curiously at variance with the established facts of South African life.

'Oh, there are things happening out there,' he conceded airily, 'but me and the Shadows didn't bother to delve into it. Gosh, we just didn't have time. Perhaps, on our next tour, things will be better.'

I said perhaps they wouldn't.

'Well,' Mr Richard grinned, 'that's show business.'

Now, Mr Richard's views on this subject wouldn't be worth tuppence if it were not that many thousands of British teenagers are ready to believe anything Cliff tells them. Master Richard, in this pop-obsessed age, represents some kind of god, a figure of enormous influence. In every town in Britain there are youths who ape his suits, his pout, his shoes and his hairstyle.

The idol really must realise that these kids are also ready to ape his views. He must learn to grow up and express himself on matters which intimately affect thousands of lives in other lands with care and humility and an awareness of his power to influence his worshippers.

I do not mean that Cliff Richard is a conscious bigot. I doubt if he has a single malicious bone in his body. But he is guilty of the unthinking and lethargic acquiescence in which bigotry can thrive. To insist that Africans 'don't mind' their deprived status is no different from the hunter's hoary old claim that 'the fox enjoys it'.

Mr Richard is about to embark on a tour of forty-one one-night stands in the British Isles. He will be interviewed about his African adventures by local reporters in each of these centres. Somebody should now warn the lad to stop this gabbling prep-school nonsense and show, at least by silence, that he has some respect for those South Africans of all races who are struggling, frequently at great risk, for a better and saner life in that spacious and tragic land.

16 FEBRUARY 1963

I resigned (briefly, as it turned out) from the Daily Express *when the paper declined to print the above article. The* Express *was known for its blimpish,*

reactionary politics and regarded the piece as too leftie-liberal for its readers. So I resigned from the paper (by telegram, from Uxbridge post office). I am gratified to be able to report that before the end of the day the Express's *fiery proprietor, Lord Beaverbrook, personally interceded in the dispute, and instructed the editor to 'print it and print it big'. It is fair to add that Sir Cliff Richard's career has been marked by impressive contributions to a wide swathe of charitable causes, benefiting all races and religions at home and abroad.*

Leni Riefenstahl during the shooting of her film about the Olympic Games in 1936, Berlin

CHAPTER 73

LENI RIEFENSTAHL – IN HITLER'S SHADOW

"Was I a Nazi? Well, I was one of millions who
trusted Hitler in the first years."

Filmmaker Helene Bertha Amalie (Leni) Riefenstahl, born in Berlin on 22 August 1902, was, next to Eva Braun, perhaps the best-known woman in Nazi Germany. She began her career as a dancer and actress and fell head-long under the spell of Adolf Hitler when she heard him addressing a rally in 1932. ('I had an almost apocalyptic vision … so powerful that it touched the sky and shook the earth,' she wrote.) At Hitler's request she directed her most celebrated films, Triumph of the Will *(1934), which glorified the Nuremberg Rallies, and* Olympia *(1936), celebrating the Berlin Olympics of that year. The* Economist *magazine wrote that the films 'sealed her reputation as the greatest female filmmaker of the twentieth century'. Frau Riefenstahl was dogged all her adult life by rumours that she had been Hitler's mistress and a member of the Nazi Party. She denied both charges, later admitting that her association with Hitler was 'the biggest regret of my life … until the day I die people will keep saying "Leni is a Nazi"…'*

Frau Leni Riefenstahl leaned forward in her easy chair. But there was nothing easy about her manner, which was earnest and agitated. 'I have never,' she declared, 'come across such an atmosphere of prejudice as I have found in England. Everywhere else in the world I am accepted as an artist. But in England, no! In England any German who did not actually kill Hitler is still regarded as a Nazi criminal!'

The legendary Frau Riefenstahl, at fifty-eight, is still lithe and animated. She constantly throws her head back as she talks. Her tawny hair shimmers and tumbles. There are, even today, echoes of her former radiance. Her accent is guttural, gravel-hard. She stumbles through

English sentences with difficulty. But there is no doubting the passion of what she has to say.

'People in this country,' she places her hand on her chest, 'do not want to know the truth about me. They have this image of me – like the foolish story that I was once Hitler's mistress – and they will not accept the truth. What more can I do? I have not come to England to defend me ... I do not go to any foreign country to defend me!'

Nervously she fingers a large gold ring on her wedding finger.

'I have been cleared by all the courts in Germany. They kept me in prison for three years while they investigated my past. They found nothing. But in England, even the journalists put me on trial. They regard themselves as a tribunal.'

Riefenstahl had agreed to see me in her Bond Street hotel on the condition that a third party was present during the interview.

And so it was that a London film man, Philip Hudsmith, sat around, quietly smoking filter-tipped Gauloises, while Riefenstahl surveyed for me her eventful life, emphasising her artistry and innocence, denying that she was ever intimate with the Nazi leadership.

She was certainly a personal friend of Hitler's. She was frequently reported to be a key figure in his love-life too – 'the Dubarry of Nazi Germany'. Reporters in the '30s quoted her as saying of Hitler, 'He is radiant and wise. He is the greatest man who ever lived.' She was photographed receiving flowers from Doctor Goebbels, Hitler's propaganda chief, with a smiling Führer looking on. Her 1934 film *Triumph of the Will* has been described as 'all-out, starry-eyed adulation of the Nazi movement'.

England, she complains, has never forgiven her or forgotten her. Earlier this year, she was invited to lecture in London to the British Film Institute. After strong protests, the invitation was withdrawn. Now she sits before me in a London hotel. She is dressed simply in black. A gold necklace gleams against her tanned throat. Gold bracelets circle both wrists. She sips a cup of coffee, lights a cigarette. She's proud, but eager to please. She says she has nothing to hide.

'The real Nazis,' she says, 'went to prison.'

'I was never found guilty of anything. How is it I am still free? I was never a member of the Party. Was I a Nazi? Well, I was one of millions of Germans who trusted Hitler in the first years. When I met him, I was impressed by him, trusted him. I thought he was an unusual personality. I never called him "beautiful" because I never thought he was. I never called him "wise". I probably called him "clever". There were millions like me. Why am I held responsible? Why do people point the finger at me? I was an artist. I lived for my work in the cinema. How could I – how could anybody – see the evil that was to come later? In the early '30s, the Nazi flag was not a criminal flag. It hung outside the German embassy in London. Even Churchill spoke admiringly of Hitler in the '30s. I have the documents to prove it. Why then must I be blamed for photographing swastikas in my film *Triumph of the Will*? It was just the flag of the time. Nothing more. I didn't want to make that picture anyway. Hitler ordered me to make it. He promised me that he would leave me alone afterwards to produce the films I really wanted to make. I accepted the bargain. I was young. My political views were cosmopolitan. Of course, as an artist, I was sorry to see so many talented Jews being expelled from Germany.'

Frau Riefenstahl's pity, it seems, did not extend to the untalented Jews who were expelled from Hitler's Reich.

'People say that my Olympic Games film glorified the Nazi ideal. Ridiculous! On the contrary, I got into a lot of trouble with the Nazi Party over that film. They tried to force me to leave out the shots of victorious American negro athletes, like Jesse Owens. I refused to comply with that edict. Goebbels tried hard to ruin my film. I decided to leave Germany as things were getting unbearable for me. The French newspapers got hold of the story. Hitler saw that if I went away it would mean a big prestige loss for Goebbels and a scandal abroad. So he arranged for this photograph to be taken of me receiving flowers from Goebbels. These pictures appeared a few days later in the world press. I was ordered to have those photographs taken. It was never my idea! After the war, I was kept in eight different prisons for three years while everybody – the Americans, the French and the Germans – investigated my past.'

Ironically, it was a French film producer – and a Jew, at that – who took up the cudgels on behalf of the imprisoned Leni Riefenstahl.

'This man,' she told me, 'saw parts of a film I was making in Germany during the war. *Tiefland*, it was called.'

'He appreciated the beauty of my film, its absence of any political motive. He and his wife hired an advocate in Paris to fight for my freedom. They worked hard for me. This man was finally called "a swine" by his fellow Frenchmen because he was "helping a Nazi". Eventually, because of this, he had to leave France and work in Canada.'

I asked Frau Riefenstahl to name this benefactor who had ruined his own career to help her. I imagined that his name would have been written across her heart for all time. However, it seems that Riefenstahl could not quite remember his name. She hunted for her spectacles, rummaged through various address books, finally found his surname: Desmarais. She had no idea of his first name.

'I never knew about the concentration camps until after the war,' Riefenstahl assured me.

'At first I didn't believe it. Then I was shown pictures of the camps, of the corpses, and I had to believe it. I was so horrified, so ill … How could I have known about these things? What could I have done? I only saw Hitler twice during the war. Once when I was looking for news of my husband, Peter Jacob. I had heard he was wounded in the fighting in Greece. The second time was when Hitler invited my husband and myself to his home in Berchtesgaden after my husband had been decorated. As for my being Hitler's girlfriend, this was always a lie. It was just a story to sell. I didn't know about this so-called romance for years because of press censorship in Germany.'

Fifteen years have gone by since the guns of the Second World War fell silent. But for Leni Riefenstahl the war goes on. Rumour and half-truth still cloud her name, bringing unwelcome notoriety. She is still the woman the world loves to hate. She has fought hard to clear her name. She has won, she says, fifty libel cases against magazines and newspapers who have accused her of particularly heinous activities, like callously watching a massacre in Poland, or filming concentration camps.

She has completed only one film since the war – an Italian version of her pre-war success *The Blue Light*.

'When will people believe the truth about me?' she asked. 'They will believe the truth only when I am no longer here. Only when I am dead.'

18 December 1960

Unable to find work in the film industry after the war, Riefenstahl turned to photography, winning universal respect with her photographs of the Nuba tribe in the Sudan. Riefenstahl, who married twice, died in her sleep in her Bavarian home on 8 September 2003, aged 101. She had been suffering from cancer.

Leni Riefenstahl with Adolf Hitler

Randolph Turpin and Sugar Ray Robinson

CHAPTER 74

SUGAR RAY ROBINSON AND RANDOLPH TURPIN – THE GLADIATORS

"I was a prize muggins … stupid, that's all…"

On 10 July 1951 two black prizefighters advanced towards each other in a boxing ring in London's Earls Court. At stake on that summer night was the middle-weight championship of the world. One of the contenders was considered the best-looking and most admired black man in America. The other man was a dim, gullible Briton named Randolph Turpin who had little idea of who he was. Turpin utterly lacked self-esteem. He was angry and knotted and anybody could play him for a sucker, and did. The fight was considered little more than a keep-fit exercise for the glamorous American, who was expected to dispose of the black Englishman at any moment of his choosing.

I was in Paris when the news came through that Sugar Ray Robinson had been beaten. I was walking along the Rue de la Huchette, heading towards the Boulevard St Michel. A radio in the small Hotel Mont Blanc had been tuned to the big fight from London. 'L'Américain est vaincu!' cried the astonished French announcer. His voice, squeaky with disbelief, drifted out onto the sidewalk through the thin red curtains of the hotel window. It was, as sportswriters like to say, 'one of the biggest upsets in years'. Over the decade to come I was to meet both the fighters who had stopped me in my tracks on a Left Bank sidewalk in 1951.

I met Randolph Turpin in a sad little cafe in Leamington Spa in 1959, eight years after his famous victory over Sugar Ray Robinson. It was immediately clear that he was a blundering, confused young man with a dumb faith in others, and absolutely no idea of how to manage his life.

He was said to have earned £2,000 a minute at his prizefighting peak, but those days were over. Now he was grunting and sweating his way around Britain as an all-in wrestler with only the haziest idea of where he would be performing next … 'somewhere around Swansea tonight'.

His wrestling earned him £10 a night, 'but take away meals and hotel and all that caper,' he said, 'and it leaves me as broke as I was before, and that's as broke as you can get, mate. Altogether I must have earned £150,000, I reckon. But a lot of it I didn't see, not ever. I'd ask about the money and they would say, "Forget it, Randy, we've got an accountant working on it."'

'Some fights, I didn't ever know what I was gettin'. What money I did see I spent on cars and clothes and having, like, a good time. I had clothes that would fill a wardrobe from here to there. Well, mate, it's too late to cry now. I was a prize muggins ... stupid, that's all.

They tell me I'm a bankrupt. That's one word for it. I call it broke. I'm told I owe £17,000 in taxes, but I'm not worried, because I ain't got it – not a penny.'

Turpin grinned and scratched a bare, well-muscled arm decorated with various tattooed tributes. One tattoo was in honour of his mother; others were dedicated to his first wife, Mary, to a girl named Jean, and to Cled, 'a soldier who once stopped with us'.

I talked to the ex-champ in a side-room off Gwen's Transport Cafe, a three-table joint owned by Mrs Gwen Turpin, Randolph's second wife and the mother of his three dark-eyed daughters. The family lived above the cafe in Russell Street, perhaps the shortest and ugliest thoroughfare in Leamington Spa.

Turpin was trying to tell me how his new interest in wrestling had saved his sanity and his marriage. He screwed up his fist and pushed it against the stained sweatshirt covering his belly. 'I felt I was going mad,' he said.

'I had all that power boiling up all the time, a kind of fury. I'd be cooking in the cafe kitchen, some geezer would complain about the tea, and I felt I could kill him. I had to stop myself from clouting the kids ... my own kids! Sometimes when I was like that I would go down to the gym, but I wouldn't go in the ring, because I felt I might go mad and cut up some kid real bad.

Becoming a wrestler's the best thing I ever done. I get everything out of me that way. I come home from the wrestling lark and everything is, like, nice, and I don't want to hit nobody no more.

I was never afraid of anyone in the ring. My biggest fear is that something might happen to my kids, like being knocked down by a car, something like that. I'd blow my top if anything ever happened to them or my wife.

A long time ago, everybody they was slapping me on the back and borrowing my money. Those friends, I never see them now. They were around only when I was the champ. Well, it's no good feeling bitter now. I could beat the hell out of them but it would only get me in trouble with the police.

I really don't care, see? I don't miss the glory. I never even looked upon myself as a champ. I'll tell you something. Four days after I won the world championship, guess where I was? At the boxing booths at Kenilworth, taking on all comers.

Even when I went to Earls Court for the title fight against Sugar Ray, I went by public transport!

My life was boxing, only boxing. I trusted anybody like they was my father. I am thirty-three but I feel like a kid of sixteen. I have never considered myself to be a grown man.'

5 FEBRUARY 1959

Randolph Turpin shot himself through the head and heart in a bedroom over Gwen's Transport Cafe on 17 May 1966. A gun was discovered next to his body. His youngest daughter, Carmen, aged seventeen months, was taken to hospital with two gunshot wounds. Turpin left two suicide notes. One, to his wife Gwen, said: 'It is just that there is some money the tax want, and I have had to carry the can for it.' Another note named a former manager. The inquest jury was instructed to treat its contents as confidential. The coroner, Dr H. S. Tibbitt, told them, 'It is not for you to judge about money being owed, and whether it was owed or not.'

"The only thing I'm an authority on is Sugar Ray Robinson."

I was kept waiting for seventy minutes by Mr Walker Smith. His manager shrugged. 'That's how fighters are,' he said.

Finally Mr Smith arrived, shining with good cheer and good looks. He shook my hand hard and looked into my eyes for forgiveness. 'Man, I'm always doing this. I talk to too many people. I can't say no.'

'I keep getting lost. I went for a training run in Hyde Park the other day and ran out of the wrong end and forgot the name of this hotel. I stopped people in the street and asked to be directed to the Cucumber Hotel.'

He laughed out loud.

We entered the lounge of the Cumberland Hotel in search of coffee. Pale English waitresses, flustered by his fame, thrust paper napkins at him to sign. Mr Smith graciously obliged them all, signing himself 'Sugar Ray Robinson'.

He explained that years ago, when he was an under-age teenager in Harlem, he had borrowed the birth certificate of a bartender named Ray Robinson in order to qualify for a boxing contest. He decided to keep the name. Sportswriters later added the Sugar.

Like other intelligent boxers I have met – Gene Tunney, Muhammad Ali – Sugar Ray hated the fight game. 'It's a livelihood. I was born poor. I started out to provide for my mother. We were reared that way. These things count.'

Now he was the reigning middleweight champion of the world.

'I have been a blessed man. I never got a bad beating. I never got my face punched up bad. I thank God for that. I thank God all the time. I pray anywhere. I pray in my room. I pray in the ring. I'm even kind of praying right now for God to give me the right words.'

He was buoyant and brainy, but his contagious joyousness did not inhibit his killer instinct inside the ring or his business sense outside of it. 'The way I look at it,' he said, 'if I am due a dollar why should I take 99 cents? Look what happened to Randy Turpin, that poor, sweet guy. If you don't make it when you can, when the hell are you going to make it, man?'

'Things happen for a reason,' he concluded.

'Experience is the only source of wisdom. Nothing is to be regretted. People think of me as an authority on boxing. The only thing I'm an authority on is Sugar Ray Robinson. I know him better than anyone else, or anything else, in the world.'

10 SEPTEMBER 1962

Sugar Ray Robinson died of Alzheimer's disease on 12 April 1989, aged sixty-seven. He had been five times the middleweight champion of the world and is still often referred to as 'pound for pound the finest boxer of them all'. He died in relative poverty after an unsuccessful career as a song-and-dance man. A US postage stamp was issued in his honour.

Sugar Ray Robinson

Richard Rodgers

CHAPTER 75

RICHARD RODGERS –
TALKING ABOUT CANCER

"Without a larynx, you know,
you have to learn to speak all over again."

Richard Rodgers, my favourite songwriter, wrote close to a thousand published songs and some forty Broadway musicals. He was born into the Jewish family of a successful New York physician on 28 June 1902. While still in his teens he formed a creative partnership with lyricist Lorenz (Larry) Hart, which would last until Hart's death in 1943. Their first hit song was Manhattan *(1925). Rodgers's second significant partnership was with Oscar Hammerstein II and would last from 1943 (*Oklahoma!*) until Hammerstein's death from cancer on 23 August 1960, aged sixty-five.*

'Cancer,' said Richard Rodgers with a sudden and unexpected smile, 'is a word that does not make me go pale. We are old friends.' He spoke in a voice that was little more than a guttural, bass croak. I had to lean close to hear him at all.

Rodgers lost his entire larynx in a cancer operation a year ago. Before that, the left side of a cancerous jawbone had been removed and replaced by a muscle from his chest. Add to that one cardiac arrest, and you have a man who has thrice stared death in the face and survived.

'The worst thing you can do with cancer,' he said, 'is not to speak about it. People are afraid to use the word. But everybody in the world has been touched by it, if only by the death of a friend or a loved one.'

I met Richard Rodgers in Suite 1406 of Washington's infamous Watergate complex. Broadway's Grand Old Man is in the American capital to oversee his newest musical *Rex*, based on the life and loves of the much married, head-hunting Henry VIII.

Rodgers is a frail seventy-three now. He walks slowly with a stick, a durable genius who composed a clutch of mammoth hit musicals like *Oklahoma!, South Pacific, The King and I, Carousel* and *The Sound of Music*. A lesser man would have retreated into silence and depression years ago.

But Rodgers told me: 'Not me. I'm still up to here' – he held a hand inches above his greying head – 'in shows and songwriting. And I'm enjoying every moment of it.'

'My doctors tell me the reason I pull through these crises each time is because I plunge right back into work. I'm too busy for self-pity. I suppose I could go away somewhere and just look at the trees, but a weekend is about all I could stand of that. I don't know of any other way to stay alive, and that's an ambition in itself. Without a larynx, you know, you have to learn to speak all over again. Most people think you have to belch the air up. That's not how it works. The air is stored in the oesophagus all the time, and it's just a question of using it. If I'm eating a sandwich I have to wait for the food to go down before I can say a word. That makes dinner party conversation rather difficult as you can imagine! But I don't allow people to treat me with concern. I insist they treat me as if there's nothing the matter with me.'

Nearby stood a grand piano. Rodgers is still re-writing *Rex*. I had heard that he was a taciturn man who resented younger rivals, but my experience of him dispelled any such notion. He spoke, for instance, with great admiration of Marvin Hamlisch, a young New York songwriter whose show *A Chorus Line* is the season's biggest Broadway hit.

'I've never met Hamlisch,' said Rodgers, 'but I have the greatest respect for him. If we can develop a boy like that every five years we're doing awfully well.'

I said it was a generous thing for him to say.

Replied Rodgers: 'Anybody who can't do that must be frightfully insecure.'

As he talked, he sipped a glass of water. 'This is all I need to keep me talking,' he said.

'I have no complaints and I feel no despair. The exhilaration of this life is tremendous. Of course, I'm given to nostalgia – who isn't? – but I shall never give up. I hope to go on writing songs as long as I live. I'm not ready to quit. Maybe I'm too old to quit.'

10 MARCH 1976

Richard Rodgers died four years later on 30 December 1979, aged seventy-seven. He was cremated and his ashes were scattered at sea. In 1990 the Forty-Sixth Street Theatre on Broadway was renamed the Richard Rodgers Theatre. He was in my estimation the most consistently inventive and melodic composer of the twentieth century, the heyday of the Great American Songbook.

Peter Sellers in *I'm All Right Jack*

CHAPTER 76

PETER SELLERS – THE UNSATISFIED MAN

"Things had to be perfect – and they never were."

Richard Henry Sellers was born in Southsea, Hampshire, on 8 September 1925 into a family of variety troupers, who always called him Peter after a stillborn older brother. Peter was a bright lad, greatly adored by his Jewish mother Peg – 'totally smothered in maternal affection', according to his friend, director Bryan Forbes. Sellers climbed the show business ladder literally from the floor up, starting as a janitor in an Ilfracombe theatre at the age of fifteen. He taught himself to be a competent pit band drummer. In the Second World War he joined the Royal Air Force and was confined to non-flying duties because of poor eyesight. But it was as a radio performer with a gift for mimicry that he began to engage the public in the post-war years. He had wangled an audition with the BBC by telephoning a light entertainment producer and impersonating the voice of radio actor Kenneth Horne. Eventually Peter Sellers was invited to join Spike Milligan and Harry Secombe in a new surreal comic radio series, The Goon Show, *written by Milligan, which established itself as a national institution. This led Sellers directly to a career in films, bringing global fame. Sellers never looked back after* The Goon Show *and many of his films are now rated as classics, notably the Boulting Brothers'* I'm All Right Jack *(1959), Blake Edwards'* The Pink Panther *(1963) and Stanley Kubrick's* Dr Strangelove *(1964), in which Sellers played three major star roles. His last important film saw him as the robotic, simple-minded gardener in Hal Ashby's* Being There *(1979). Peter Sellers was married four times (to Anne Hayes, Britt Ekland, Miranda Quarry and Lynne Frederick) and fathered four children, one of whom, Michael, died during a heart bypass operation at the age of fifty-eight.*

I knew Peter Sellers, or rather did not know Peter Sellers, for the last twenty years of his life. When I met him in 1958 he already had a reputation as an actor and as an unknowable eccentric. He was funny and convivial, but an aura of neurosis almost always seemed to cloud the picture. He gave little of himself to his friends, many of whom, in later years, tended to talk of him in hurt or mystified tones. Though he commanded a fierce loyalty among a handful of cronies, Peter Sellers in person was not a widely popular man.

I interviewed him often, the first time in his family home in the north London suburb of Whetstone. He was married, apparently happily, to a gentle Australian girl named Anne Hayes. They had two pleasant children, Michael and Sarah. But even then there was a hint of manic desperation about Peter – the way he raced me around the house, showing off his radio sets and kitchen gadgets, endlessly seeking diversion and distraction.

All my interviews with him followed a familiar pattern. He saw himself as an uninteresting cipher, an unfinished man who had somehow been denied a definable personality. People wanted more from him than he could give. He would never be able to live up to their expectations. The challenge exhausted and bewildered him and drove him increasingly into himself.

He had not yet become a star when I met him; he was still doing 'guest spots' on other people's TV shows. Sellers always took care to send me polite thank-you notes whenever I mentioned him in my newspaper column.

His breakthrough to celebrity appeared to alarm him, giving him no place to hide. When we went to restaurants he would be careful, I noticed, to choose a chair facing a wall.

'I can't explain it. I'm a guy in search of the perfect thing; I've got a real psycho thing about it. Long ago when I was a drummer in a band I'd go crazy if there was the slightest thing wrong with the drums. Things had to be perfect – and they never were.'

He sought perfection in mechanical, increasingly expensive, things. Machines demanded nothing of him. His home was a treasure cave of cameras, hi-fi units, radios that revolved on steel turntables, coffee machines, all manner of fads and fancies. He needed to show them off; it was hard to get him to sit down. He felt exposed if he was not constantly on the move. Once he told me that he had begun negotiations to acquire a life-sized mechanical elephant driven by a Ford engine.

'I've had forty-eight cars since the war ended [thirteen years earlier]. Shameful, isn't it? Ever since I was a kid I knew that if I had enough money I would buy cars, cars, cars. I've got a Rolls-Royce now; it's a beauty; it's damn near perfect; lovely job.'

A couple of years later I had written the lyrics of a novelty song called 'Goodness Gracious Me', which became a hit for Sellers and Sophia Loren. The recording, which demonstrated Sellers' gifts as a mimic, had been suggested by Peter himself. At that time he was making a film in England called *The Millionairess*, based on a Bernard Shaw play, in which Sellers played an Indian doctor (Egyptian in the original play) who, in one sequence, becomes fascinated by the eccentric heartbeat of a glamorous woman patient (Loren). Sellers had telephoned me suggesting a duet for him and Loren which would exploit the rhythm of the heartbeat that so enraptured the physician. He reacted with enthusiasm when he first heard the song, but typically suffered an attack of cold feet and decided not to proceed with the recording. A protesting Sellers had to be practically dragged out of his bed by producer George Martin to the Abbey Road studios. The recording became a top ten hit and promoted *The Millionairess* beyond its merits.

Sellers had second thoughts about most things. Writers who were thrilled by his initial enthusiasm for their work found themselves a week later unable to reach him on the telephone. Peter Sellers let down a lot of people and dashed a lot of hopes in his time. Playwright Wolf Mankowitz once described Sellers' professional conduct as 'shitty'. Not many would argue with that.

I saw Peter Sellers from time to time over the years. Occasionally he telephoned me from some far-off movie location. But I never got much closer to him.

One day he said to me: 'I am not good-looking. Spike Milligan, at least, is good-looking.' Nothing, and nobody, ever satisfied Peter Sellers for long.

24 FEBRUARY 1958

Two years later I interviewed Sellers again. His unhappiness appeared to be even more rooted, his bewilderment even more intense.

Here is a man who has everything. He's the most successful British actor since Olivier and Guinness. He enjoys a riotous acclaim across the world. He has more money than he can spend in his lifetime – and the endless promise of more. He has a beautiful and devoted family. He's young and in good health.

Yet Peter Sellers is a man almost devoid of any capacity to enjoy the rewards his talents have produced. As the clamour for Sellers' services rises in volume, so the man at the heart of it increasingly retreats into himself, deliberately recoiling from the world that seeks only to honour him.

Peter Sellers is becoming a haunted recluse, a million miles from the public conception of him as a happy clown.

One night this week I drove through the autumn rain to talk to him in his manor house half a mile from the Hertfordshire village of Chipperfield. We sat in his study for hours, smoking and drinking coffee. After a period of hesitation and caution he began to talk. Words poured out of him, revealing an almost brutal awareness of his own bottomless discontent.

> 'I have no confidence in myself. I have no push. I am terribly aware of my shyness and reserve. People are all wrong about me. They see me on television. They hear my records. They think I'm a terribly funny and witty fellow … so they ask me to bazaars and cocktail parties and dinner parties, and expect me to be funny all the time. I can't do it, love. I just can't. Don't underestimate the effect of this, day after day, on the nerves and the patience. I dry up. I'm afraid to open my mouth. I'm really a negative and colourless person. I avoid people as much as I can. I have nothing to offer. I guess I hide behind a lot of things. If I can hide behind something – like a voice – then I tick over. I become articulate. I'm at my best when I'm not being myself. I wish I could be some of the people I portray instead of this Peter Sellers talking to you now.'

As we talked we could hear the footsteps of his wife, Anne, on the stairs. She was probably going up to see if the Sellers' children, Michael and Sarah, were comfortably asleep. 'Dammit,' said Sellers, 'if I'm ever going to be happy, surely the time is now!'

> 'I've got everything, man, everything. Two lovely kids. And Anne. God, I don't want another wife. I don't want other children except my own. I know what it's like to be penniless. Well, what's wrong? Why can't I be happy now? What am I looking for?'

Sellers clenched his fist and beat a steady drumbeat on his knee. 'What am I looking for?'

When Peter readies himself for a new movie, he is practically unapproachable.

'Poor old Anne,' he told me, 'goes through a very bad time before and during every film.'

> 'I go through a black hell of depression getting myself ready for a part. Even tonight, before you arrived, I've been walking around the house – from bleedin' room to bleedin' room – trying to find the answers to the man I play in my

next film. He's a schoolmaster named Monsieur Topaze. I walk around, trying different accents, feeling my way to the character. I do this every time; stare at my own image in the mirror every evening, waiting for the other fellow – the man I'm going to portray – to emerge, to stare back at me. I'm waiting for this stranger to come into my life. When it happens, I have this flush of happiness. I know I have found him at last.'

Once Peter Sellers has sulked and brooded his way into a character, he lives the role with lacerating intensity. So complete is this surrender to the role that even the structure of Sellers' physical features appears to shift and alter as he moves from film to film.

In *I'm All Right, Jack*, as shop steward Fred Kite, Peter Sellers carries himself in a special way. His walk is stiff and foot-splayed. When he moves he appears to lean back against an invisible wall, his face as round as a foot-ball, his eyes popping like glass marbles. Says Sellers, 'It is Fred Kite himself who looks like that and walks like that. He took me over completely.'

In *Never Let Go*, in which he played a brutal lecher named Lionel Meadows, Sellers' head appears to be elongated, the very depth and length of the jaw uncannily more pronounced.

'Sometimes,' Sellers told me, searching awkwardly for the words, 'I have a feeling that the film character enters my body ... as if I were a kind of medium.'

'I get so damned deep into it I become another living person. When I played Lionel Meadows in *Never Let Go* I *was* Lionel Meadows. I snapped everybody's head off. I talked like him. I thought like him. I would come home at night from the studios and not speak to anybody – not to Anne, not to the kids – not to anybody. In *The Millionairess*, my last picture with Sophia Loren, I played an Indian doctor. I tell you, man, I practically became that Indian doctor. The real Indians in the cast accepted me as one of their own. They talked to me in the studio as though I were not an Englishman. For the first time I became actually frightened of this power I seem to have. I even began to feel that I could heal people...'

Sellers will direct his next picture, *Mr Topaze*, himself. 'No picture I have made has satisfied me,' he said.

'I can always see what's wrong with them. I get the feeling it can be done better. That's why I must now direct a picture for myself. Perhaps by drawing great performances from other people I can get this thing, this despair, out of myself. I don't know, love, I am looking for the impossible. I'll never find it, but I'll spill my blood trying. It's a way of life. Unfortunately it will always deny me any kind of happiness. I realise that and I regret it. But it's my life, isn't it? I am not a happy person. I am what I am. I must do what I must do. And I hope to God it all comes out right.'

25 SEPTEMBER 1960

Peter Sellers died of heart failure in London on 24 July 1980, aged fifty-four. English stage director Peter Hall said of him, 'Peter had the ability to identify completely with another person and think his way, physically, mentally and emotionally into their skin. Where does it come from? I have no idea. Is it a curse? Often. It's not enough in this business to have talent. You have to have talent to handle the talent. And that, I think, Peter did not have.'

Peter Sellers with his first wife, Anne Howe

Peter Shaffer

CHAPTER 77

PETER SHAFFER – THE MAN OF TWO CITIES

"Farce is all about people who are afraid of being found out."

With plays like Amadeus, Equus *and* The Royal Hunt of the Sun, *Peter Shaffer has earned his place in the front rank of British dramatists. He is the identical twin brother of the late playwright Anthony Shaffer, who is himself chiefly remembered for his Tony Award-winning thriller* Sleuth. *Peter Shaffer was born in Liverpool on 15 May 1926, the son of a Jewish estate agent. He was a 'Bevin Boy' coal miner during the Second World War. As a playwright he won the 1981 Best Play Tony Award for* Amadeus. *As a film,* Amadeus *won eight Academy Awards, including Best Picture. His brother Anthony died of a heart attack in November 2001.*

'When I was a child,' says playwright Peter Shaffer, 'I suffered from a feeling of invisibility.'

'I felt I was looking at life through a plate glass window. What interested me didn't seem to interest the rest of the human race. I was evacuated all over the place during the war before I went down the mines. I felt tremendously shy and introverted. I used to envy people who could laugh out loud in a theatre. That was something I could never do. If there's been a change in my life, it's because that plate glass has begun more and more to dissolve. Writing has made the difference, especially the writing of *Equus*, which seems relevant to so many lives that it has made me feel real and visible to myself at last.'

Shaffer is briefly in London from New York, where he now lives and where he enjoys Olympian fame. Rich and successful in a city which, above all, loves a winner, Shaffer maintains a cool, intelligent detachment. He is a trans-Atlantic man, a regular London–New York commuter, observing the vagaries of both cities with an affectionate eye.

'We are most unfair about each other,' he says.

'The English see New York as a city of thugs, muggings and drugs, with everyone being held up at gunpoint. The Americans, from their side, think of us as
bankrupt, starving and finished. But when you actually go to the two cities,
you find that nothing much has changed at all. Why do we take such glee in
each other's mistakes and misfortunes? Maybe we, the English, feel slightly
envious of the USA. Americans, on the other hand, have this lingering sense
of inferiority about us. I like the American quality of open-eyed, open-hearted
niceness. I also like the slight sense of danger I feel in New York … of never
being quite safe, never being quite certain what's going to happen next. It's all
very good for a writer's adrenalin flow.'

A revival of Peter's brilliant one-act farce *Black Comedy* opened in London
last night. But Shaffer believes that farce, as a theatrical form, is losing its
clout in our permissive age. 'Farce is about people who are afraid of being
found out. But who really minds these days?'

Shaffer is not only an animated, fluent talker. He is also a perceptive
listener to the tones and language of others. 'Whenever I come back to
England from New York,' he said, 'I've this feeling I've gone deaf.'

'Have you noticed how the British mumble … a kind of murmur? I hear it
everywhere. Whereas Americans are very anxious to communicate, to spell
it out, to get it right. New York's wisecracking verbal style, represented by
playwright Neil Simon, is really about hostility, about the awfulness of getting
through another hard day in New York. New York is a city of depressives.
Neil Simon's one-liners feed that communal depression and that slight, but
constant, sense of paranoia. There's a tremendous optimism and, at the same
time, a tragic quality about America that is marvellous.'

Peter Shaffer is fond of the word 'marvellous'. It is part of his ungrudging
enthusiasm for the work of others, like that of his British contemporaries Tom Stoppard and Harold Pinter. Like them, Shaffer is disinclined to
explain his own plays. Critics and psychiatrists have had a field day debating
the meaning of *Equus*, with its story of a boy who blinds horses, and its
central themes of adoration and worship.

'I wrote *Equus* for myself,' says Shaffer. 'It took me two years to hammer it
out. What does it mean? It means what it says. I'm not saying that my work
is anywhere as important as Mozart's, but you cannot talk about a Mozart
symphony. All you can do is play it.'

Yet Shaffer does not disguise the pleasure of being celebrated, even lionised. 'The American worship of success is awful,' he concedes, 'but when you have a spectacular success in New York like *Equus*, everyone makes a huge fuss of you, which is marvellous.'

'I don't bask, or pose about as a celebrity. In fact, I don't go out much. But it would be churlish not to acknowledge that we all need a little ego-massage now and then. Graham Greene says that success is an aphrodisiac and I think he's right. For a limited time one may enjoy it – but one must never believe it. As long as you can say to yourself, "I really did try to the best of my ability, to make the journey," then you can escape the feeling that you're a fraud who is getting away with something. Getting through to people is the most marvellous thing in the world. On the first night of *Black Comedy* in Chichester I kept my eye on a somewhat stern man sitting just in front of me. I thought, if I could reach him, I'm home. The man didn't move a muscle for a while, but presently he began to shake his shoulders with laughter, like a volcano simmering. Eventually, this man actually tumbled helplessly into the aisle, holding his hand up, crying, "Oh stop, please stop!" That was the most wonderful moment I've ever had in the theatre. It was adorable.'

29 June 1976

Peter Levin Shaffer was knighted in the 2001 Queen's Birthday Honours List.

Moira Shearer with her husband Ludovic Kennedy

CHAPTER 78

MOIRA SHEARER – REDHEAD IN RED SHOES

"Ballerinas are terrible when it comes to doing the foxtrot.
We tend to bounce about and create havoc."

Moira Shearer was born in Fife, Scotland, on 17 January 1926, the daughter of an actor. Though she never wanted to be a dancer ('When you're ten you don't have much say in the matter'), she eventually became one of the most celebrated ballerinas who ever lived, thanks to a starring role in the British dance film The Red Shoes *(1948). She married writer, TV broadcaster, activist and ex-Royal Navy officer Ludovic Kennedy in 1950.*

Moira Shearer, the ravishing redhead ballerina whose film *The Red Shoes* danced her into a kind of immortality, is going back to the stage after a retirement lasting twenty years. She is fifty-one, yet retains that cool-skinned, grey-eyed, Titian-maned beauty that invites any man to fall in love with her at first sight.

Later this month she opens in the daunting role of Madame Ranevsky in Chekhov's *The Cherry Orchard* with the Royal Lyceum Company in her home town of Edinburgh. She lives there with her husband, TV man and author Ludovic Kennedy (can there be a more handsome couple in the land?) and their four children, who are beginning to grow up and scatter. That's why Moira is going back on the boards.

She talks about her comeback in a warm, hurried voice, using plain words. She occasionally combs her fingers through her splendid hair, which is unmarked by even a hint of grey.

She can address herself with intelligence to political and social topics. At other times she reverts to a sort of heavily italicised youthful verbal style. For instance, describing her performance as Madame Ranevsky after the first day of two rehearsals, she confesses: 'I'm *terrible* in it, I promise you … it's *pathetically* bad just now … *abysmal!*'

She retired two decades ago after a brief career as a straight actress. She had not repeated her ballet successes on the speaking stage. Drama critics acknowledged her allure and personal impact. 'Still feeling her way,' one wrote. Another said: 'Irresistible, but I doubt if she will ever be a major actress.'

Moira herself says:

'I didn't give myself long enough to be accepted. The British are prejudiced against people travelling outside of the pigeon-holes they've been put into. I was a ballerina, so what was I doing in a play? But I am not going back to the stage to prove anything to anybody, or put myself back on the map or anything like that. I've loved my life as a wife and mother raising my family, but from time to time I've positively hankered for the stage. I always felt that one day I might emerge again as a white-haired old character actress. But the time was never right. Two years ago they asked me to take over from Jean Simmons in *A Little Night Music* but we were shifting children from one school to another, and anyway, Ludo and I never want to live in London again, except maybe for short periods.'

The Kennedys are proud Scots, linked by blood and culture to Scotland's history and mystery. 'I feel at home here in a way I never do in England,' she said. 'We have put down roots here. We want to keep them.'

Moira Shearer acknowledges without hesitation that she is a happy woman. 'What's more,' she said, 'I get infinitely happier as I grow older.'

'When I was young I fussed over so many things … oh dear, oh dear, the agonies I went through over nothing. The theatre is not a good place for growing up in. People get so fussed over themselves and their own performances that they don't see much else. One becomes so terribly self-centred. I'm terribly grateful to my dear old man [she means Ludovic] who opened my eyes to countless things that I hadn't had time to do … or see … or read … He taught me everything, really. I met him at a ball. I'm afraid I kicked his shins blue when he asked me to dance. Ballerinas are terrible when it comes to doing the foxtrot. We do tend to bounce about and create havoc. Heavens … what years ago … goodness!

Ludo used to come and see me at the ballet. He always fell asleep. I'd see someone under the *Evening Standard* in the stalls and I knew it was Ludo having a quiet kip. I am delighted to be fifty-one. I cannot understand women who won't say their age. It's so nice to get old! I'm so looking forward to being old enough to say absolutely everything I feel and think.

There's nothing but good to be gleaned out of getting older. Look at Sir Thomas Beecham. Look at the things he said and got away with when he was eighty!'

3 OCTOBER 1977

Moira Shearer and Ludovic Kennedy were married for fifty-six years. The couple had one son and three daughters. She died at Radcliffe Infirmary, Oxford, aged eighty.

Neil Simon

CHAPTER 79

NEIL SIMON – THE SOUND OF LAUGHTER

"My quest is to write the perfect play … I'll never do it."

Neil Simon was born on 4 July 1927 in the Bronx, New York. The most popular comedy playwright alive is the son of a garment salesman who several times quit the family home. Neil enlisted in the US Air Force Reserve and was discharged as a corporal in 1946. He began writing comedy material with his brother Danny. Their work caught the attention of the great Sid Caesar, star of the TV comedy series Your Show of Shows, *whose stable of writers already included Woody Allen and Mel Brooks. In 1959 Phil Silvers employed Neil Simon as one of his writers for another '50s hit comedy TV series,* Sergeant Bilko. *Two years later Neil Simon wrote* Come Blow Your Horn *and, five years later, he had four hit comedies running on Broadway simultaneously – an unprecedented achievement.*

Neil Simon is the most successful playwright alive. Dozens of productions of his plays are staged all over the world every night of the year and consistently they strike gold.

'The most successful dramatist since Shakespeare,' gasped one American newspaper. This week's issue of *Time*, reviewing the 1969–70 Broadway season, asks itself in awe: 'The big question is: Can Neil Simon ever write a flop?'

His unbroken line of success includes *The Odd Couple*, *Sweet Charity*, *Barefoot in the Park*, *Plaza Suite* and the current Broadway musical *Promises, Promises*.

Neil Simon, always called 'Doc' (a boyhood nickname that stuck), is in London for tonight's opening of *Promises, Promises*, which he fashioned from Billy Wilder's film *The Apartment*.

Doc Simon is a quiet, donnish, sweet-tempered New Yorker whom everybody likes on sight. He looks ten years younger than his forty-two years, seldom talks above a murmur, does not feel impelled to throw wisecracks around, sees himself as an ordinary guy.

'What I think is funny,' he said, 'is what most people think is funny. It's just that I'm able to point it out.'

Behind that modesty, however, lurks a ferocious drive to keep working.

> 'I'm always writing my next play while the last one is in production. I'm a fatal-
> ist. I only have so many years of life, so many years of productivity. My quest
> is to write the perfect play. I'll never do it. Nobody ever does it.'

He takes little pleasure in being famous. 'You can kill an old lady by throwing her down the stairs, get your picture in the papers and become a celebrity. Big deal.'

His income has been reckoned at around £6,000 a week from stage royalties. He doesn't know.

He said:

> 'The only time money meant something to me was after I wrote *Come Blow
> Your Horn*, and I knew I didn't have to grind out any more TV and radio gags
> for a living. When I have a success I never say, "Wow, I'm going to make more
> money." I never think about it any more. Everybody I know in the world is
> looking for happiness. But hardly a soul ever stops to ask: what is happy? I
> am only happy when I work. I can't imagine myself not working. I really do
> it for me.'

During the past weeks he has spent every waking moment at the Prince of Wales Theatre watching over the progress of *Promises, Promises*.

'Writing a book for a musical,' said Neil Simon, 'is the most thankless thing a writer can do. You keep leading up to the big moment and then somebody sings it! You're always robbed of that big emotional moment. Promises will probably be the last musical I'll ever do.'

He dislikes being known simply as a comedy writer, and resents critics who, he says, 'don't take seriously what people laugh at. They take the line that if it's funny it can't be serious.' He points out that the mismatched males in *The Odd Couple* were really pathetic failures, and that the phoney Hollywood producer he depicted in *Plaza Suite* was a tragic character whose life had been one long, sustained lie.

> 'To me the ideal would be to write one of the great tragedies of all time, a deeply
> moving play that would make people laugh helplessly all the way through until
> the very end, when the true meaning would really hit them. I see comedy in
> tragedy, in the dilemmas of other people, in the concerns of my own life. The
> only thing I do in my life is to get people to recognise the absurdities of living,

to laugh at themselves. I laugh at myself too. It's the only thing that keeps me sane. When I am writing I am full of ego, and I feel that everything I am saying is worth the attention of thousands, even millions of people, that what I am putting down is true, touching, honest and important. The moment it is all down, however, I lose that feeling and never regain it. As I walk through the streets I become so objective that I literally feel myself becoming invisible, not being part of it, looking at the world through a two-way mirror, outside of it all. It's a good thing for a writer to be able to do, but rotten for a person.'

When Neil Simon turned forty, two years ago, he underwent a severe shake-up of confidence, as most men do at that age. Life was speeding by. Where was he going?

'Turning forty,' said the funniest writer in the world, 'is the least funny thing that ever happened to me. I hear turning fifty is much better. You just kind of glide into it. But forty was a horror. I even went back to my psychoanalyst, but I quit after a month because I got so bored talking about me, me, me.'

He wrote a play about it instead. It is called *The Last of the Red Hot Lovers*, which opens on Broadway next autumn.

'It's about a man in his forties who owns a seafood restaurant in New York. He has lived a very mundane life. He is married to his schoolgirl sweetheart and has never been unfaithful. Suddenly it occurs to him that life is passing him by and how little of it he has tasted. He complains that he has never been hit by another man. Life has not only not touched him, it has ignored him. So he has an affair with three women, one in each act of the play; he learns a lot about himself and is able to go on living.'

Neil Simon himself is happily married to an ex-dancer ('she's the best there is') and has two daughters.

'I am an optimist,' he said. 'I have a feeling that a good fairy will always look after me. In any case, the best way of getting over being forty is to hang around with people who are fifty.'

2 OCTOBER 1969

Neil Simon married five times, fathered two daughters and adopted another. He wrote over twenty screen-plays. Notable stage plays include The Sunshine Boys, Brighton Beach Memoirs, Biloxi Blues, The Goodbye Girl, Plaza Suite *and* California Suite. *In his honour, Broadway's Alvin Theatre was renamed the Neil Simon Theatre.*

Frank Sinatra

CHAPTER 80

FRANK SINATRA – OL' BLUE EYES

"Nerves? I had 'em cut out years ago."

Outside a brief five-minute meeting in the Sporting Club in Monte Carlo in 1958, I did not get to interview Frank Sinatra. But when he retired for the first time, I wrote a short appreciation, which follows below. Sinatra hated being interviewed and had a poor opinion of British popular newspapers. All the more remarkable, then, that he should have responded unbidden and so warmly to the words I wrote.

He used to play shy young sailors in Hollywood musicals, dropping his hungry little head sideways in a gesture of charming submissiveness. One lean finger would tinkle out a melody on a piano and the scene would be set in a dawn-empty New York café. 'I fall in love too easily…' Sinatra sang, and the women of the world, in their multitudes, gathered the sparrow-boned urchin to their matronly bosoms, urging solace.

Sinatra was discovered by women.

Did they suspect, even then, that the emaciated boy they were cradling in their infidel dreams would grow up into a dominating, somehow dangerous maverick, quick to fury, slow to placate, the toughest guy on the block?

Sinatra has been around for so long, and at so potent a level of celebrity, that he seems to have grown old with half the world, familiar as cornflakes. The singer he was, the songs he sang, have fused themselves into the lives of ordinary people in a manner unprecedented in our time or any other.

How many anonymous millions there must be who will forever associate a Sinatra song with a time in their lives when hopes ran high, or were dashed low. Sinatra had a song for both. I listen to Tony Bennett and Bing Crosby with pleasure, but without a tremor of nostalgia. But I cannot hear the nut-brown voice of Sinatra singing the words of 'Without A Song' without instantly remembering a girl with black hair who lived on a hill in Johannesburg and who made me very unhappy for a while. A London woman I know is regularly embarrassed into quiet tears in public places by the unexpected playing of Sinatra's 'Change Partners'. Sinatra is able to wield such power because what he has more of than other singers is an innate, unquestioned authority, or command, called arrogance by those who resent it or fear it.

Many entertainers take the stage begging for applause, blowing kisses, dropping curtseys. No such cringing for Sinatra, who refuses to indulge himself in such humiliating games with his audience, and thus elevates both.

Singing close to the mike, feeling the phrasing from note to note, lost in a ballad, he projects something that is at once polite but remote, the image of a man who has come to terms with himself, beaten his fears and won't kiss boots. These qualities appeal equally, of course, to men, who can recognise a proud man when they see one, a private man who won't be jostled.

It is this quality of command ('Nerves?' he once answered Princess Margaret. 'I had 'em cut out years ago.') that gave his voice its enduring resonance and separated him from the rest of the field.

Most of us have a special feeling for Sinatra because we recognise him as a good man who doesn't give a damn for the world's opinion, and so earns it.

In that sense, at least, the self-esteeming lyrics of one of Sinatra's last hits do seem to speak true. Sinatra has done it his way, taking the blows ... and throwing a few him himself.

22 May 1971

Sinatra (born 12 December 1915) began to show signs of dementia in his later years. He suffered a heart attack early in 1997 and made no further public appearances thereafter. Cause of death was officially given as complications from senility, heart and kidney failure and bladder cancer. He died in the Cedars-Sinai Hospital in Los Angeles on 14 May 1998, in the presence of his wife Barbara. His last words to her were 'I'm losing...' He is buried in Palm Springs, California.

Frank Sinatra

June 7, 1971

Mr. Herbert Kretzmer
Daily Express
London, England

Dear Mr. Kretzmer:

One of your readers has just forwarded
me your May 22nd article and I would like
to thank you for the very kind words.

Your column was most compassionate and
sensitive and I am most grateful to you
for it.

Again, my most sincere thanks.

Cordially

Frank Sinatra

FS:lil

Terence Stamp, Los Angeles, December 2008

CHAPTER 81

TERENCE STAMP – A NAME TO REMEMBER

"It's all happening. It's all swinging."

What follows is an account of my first meeting in 1962 with a beautiful Cockney lad who would later be seen as an embodiment of the so-called swinging, classless Sixties. He had just completed his first two films, neither yet released. Stamp was unknown when we met. We would go on meeting for the next fifty years (and counting).

Show business, like any other business, casts out its aged and replenishes itself from the young. So rapid is the recruitment, so quick the turnover, that names like Finney and O'Toole are already beginning to be classified as veterans, the old guard of the new wave.

But there are young ones coming up. Terence Stamp, for instance. A name to remember. A face almost too beautiful for a boy. Peter Ustinov discovered Stamp acting in a minor play called *Why the Chicken* and shoved the bewildered, delighted youth into the leading role of his film *Billy Budd*.

Since then Terence Stamp has also had a part in the new Laurence Olivier film, *Term of Trial*. Neither film has yet been released, but Mr Stamp, aged twenty-three, is clearly on his way.

He is, of course, working class. I can't think of a worthwhile male actor who has come up in recent years who isn't. He was born in Cable Street, Stepney. His father, Tom, drives a Thames tug. 'In the war my father was torpedoed while in the Merchant Navy and his hair went white overnight.'

Lithe, slim-hipped, with eyes of the palest blue, Terence Stamp talks a sort of soft Cockney peppered with the cool clichés of hipdom. He throws his arms out wide. 'Suddenly,' he cries, 'there's so much talent in the working class, man, it's exploding all over the place.'

'We've always had great men, but they've never broken through before. Now, look. The O'Tooles and the Finneys and old Lionel Bart and Willis Hall and all those cats coming down from the north. Man, it's too much.'

Stamp left school in his early teens, became an assistant professional golfer at Wanstead, then a typographer for an advertising agency, earning about £20 a week.

'But something was missing. My family kind of smothered me. They were obsessed with security. My father always talked about the slump. I was earning more money than he ever earned. He couldn't understand me. Finally I left home…'

Terence Stamp is eager to liberate himself from his origins. 'People in the business think I'm some kind of cockney idiot picked up by Ustinov walking down Cable Street, and just good for one picture. It's very degrading.'

Stamp subscribes to no acting philosophy, no method. 'I'm always watching people. I'm one of the world's observers.'

He pulled on a sheepskin coat and we walked along the chill streets of Victoria. He puffed at a cigarette, looking at girls. 'Birds,' he said approvingly, 'crazy.'

The world was wide open for this joyous, confident youth. He looked at me happily. 'It's all happening,' he said. 'It's all swinging.'

19 APRIL 1962

Seven years later, in 1969, I wrote about Stamp again.

He lives in Albany, probably the most exclusive, hard-to-get apartments in London, a hushed and hidden place 100 yards from Piccadilly Circus. His neighbours include the Hon. Edward Heath, Leader of Her Majesty's Opposition, whom he calls Ted.

Terence Stamp is everyone's idea of a new showbiz aristocrat, one of the myth-heroes of the pop age. Like Michael Caine and David Bailey, Terence Stamp has come to embody the idea that any Cockney kid can make it big in the new, classless Britain of the fast-changing Sixties. In mid-decade he was closely identified with the 'Swinging London' mystique fostered by *Time* and *Esquire* magazines.

The popular conception of Stamp pictures him as a smartly dressed peacock male, escorting London's prettiest, slimmest blooms (Jean Shrimpton, Julie

Christie) to world premieres in Leicester Square and thereafter to cool, tiled Italian restaurants along the King's Road.

That image of Stamp was largely a frolicsome invention of magazine writers looking for simple symbols. He was always shy and not much of a gadabout. His relationships with girls tended to be extended and complex.

Now in his thirty-first year, Terence Stamp lives quietly and alone, far from the madding crowd, relishing study and solitude.

He keeps himself in superb physical trim. He does not smoke or drink or take stimulants of any kind. He is a vegetarian and fasts a whole day every week, usually on Thursday. As a boy he had one of the highest IQs in his dockland school. His conversation remains alert and wide-ranging. He has studied Buddhism and seeks self-awareness with the dedication, but hardly the solemnity, of a novice monk.

Apartment D1, Albany, is a treasure house of antique French furniture and paintings of massive dimensions. Equipping this superior pad took all the money Stamp had at the time. A writing table by the eighteenth-century cabinetmaker André Charles Boulle – there is another in the Palace of Versailles – is strewn with film scripts, magazines, photographs, hippy bead necklaces and a bronze bust of Socrates wearing one of Stamp's black velvet hats. His two enormous fireside chairs may cost something like £1,000 apiece (Stamp won't say) but they are lived with, sat in, flopped on.

'Everything in this place,' he says, 'is used, everything works. I am not a collector. I hate museums.'

He talks with a subdued, classless accent, but in moments of enthusiasm he tends to lose control of it and comes out with shocking Cockneyisms, like 'froo dere' instead of 'through there'. I have heard him launch into stories beginning: 'My uncle, whats name is Jim, and aunt, whats name is Mary...'

He often refers to himself, with every indication of pleasure, as a 'hobbidy', a name still given to rough little urchins born east of St Paul's who wipe their noses on their sleeves.

'My boyhood,' he says as he sinks his body into several thousand pounds' worth of French furniture, 'was interesting but mostly kind of horrible.'

He remembers street gangs, lots of fights, playing in bomb craters, knocking at doors at night and running away, skipping school, worrying about not being able to waltz, or foxtrot, or talk to girls, feeling depressed and not knowing why, one-and-tuppence weekly pocket money, bunking into the pictures on Saturday, Camp Coffee, darned socks and Brylcreem.

He dreamed of being famous and living in Albany. He got both, and is not at all thrilled.

'I haven't changed. I'm surrounded by things that cost more money, that's all. I don't feel any happier for all my expensive surroundings. In the same way I am supposed to have become famous, but I don't feel famous, though I consciously know what it's like to be looked at, hard, all the time.'

He concluded sombrely that 'it is better to forgo all fantasies' and went off to brew up a couple of cups of clear tea and honey. 'The best part of the flower becomes honey,' he said, 'and when I eat honey that flower becomes a part of me.'

'Not enough people realise that we are, literally, what we eat. We are made up of pie and mash, sauce and sweets, mostly rubbish. You might say I'm a food reformist. All the food I eat is unrefined, untinned, unprocessed and what I refer to as —'

Stamp stopped suddenly in mid-sentence and laughed aloud. 'Enough! I don't want straight-eating people writing me off as eccentric.'

Though he can hardly be described as a recluse, Stamp spends more time totally alone than any man I know. He recently sent back his rented television set and sold his Rolls-Royce.

'Being alone is something I've only recently discovered. I was always frightened of solitude. Simple as it sounds, you have to learn to be happy with yourself before you can hope for happiness with anyone else. Besides paying rental on my TV set, I was condoning a felony, encouraging them to put on all that garbage. Driving a car brought out the worst in me, as it does in everybody. It doesn't matter to me that everyone is rushing somewhere. By walking at half the speed you become aware of four times as much, so there's 200 per cent profit, which is good business.'

Terence Stamp is, in many ways, typical of a whole hip new generation with its emphasis on kindliness, its preoccupation with the occult, and its comprehensive rejection of known political structures.

'It is not desirable,' he said, 'to become a spiritual chipmunk, a creature forever darting from one bizarre cult to another, with increasing impatience and increasing terror. My own feeling is that one cannot seek a guru. I have read that, when the pitch of your cry is right, a teacher will come to you.'

Stamp decided recently that it was 'not desirable' to eat yoghurt. 'I found myself in the film studios actually looking forward to tasting the cool lovely stuff as soon as I got home, and I thought: "My God, I'm getting to be like those Americans who can't wait for that first martini!"'

Stamp is always putting himself through little personal tests like that. They keep him aware of himself, he says, and prevent him sliding into a life dictated by casual habits.

'I figure I get paid good money as a film actor and that I owe whoever I'm working for to be in good physical shape. Julie Christie put me on to yoga. It's the only form of physical exercise I have experienced that seeks to clear and direct the mind as well.'

He maintains an excellent relationship with his parents, who have just moved to Blackheath into a house acquired for them by Terence and his brother Chris, a successful promoter of pop groups and recordings.

Terence Stamp sees himself as a voyager, always moving on. He seeks a kind of perfection. This is not a weekend hobby or a fashionable way of spending his hours of leisure. It is the central thread of his life, its dominant theme.

2 APRIL 1969

*Terence Stamp is the author of three volumes of memoirs (*Stamp Album, Coming Attractions, Double Feature*), a novel (*The Night*), and co-author with Elizabeth Buxton of the* Stamp Collection Cookbook. *He has made some sixty films, including* Poor Cow, The Limey, Superman, Modesty Blaise, Theorem, Far From the Madding Crowd, The Collector *and* Priscilla: Queen of the Desert. *In latter years he has appeared in roles in films starring Tom Cruise (*Valkyrie*),* Jim Carrey (*The Yes Man*) and Matt Damon (*The Adjustment Bureau*). In 2002 he married Singapore-born pharmacist Elizabeth O'Rourke; the couple were divorced six years later. In Stamp's latest film,* Song for Marion *(2012), he stars opposite Vanessa Redgrave.*

Tommy Steele

CHAPTER 82

TOMMY STEELE – CABIN BOY

"You know what? I'd like to die on the stage."

Thomas William Hicks was born in Bermondsey, London, on 17 December 1936. Renamed Tommy Steele, he was Britain's first teenage idol singing star. After a stint as a merchant seaman he was discovered by PR man John Kennedy, and rapidly rose to fame leading a group called the Steele Men. Their first hit record was 'Rock with the Caveman' (1956).

The lean young Londoner with the fluffy halo of fair hair springs up from a chair, supports himself momentarily against the chimneypiece, then falls back on the bed, bouncing. 'I'm thinking abaht it,' he says, assuringly. Having thought about it, he says finally: 'Yes. OK. I've got it. The only change that getting married has made in my life is a change of address. Got that? A change of address.'

He lights a cigarette. He is frail, eager and friendly.

Probably Britain's highest-paid stage performer, Tommy Steele is no longer a teenager, no longer a teenage idol. He recognises, with apparent relief, that the squealing years are over for good.

He's twenty-four. Eight months ago he married Ann Donoghue. 'I'm just as happy married as ever I was single.' He sounds surprised. 'Marriage is supposed to bring you down, don't it? Everybody says that. In my case, it ain't true. I love my wife. I love her so much. It's a thing you can't talk abaht.'

The telephone rings at his elbow. Someone has got the wrong number. 'No, this is not the Westminster Bank, missus,' says Tommy Steele. 'Do you want to borrow a few bob?' He laughs kindly into the mouthpiece. 'Missus, I hope the bank gives you everything you want. Good luck.'

He talks in a quick, husky, Cockney voice. Some of the finesses of the English language still baffle him. 'I've got a pain in me toof,' he says; and 'we've got to stick togevver.'

He has never lost the common touch. He has a genuine feeling for the cloth-cap stratum of his audience. He loves those mums and dads. He says, 'Mr and Mrs Bloggs. They are my people.'

Steele has already outlived scores of guitar-plucking grunters who were hailed in their time as discoveries and idols. Now, his wide, blue eyes are aimed at wider horizons. Last year he joined the Old Vic Theatre Company to play Tony Lumpkin in Oliver Goldsmith's *She Stoops to Conquer*. He has been invited to return to the Vic as Puck in Shakespeare's *A Midsummer Night's Dream*.

'When I first started,' he says, 'all I had to do was to play a loud guitar and jump all over the stage, and I got all that high-pitched hysteria, like.'

> 'That's not good enough anymore. Today they want to see an act. Those days all me fans were aged fourteen to eighteen. They sent me letters. Tommy, I love you. That kind of caper. Mobbed wherever I went. Murder!
>
> Nowadays me audiences are different. Old grannies of eighty. Little children. It's harder work for me. Thank God.'

He bounces off the bed, plunges his hands deep in his trouser pockets. 'I'll tell you something straight,' he says.

> 'I wasn't a stage-bitten kid. Never. I came in because it was an adventure, like. I thought I'd last six months, that's all. I thought to meself: Enjoy it. Make a couple of hundred quid and get out. Back to the sea, where I'd started as a cabin boy.
>
> I decided to follow the example of Donald O'Connor [Hollywood all-round musical performer]. He was my boyhood idol. Still is. Dance, sing, comedy, the lot. Branch out. Think big. Don't be a flash-in-the-pan.
>
> I went to the Old Vic for the experience and the honour. Certainly not for the money. All I got was sixty quid a week. But the experience – man, you can't count it on your fingers!
>
> When I'm thirty years old, and forty, and fifty, I want to go on doing what I'm doing now. You know what? I'd like to die on the stage. S'matter of fact, if I died tomorrow I think I've lived a full life. That's straight. That's the troof. I love it. I'd give anything to be able to say that there isn't a man I ever met who I didn't like.
>
> I'm always asking my agent, my manager, my friends: "Do I have any enemies? Who doesn't like me?" I always feel I've got to be liked. It's becoming an obsession with me, like. My wife is always on to me abaht it, saying I worry

too much about what people think. I know it's silly, believe me, but what can I do? That's me.

It's not like I was starved for love as a kid, anything like that. In the Merchant Navy it was different. I talked too much, tried too hard to impress. "Old Mouth and Trousers" they called me. When the lads went ashore and invited me along, I was so pleased, so proud. I felt I was wanted.

You've gotta have a philosophy, see? By getting married, like, I've started on three things. Planting a tree. Taking a wife. And giving the world a son. That's from a very old song by Tennessee Ernie. It goes: "There are three things a man must do before his days are done. He must plant a tree and take a wife and give the world a son."

Marvellous, ain't it? You're born in the world with nothing. Everything that happens to you after that is sheer profit.'

Tommy Steele lights another cigarette and talks about books, and what they do to him.

'I'm reading four books. One is William Shirer's *Rise and Fall of the Third Reich*. The other three are all about gangsters like Lucky Luciano and the mobs. I get a terrific excitement reading about people getting shot all time. I can never believe that people can be so bad. I tell you straight, it excites me so terribly I can actually feel my heart skipping a beat! I feel sometimes I want to be an undercover agent, in charge of a special patrol, hunting down the mobs. I was never a sex symbol like some of the other singers. I've never been sexy. I couldn't be. I don't think it's entertainment.'"

He searches in his mind for a more precise symbol, and finds it in Shakespeare's Puck, the part he will one day play. 'Puck's a con-man, see? He's a practical joker, taking advantage of any situation. Always in and out, always dodgin' abaht. That Puck, man! He's marvellous. He's me…'

19 FEBRUARY 1961

Tommy Steele's star continued to rise. He had hits with 'Singing the Blues' and Lionel Bart's 'Little White Bull'. On stage, in London and on Broadway, he starred in David Heneker's Half A Sixpence *(1963), Frank Loesser's* Hans Christian Andersen, Singin' In the Rain, Scrooge, Dr Dolittle. *He also became a director of musical comedies. He would also become, in many ways, a tormented figure, a victim of stage fright.*

'Somebody comes into my dressing room before the show and says, "the house is jammed ... they're standing in the aisles." For some entertainers that would sound like manna from heaven. But for me it's the opposite. The bottom drops right out of my heart and right out of my toes. Boom, boom! It hits the floor – and then I hear its echo through the great emptiness in me.'

Tommy Steele speaking – the enduring, ageless wonder-child of British showbiz. Ex-sailor, rock 'n' roller, and Fifties phenomenon.

Two weeks from now, on his forty-first birthday, Tommy Steele will come bounding onto the vast acres of the Palladium stage in Frank Loesser's perennial musical *Hans Christian Andersen*. Steele is a toothy, fatless figure with a Cinemascope grin and an overwhelming desire to please.

Few among the applauding thousands will even begin to guess at the torment he feels during the hours before he walks out onto the boards. Nobody beyond his family and near associates will know that the sheer terror of the challenge has often seen him doubled up in his dressing room, literally spilling his guts into the hand-basin.

'It's always been the same,' Tommy told me yesterday, 'and I am resigned to the fact that it always will be the same. That is the deal I've made. I don't want to be anyone other than who I am. If that means being sick all night and having headaches all day and being absolutely dead scared all the time ... okay, that's the contract, and I have signed it.'

Yesterday I watched him rehearsing the *Andersen* musical. He supervises everything. His blue eyes don't miss a thing. His personal style is friendly and easy-going. But nobody in his company is in any doubt that Tommy is the boss, the ultimate authority.

'Every day before a show,' he says, 'round 'bout four in the afternoon I begin to tense up. I feel that nausea welling up in me. My eyes go dead and I retreat into myself. I start rehearsing that night's show in my private mind. I go over it and over it. I lose myself in my stage character. If I was playing a killer I feel I might even kill ... Look at this, for God's sake!' he says as his hands push back the thick golden hair on his head, revealing a scalp that is covered entirely in dry, scaly skin. 'I've been to countless doctors about it,' he confesses.

'The flaking begins on the first day of rehearsals and goes on until the fifth or sixth day into the run of the new show. It itches so badly that I don't sleep at night. I've learned to live with it. I love the work I do; I adore and respect the audience. It's the last thing I think of at night, first thing I think of when I wake. It's a magnificent obsession. There used to be a family high-wire act in the circus. They lost about six or seven lives in death falls. The old man, leader of the troupe, was asked why he continued in the face of all those tragedies. He replied, "Because to be on the wire is to live – the rest is just waiting." That, for me, is the most beautiful quote in the world. Blimey, I understand exactly what the old man meant.'

Tommy Steele is a happily married man. He regards his wife Annie, his eight-year-old daughter Emma, and his mother and father as his only true friends in the world.

'They are the only people I can absolutely rely on to be always there … at the end of a telephone wire … or the end of a scream.'

When he feels that other people have let him down, Steele's rages can be awesome. Those who work regularly with him have divided his furious outbursts into two categories. A Number One Rage and Number Two Rage.

'Number Two,' he says, 'can be pretty electrifying.'

'But a Number One is something else. I go black. I scream with fury but I remember nothing afterwards. People scatter … I divide people into Believers – those who believe in what you are doing – and Passengers – those who get on my back for the ride. If I catch them out I go mad.

My home and my family are my rock and my haven. Annie and I don't drink. We don't smoke. We don't go to parties. My marriage is the epitome of bliss. For all the doubts, rages and terrors of my life, I love it … I love it all. I am the luckiest man in the world.'

1 DECEMBER 1977

Now seventy-five, Tommy is still active in the business.

John Steinbeck

CHAPTER 83

JOHN STEINBECK – CALIFORNIAN GIANT

> "I wish to God I knew as much about writing now
> as I did when I was nineteen."

John Ernst Steinbeck was born in Salinas, California, of German and Irish descent, on 27 February 1902. Saluted as one of the literary eminences of the century, he was awarded the Pulitzer Prize for The Grapes Of Wrath *(1939) and the Nobel Prize for Literature (1962). He wrote sixteen novels, mainly about the disadvantaged rural poor, six non-fiction books and five collections of short stories. As a youth he spent his holidays working on California ranches. He attended Stanford University but dropped out without a degree, served as a war correspondent in the Second World War, accompanying commando raids on German-held territory in the Mediterranean. He married three times and fathered four children. The publication of* The Grapes Of Wrath, *while exciting universal acclaim, was condemned by self-serving conservative opinion as a biased socialist account of working conditions in American agriculture. The book was briefly banned by some school boards. Steinbeck wrote of the controversy, 'The vilification of me out here from the large land owners is pretty bad ... I mean a kind of hysteria about the book that is not healthy.'*

Six feet tall and rock-solid, John Steinbeck seemed to fill the room. Everywhere you looked, he was there. He lit a cheroot, poured a shot of whisky, crinkled his Pacific-blue eyes. Public curiosity about him has been strong ever since the publication of his Pulitzer Prize-winning novel *The Grapes Of Wrath* (1939), which describes the plight of the American rural poor in the years of dustbowl and depression.

Steinbeck did little to satisfy the inquisitive and rarely sat down to an interview. As a boy in California he had been chronically shy. When he was first touched by fame a stranger recognised and hailed him in a street in San Francisco. The experience, Steinbeck said, 'sickened' him.

'It is not that I abhor publicity,' he said when we met at the Dorchester Hotel in London, 'I see no point in it. The business of being a celebrity has no reference to the thing I am interested in, and that is my work.' Steinbeck's voice, deep and resonant, seemed to rumble up from an underground vault.

'I know no sadder people than those who believe their own publicity,' he said. 'I still have my own vanities, but they have changed their face.' His smile was sudden and disarming. 'Also, it's nobody's damn business how I live.'

He had recently been awarded the Nobel Prize. 'I do not believe that age produces knowledge or wisdom,' he said.

'I wish to God I knew as much about writing as I did when I was nineteen. I was totally certain about most things then, and I suspect, more accurate. I have lived too long. Preferably a writer should die at about twenty-eight. Then he has a chance of being discovered. If he lives much longer he can only be revalued. I prefer discovery.'

Steinbeck was constantly being revalued, and was currently considered an unfashionable writer whose best work – *The Grapes Of Wrath*, *Tortilla Flat*, *Cannery Row*, *East of Eden* – lay behind him.

He did not appear much concerned. 'Literary critics,' he said, 'really write about themselves. A critic is interested in his own work, his own career, and properly so. I don't care what is said about my books. I do care, however, what is thought about them.'

He laughed in a craggy, infectious manner. 'I am an ordinary man,' he said, 'scared and boastful and humble about my books.'

'I love compliments but am not thrown by insults. Like everyone else in the world I want to be good and strong and virtuous and wise and loved. I am a solitary man. Unless a writer is capable of solitude he should leave books alone and go into the theatre. What some people find in religion a writer can find in his craft – a kind of breaking through to glory. I write because I like to write. I find joy in the tone and texture and rhythm of words. It is a satisfaction like that which follows good and shared love. When I finish a book I have a sense of death. Something that has been alive no longer exists. I feel the same sense of loss when a friend dies. I never re-read my books with any satisfaction. That thing between hard covers is a tomb.'

He poured another drink and rubbed the back of his hand against his grey, trimmed beard. He raised his whisky glass and said, 'This proves I'm on vacation.'

He stood at the window staring down at the late-afternoon traffic in Park Lane. He looked like a windswept giant.

'Actually I am an inch shorter than I was,' he said. 'You get older, you get shorter. You dig deeper into the grave, I guess.'

He laughed again. Laughter bubbled endlessly in this austere, attractive man. He saw me to the door. 'Call me in New York,' he said as I walked away from his suite towards the lift. 'I am the only Steinbeck in the book.'

15 JANUARY 1965

Eleven years after his death, Steinbeck's face appeared on a US postage stamp. Steinbeck, a smoker all his life, died on 20 December 1966 of congestive heart failure, an autopsy revealing nearly complete blockage of the coronary arteries. His body was cremated and his ashes buried in the Steinbeck family plot in Salinas. As a long-serving interviewer, I am sometimes asked to name the 'most impressive' person I have met. I always unhesitatingly name John Steinbeck. (And, no, I never summoned up the nerve to call him in New York, even though he had so generously invited me to do so.)

James Stewart

CHAPTER 84

JAMES STEWART – ALL AMERICAN

"Danger is an elusive and abstract thing and it totally fascinates me."

James Maitland ('Jimmy') Stewart, born on 20 May 1908, was Hollywood royalty. Over a professional career spanning seventy years, he starred in a string of classic movies including The Philadelphia Story *(1940),* It's a Wonderful Life *(1946),* Rear Window *(1954),* Vertigo *(1958),* The Man Who Shot Liberty Valance *(1962). He was also an accomplished stage actor, appearing many times on Broadway and in London's West End where he notably played the role of Elwood P. Dowd in* Harvey, *a comedy about an invisible 7-foot-tall rabbit. Son of a Pennsylvania hardware store owner, Stewart was descended from veterans of the American Revolution and the Civil War. Princeton-educated, he was the first major Hollywood star to join the services in the Second World War. He had a distinguished military career as a bomber pilot.*

James Stewart lives clean, votes the conservative ticket and refers to his wife, Gloria, as 'Mrs Stewart'. He is a lanky, blue-eyed hometown boy of Pennsylvania WASP stock who has made good in the big town, banks his dollars, fought bravely for his country, does not smoke, goes to bed early, and remains a member of the Los Angeles Board of the Boy Scouts of America.

As a young movie actor he slurred and goshed and gasped his way through a succession of well-remembered films in which he played modest and upstanding young fellows just like himself. Jimmy Stewart had what every American mother desired in a son, and that made him a millionaire and a star.

When we met for tea at Claridge's he wore an old-fashioned gold pin, which linked the points of his white shirt collar. His shoes were plain and laced up.

As a wartime USAF Colonel, Stewart commanded a bomber squadron based in England. He led many sorties over Germany, and was twice awarded the Distinguished Flying Cross.

'I have always been afraid of flying,' he said.

'As a teenager I nearly broke my neck trying to fly my own version of an airplane. The more I got to know about flying, the more afraid I became. You become aware of all the things that can go wrong. Danger is an elusive and abstract thing and it totally fascinates me. If people were honest everyone would admit to being afraid. I know I do. At the same time I believe that it is allotted to some people to shake fear off, and it is that conquest that I find so exhilarating.'

He told me that he was in London on his way to India, where he planned to join a tiger hunt. He figured that there might be an opportunity there to feel some fear and conquer it.

'I have felt fear as an actor before going onstage, in front of film and TV cameras and radio microphones. When I was piloting bombers here during the war I was always afraid I would make a mistake at the controls. A lot of guys depend on you when you are in charge of a Flying Fortress. Fear of making a wrong decision was always stronger than fear about my personal safety.'

Stewart closed his lips, then popped them apart. 'That terrible dry feeling in the mouth,' he said. He reached forward and sipped a mouthful of hot tea. 'I have a very real fear of being in a motor accident,' he said.

'I often dream of being in a smash-up. It's a kind of premonition. Mrs Stewart says I am not a good driver, and so do many of my friends, so I guess it must be true. I don't seem to be able to concentrate on driving. I have this terror that I will one day drive into something. Lots of times I have been grateful to drive into my own garage. It's a thing I will have to learn to live with because I imagine the automobile is here to stay. Fear is something you must accept and deal with; otherwise you might as well stay at home and spend the rest of your life in bed. Now, having a tiger charge at me is so beyond my comprehension that I am absolutely thrilled just thinking about it. The psychiatrists may say that I am mixed up. But I don't think I am, and that's what matters.'

James Maitland Stewart stood up, shook my hand and said he was off to have dinner with Alfred Hitchcock.

15 JANUARY 1959

James Stewart died of a pulmonary embolism on 2 July 1997 (one day after the death of fellow star Robert Mitchum). President Bill Clinton said, 'America lost a national treasure today.' James Stewart was married only once, to Gloria Hatrick McLean. Stewart adopted his wife's two sons, one of whom, Ronald, became a Marine Lieutenant and was killed in action in Vietnam, aged twenty-four. The Stewarts had twin daughters, Judy and Kelly. Stewart had a passion for gardening and for writing homespun poetry, which on one occasion caused TV chat show host Johnny Carson to weep on air. Like his best friend Henry Fonda, James Stewart continued acting until late in his life and was regularly listed as one of the great screen actors of all time.

Jule Styne

CHAPTER 85

JULE STYNE – A SONGWRITER COMES HOME

"There was a sweet shop on this corner, a fire station over there."

By the time he reached his tenth birthday, Jule Styne had already appeared as a piano soloist with the Chicago, St Louis and Detroit Symphony Orchestras. The child prodigy discovered his true vocation, however, as one of the great Hollywood and Broadway composers, whose hit shows and songs included such all-time winners as 'Diamonds Are A Girl's Best Friend', 'Just In Time', 'Make Someone Happy', 'The Party's Over', 'Three Coins In The Fountain', and Barbra Streisand's hits 'People' and 'Don't Rain On My Parade'.

D ucal Street, which once rang with the cries of children of the immigrant poor, is dead and gone. A cluster of council flats now sprawls bleakly across that vanished byway in London's East End. Yesterday, a famous man came home again, searching for a trace of his long-ago childhood. The record shows that Jule Styne is the composer of more than 900 popular songs. The kind of songs that stick. Some of them, indeed, have become part of the language we speak: 'Everything's Coming up Roses', 'Don't Rain On My Parade'.

Jule (pronounced Julie) Styne is also the indefatigable composer of a list of Broadway musicals of the highest pedigree, including *Gentlemen Prefer Blondes*, *Bells Are Ringing*, *Funny Girl* and *Gypsy*.

A permanent US resident, Styne is in London keeping an eye on the long-delayed West End opening of *Gypsy*, which will star Angela Lansbury in the role made famous on Broadway by Ethel Merman.

I took a ride with Jule yesterday to look for the street where he was born in 1905. Piquantly, the man whose name has become synonymous with the all-American glitter of the Broadway musical actually started life in a lowly street in the London suburb of Bethnal Green, where his Ukrainian-Jewish parents kept a butter and egg shop.

Jule is sixty-seven now, but still the little go-getter. No sign of slowing up. His mind spins with ideas and projects for future shows. He plans to live and work in London for the next few years. He sees Britain now, despite the scare talk of depression, as a country bristling with the promise of boom times, rich in theatrical life and talent. He wants to be part of it. It is a kind of homecoming.

We could not locate his birthplace at first. It is no longer there. The house and the street have been blitzed and bulldozed into the ground. The Bethnal Green police station saved the day by digging up an old map of the territory. We were thus able to pinpoint the site of his birthplace exactly.

Minutes later Jule Styne stood, a small man lost in a concrete wasteland of unyielding council-dom, trying to remember how it used to be.

'There was a sweet shop on this corner, a fire station over there ... and here must have been our front door ... just about here.' He pointed at a grim brick wall enlivened by a graffiti message urging Spurs for Wembley.

Jule Styne kept lighting up a stream of cigarettes, darting around corners, pointing this way and that. He was excited to be exploring the London he last saw when he was eight years old, before the First World War, when his parents followed the immigrant wave to America.

> 'When I used to live here I was a child entertainer, a precious little prat who used to do an impersonation of Harry Lauder, the great Scottish performer. That was my whole act. When I was five or six years old I once actually jumped from a box on to the stage while Sir Harry was performing. I announced I could sing just like him and I sang "That's My Daisy", with Lauder standing right next to me! After the show my father whacked me hard outside the theatre and made me go back to apologise to Sir Harry, who gave me some wonderful advice that night. "My boy, never impersonate anybody," he said. "And learn to play a musical instrument."'

A cold wind whistled along what once was Ducal Street. Jule Styne pulled on a raincoat, engaged several passersby in conversation. 'Hullo,' he greeted them. 'I used to live around here...'

Before he returned to the car he took a last look around at the barren surroundings. 'The world changes, feller, it all changes...'

Riding back to Park Lane he kept up an unstoppable flow of talk about the old days, the old values.

'We believed in families then. The greatest glow I ever had in my life was giving my mother the first money I earned. Today we've lost that feeling. Parents don't spank their children any more, even when they burn down the house. Children are encouraged to get their own way. There's no generation gap. There's only neglect.'

Through his shaded spectacles he gazed at London speeding by on a cloudy spring day. 'A good town,' said homecomer Jule Styne. 'A breath of sanity.'
10 MAY 1973

Julius Kirwin Stein was born on New Year's Eve 1905 and died in New York on 20 September 1994, aged eighty-eight.

Kenneth Tynan and his wife Kathleen Halton

CHAPTER 86

KENNETH TYNAN –
HOW DO YOU FOLLOW *OH! CALCUTTA!*

◇◇

"There are people who think of sex as a chamber of horrors."

Kenneth Peacock Tynan (born in Birmingham on 2 April 1927) was afflicted with a childhood stammer, which stayed with him all his life. He was born with a precocious intelligence, which, combined with good looks and a flamboyant sense of style, made him one of the most famous Englishmen of the century. A schoolteacher said of him, 'He was the only boy I could never teach anything.' Tynan dodged National Service by showing up for his initial interview with painted fingernails and reeking of perfume. He was, as he had planned, rejected as 'unfit for military service'. At Cambridge Tynan's impact was such that he instantly became 'the most talked of person in the city'. Despite his stammer, he was a supremely witty and provocative debater. In 1951 he married American writer Elaine Dundy. Their daughter Tracy was named after the film actor Spencer Tracy. Katharine Hepburn was invited to be the child's godmother and accepted. Tynan found his true calling as a theatre critic, first on the London Evening Standard *and later, more significantly, on the* Observer *and the* New Yorker. *He was the first critic to welcome John Osborne's* Look Back In Anger *as an example of a new radical wave in the British theatre, sweeping out (or so he thought) the conservative conventions of the polite West End stage. As a critic Tynan's slogan was 'Rouse Tempers, Goad and Lacerate, Raise Whirlwinds'. Tynan was the first to use the 'F' word on British television. English historian Paul Johnson described Tynan's behaviour 'as a masterpiece of calculated self-publicity'. Tynan produced two erotica-based stage reviews:* Oh! Calcutta!, *a notorious hit in the West End and Broadway, and its pale successor,* Carte Blanche. *Tynan became literary advisor to Britain's National Theatre. The stage director Michael Blakemore, in his memoirs, offers the following vivid picture of Tynan's charisma: 'He liked to mix socially with theatre people and I would often see him at some party, always in the company of one or two pretty women and sometimes with a New York celebrity tagging along. He and his party stayed only as long as the occasion held his interest. Then they were off, with Ken breathing*

disdainful smoke over the gathering from a cigarette held with calculated affecta-
tion between his middle fingers ... I would have given anything for a good notice
from him, because as a critic he was incorruptible.'

Kenneth Tynan meets me in a London pub, puffing a cigarette he shouldn't
be smoking at all because of a chronic chest complaint that he knows may
one day kill him. On the other hand, what Tynan stands for above all is allow-
ing people freely to choose their own pleasures as long as they do no harm to
others. So he talks away and smokes away, a luminously intelligent and stylish
man who also happens to be the most readable theatre critic of his time.

Seven years ago *Oh! Calcutta!*, the sex revue devised by Tynan, provoked thun-
der storms of protests. Next week sees the London opening of *Calcutta's* successor, again assembled by Tynan, called *Carte Blanche*. But this time there is no fuss
and little excitement. Tynan regards this as an encouraging sign of progress in
British attitudes. 'Last time,' he says, 'the jungle drums were pounding.'

> 'Protest groups outside the theatre, that kind of thing. We had to chase around
> for rehearsal rooms because landlords were persuaded that we were using their
> premises for dishonourable purposes. There's nothing like that now. I don't accept
> that there is a puritan backlash. The pendulum never swings all the way back. It
> creeps forward a little with each swing. Since *Calcutta* there has been a welcome
> change here. The air is quite good to breathe. Seven years ago it was a bit noxious.'

Wearing a casual dark blazer edged with a narrow red ribbon, Tynan sips
gin and ginger ale, lights up another forbidden cigarette. He is a friendly
but private man who is sometimes credited with having single-handedly
launched the Permissive Society when he spoke the 'F' word on live
television for the first time ever. Tynan dislikes the phrase 'Permissive Society'.

'It's so typically English,' he says. 'It implies that you have to ask someone's
permission to enjoy your own body, like obtaining a chit from the headmaster. *Carte Blanche* is not a show that should outrage anyone. We make
no evangelistic claims for it. We are not in the business of propaganda.' He
pauses for a few seconds to frame his thoughts.

> 'It is a form of pastime for people who have accepted the idea that sex is a subject
> fit for public presentation and debate. It is a more ambitious show than *Calcutta*,
> which had inevitable crudities, which had to be more aggressive, because it was
> trying to establish a beachhead. When we did *Calcutta* all the puritan crusaders
> said it would open the floodgates for sex shows. In fact, there's been barely a

trickle. Apart from *The Dirtiest Show in Town* and *Let My People Come* – both American shows – there have been no local experiments in the field at all.

It is extremely difficult to put a show together that illuminates the question of sex. It's not just a question of calling up half a dozen writers and asking them to have a go. It's taken a couple of years to put together the final selections for *Carte Blanche*. It's not an easy mark, not an easy thing for writers and choreographers to translate their own private ideas about sex into a form of public entertainment. The cheap continental soft-porn films have made sex look like a job for amateurs. To do this kind of thing properly requires a knowledge of all the nuances of sexuality. It can't be done on the cheap and it can't be done without great skill.'

'Some of the tableaux of *Carte Blanche*,' Tynan promises, 'will be funny, some will be disturbing, and some will be simply beautiful. There are people in this country who think of sex as a chamber of horrors. We regard it as a palace of delights. All we can hope to do is offer a guided tour of some of the rooms of that palace.'

Soon after *Carte Blanche* opens at London's Phoenix Theatre, Tynan is leaving England to work in California. But he insists, 'I am not shaking the dust of England off my feet.'

Tynan may be disgusted by what he calls the deadlock in British political life, but clings to the 'possibility of change because we're a small country. Super-powers are virtually unchangeable. I would not live permanently in a super-power. Besides,' says Tynan, fifty next birthday, 'I have bronchitis and England is a plague spot for bronchial sufferers. The further away I go, the better I'll be when I come back.' Tynan stubbed out his cigarette.

He hurried back across the sunny street to rehearsals of *Carte Blanche*, a show he originally intended to call 'Soft Anvil'. It's a quote, he explained, from a poem by the Earl of Rochester and refers to the female generative organ:

> *This is the workhouse of the world's chief trade*
> *On this soft anvil all mankind was made.*

'We scrapped the title,' Tynan said, 'because "Soft Anvil" sounded like just another pop group.'

14 SEPTEMBER 1976

In 1967 Tynan married Canadian writer Kathleen Halton. A decade later he moved to California, hoping to halt the increasingly severe effects of his hereditary emphysema, not helped by his lifetime smoking habit. He died of the disease in Santa Monica, California, on 26 July 1980.

Jimmy Webb

CHAPTER 87

JIMMY WEBB – UP, UP AND AWAY

"We were forbidden to go swimming with girls in case
we caught a glimpse of their thighs."

*Jimmy Layne Webb was born on 15 August 1946 in Elk City, Oklahoma,
son of itinerant Baptist minister Robert Lee Webb. As a boy, Jimmy was
allowed to listen only to white country music and white gospel songs. In
1964 the family moved to California, where his beloved mother died a
year later. By the mid-60s, with the exception of the Beatles, Jimmy Webb
was the hottest songwriting talent around ('Wichita Lineman', 'Galveston',
'Didn't We', etc.).*

Three years ago he drifted around Los Angeles, just another small-town boy far from home. Now people everywhere are talking about Jimmy Webb, songwriter of the year, the wonder boy from Oklahoma who wrote the buoyant 'Up, Up and Away', and the hot-selling Richard Harris pop hymn 'MacArthur Park' (Someone left the cake out in the rain…).

Just twenty-two years old, Jimmy Webb is already a world celebrity. His music and words are quirky and personal, usually wrapped in a lush symphonic package (he is a superb arranger) that makes them esteemed on both sides of the generation gap.

Last week in London he was writing words and music for MGM's multi-million-dollar movie based on J. M. Barrie's *Peter Pan*, shooting next year with Mia Farrow. In all Webb's work there is an uncorrupted grace, a sweetness of spirit. He is a fragile, lanky, 6ft 1in beanpole of a boy, good looking in that soft-eyed, even-featured American collegiate way.

He was staying in Park Lane in the penthouse of the Playboy Club's adjoining apartments. He had just taken a bath and was dressed in an ice-blue dressing-gown. Barefooted, he looked like an Olympic swimming finalist quietly certain he was going to win the big race.

Webb enjoys good, expensive things and can now afford them after a lifetime of almost bizarre religious self-denial. But he still neither drinks nor smokes, claiming to have tried them both. One tasted awful and the other hurt his throat.

Jim Webb is one of the five children of a restless, pulpit-pounding Baptist minister of the old school who looked on the ways of the world as wicked, regarded parties as sinful, songwriting as evil, but has now been converted by his son and is today the administrator of Jim Webb's burgeoning music publishing and film interests in California. 'My father has come a long way,' Jim says fondly.

Jim Webb's paradoxical relationship with his stern but loving father, and all his father stood for, is at the heart of his own elusive personality. 'My home life was very happy, but I suppose it was happy because we didn't know any better.'

Webb grew up in a series of one-horse towns in Oklahoma and Texas where his father built churches, preached the good word, was sometimes paid in groceries by poor congregations and then, his work done, set out to find yet one more hick town to build yet one more church.

'He felt the Lord would always bless us,' says Jimmy Webb, who, for eighteen years, never missed a single Sunday in church. 'Even when I was ill, somehow I held myself erect in the pew. Every New Year's Eve all of us had to go to church to pray the New Year in…'

Predictably that kind of early experience has left its quota of guilt and inhibition on Jimmy Webb, which still bedevils his personal relationships, especially with girls.

'Everything was in its place. Too bad I didn't fit in…'

So runs a line in a song from Webb's album *A Tramp Shining*, sung by Richard Harris.

'Sexually,' Webb says, 'I suppose we, as Baptist children, were done the most harm having this aura of "sin" placed around what should be normal and wonderful. We were forbidden to go swimming with girls in case we caught a glimpse of their thighs. That kind of teaching is as much a perversion of an idea as a Black Mass; it's wrong and it's sick.'

When the small boy began writing pop songs he took to hiding away in the garage to escape his father's wrath.

'My father felt I should devote my life to playing the piano and organ in church.

He went to extraordinary lengths to discourage my songwriting, applying economic harassments, and so on. You can't have this. You can't have that. You can't have the car. Daddy had, as a young man, played the guitar in a hillbilly band, and he sang country songs to us when I was growing up. But he didn't understand what I was doing. "Nobody will listen to your music, son, you're just breaking your heart…"'

Webb's mother always took his part, soothing her husband ('Jimmy's not a bad boy…'). She was only thirty-six when she died, four years ago, of a brain tumour.

'She was beautiful, she was beyond description,' Jim says.

'I went in to see her just before she died and she looked up and called me by my full name – Jimmy Layne. Those were almost the last words she spoke on this earth. I don't remember her with any sadness. She was one of the nicer things of my life. I still recall her standing by the ironing board tidying up my mind after a long day in school. I've written a sequence about her on the new Richard Harris album, *The Yard Went On Forever*.

It goes like this: "There were houses, There were hoses, There were sprinklers on the lawn, There was an ironing board, And she would stand amid her understanding, And ask the children what they'd done at school that day, And the yard went on forever."'

After his mother's early death Jimmy Webb dropped out of college, cut his ties with his father's world, and tried to make it on his own. His father gave him $40 and a week's rent, and wept for his son.

Jim remembers: 'Two big tears rolled down my father's cheek and he said: "Well, son, this is the hardest thing I've ever done in my life." I swear to God we just stood there and cried. I think he felt at that point that I was terribly lost.'

Jim hung around Los Angeles for a year writing songs, waiting for a break. He tends to dramatise the story ('I swept foyers…'), but the Jim Webb story is not really a rags-to-riches saga. His talent was too spectacular to remain long hidden.

His first hit was the haunting 'By the Time I Get to Phoenix'. After his next success, 'Up, Up and Away' (based on a publicity flight in a balloon to advertising a newly opened hot-dog stand), Webb was into the big time and the big money.

Today he is the most successful and potentially the wealthiest composer since Lennon-McCartney.

Jim Webb is polite and well mannered to a degree no longer common in this crass world. Last week he phoned my home and spoke to my wife, calling her 'ma'am' throughout the conversation, the way boys were brought up to do in another world, at another time. She was deeply touched.

Webb is aware that his innocence is what distinguishes his giftedness.

'I have a curious sense of detachments from the affairs of the world. I am lucid. I am free of prejudice. If I began to play everybody's game I'd lose my capacity to discern what is delicate and what is boorish. I will participate only up to the point that it changes me. I don't want to be part of the jet set – the groovies, the trendies, the celluloid people, the in-crowd. The moment you decide you're in, man, you are out. The world is full of mutants who no longer fall in love. We are witnessing the dehumanisation of man.

I would very much like to believe in God, as my father did – and still does. That would be a great emotional cushion for me to sit on. But I don't have the luxury, not any more … I am appalled by the apathy and defeatism that run rampant in the world. People are already telling me I'm through, that this is the end. As far as I am concerned I'm at the beginning. All my best songs are to come. I would die if I didn't believe that. At school my teacher wrote on my report: "Your son Jimmy is too inclined to daydream." When I marry and have a son I will teach him, if I can, to daydream. More than mathematics or English literature I'd like my son to learn to dream.

I don't protest. The only political machine that counts is the machine that exists in each human being individually. We must learn to master that machine before we freak out in Hyde Park.'

Then Jim Webb played some songs from *Peter Pan* for me on the piano. His thumped gospel chords, his hair flying, his thin arms a blur across the keyboard. He sang a song about Peter Pan 'floating on air with the grace of an innocent swan'.

I love Jimmy Webb. He is one of the good guys. As another writer of notable lyrics laid it out in *Measure for Measure*:

'How far that little candle throws his beam. He shines like a good deed in a naughty world.'

10 MAY 1973

In 1974 Jimmy Webb married Patsy Sullivan (five sons, one daughter). The couple split after twenty-two years. Between 1982 and 1992 Webb wrote film scores and classical music, but he was never to repeat the run of outstanding popular hits that marked his career in the 1960s. He married broadcasting executive Laura Savini in 2004 and rediscovered religion without specifying its form. ('God is bigger than any one particular denomination.') Webb continues to perform and has recently recorded a live album Live and at Large. *But, alas, his confident prophecy that 'all my best songs are to come…' has so far not been realised.*

Billy Wilder (centre) with Walter Matthau and Jack Lemmon

CHAPTER 88

BILLY WILDER – HOLLYWOOD GENIUS

"The great pictures are the pictures that most people see."

Billy Wilder was one of the fifteen hundred or so Austrian and German Jews who worked in the German film industry and who quit their homelands in the early '30s to escape Nazi anti-Semitism. He was also, surely, the most gifted. His mother, who ran a popular cake shop and would eventually be killed in Auschwitz, named him 'Billie' to honour her hero, Wild West show-man 'Buffalo Bill' Cody. After dropping out of the University of Vienna, Wilder became a journalist and moved to Berlin, writing sports journalism and screenplays, eventually reaching Hollywood in 1934, speaking not a word of English. Five years later he co-wrote the first of a lifetime of Wilder hit movies, Ninotchka, *a mocking view of Soviet Russia starring the alluring Swedish actress Greta Garbo. The Wilder style, fundamentally European, was adult, unsentimental, constantly challenging the repressive limitations imposed by official US censorship.*

Billy Wilder is a small and sturdy American genius who thinks fast and talks fast. He also walks fast.

I was with him for ninety minutes yesterday, and for eighty of them he walked compulsively in, out, and about three rooms of his Savoy Hotel suite, covering I would guess, the equivalent of an 18-hole golf course.

He talked all the time. Sharp, astute, no-nonsense talk, delivered some-times with a cynical edge and always with a Viennese accent.

When he was in the room with me he talked softly. When he walked off to other rooms he obligingly raised his voice to a kind of subdued yell so that I should not miss a word.

Walking, talking, smoking and drinking, Mr Wilder radiated the creative force and energy of a dozen ordinary mortals. But then there has never been anything ordinary about Mr Wilder.

He is the most consistently successful writer-director in Hollywood today. With pictures like *The Apartment, Sunset Boulevard, The Lost Week-end, Some Like It Hot* and *Ninotchka* spinning out of his brain like rockets on Guy Fawkes night, Wilder has careered through a movie career of polished sophistication and gratifying rewards.

He has made twenty-four films, been nominated for twenty-one Oscars, actually winning six. Modestly he explained why he didn't win the others: 'I was robbed fifteen times.'

As a movie-maker he has constantly teetered on the brink of the implausible, the improbable and the distasteful. But Billy always gets away with it.

The Apartment, for instance, concerned itself with adulterous Manhattan executives in the midst of which Wilder nervously threw in a scene of attempted suicide. He opened *Sunset Boulevard* with a corpse floating in a swimming pool.

He based *Some Like It Hot* on the questionable hilarity inherent in the idea of two men posing as women in an all-girl orchestra.

Not surprisingly, he has become the darling of the art house sets, who see in Wilder an intellectual missionary, selling cynicism. Such talk makes Wilder want to throw up.

'Listen,' he said, 'a whole heapa rubbish is thrown back and forth about me.'

'The truth is this. I make pictures like other people make motor cars. It's a business. I'm a craftsman who knows his craft. Simple as that. I am not out to reform an audience, I am not out to better an audience. I just want to force an audience to drop its popcorn and listen. Let me put it another way. I sleep an awful lot in movie houses and I try to stop others from doing it.'

Wilder paced the floor looking like a somewhat greying old owl. 'I'm sick up to here,' he continued lifting a bare, muscular arm up to the level of his spectacles, 'with all that fancy-shmancy, high-falutin', long-hair, avant-garde, nouvelle-vague, phoney intellectual deep-dish pretentiousness. Get it?'

I said I got it.

He is, beneath the brash, trouble-shooting exterior, a man of almost palpable kindness and humility.

Wilder was born in Vienna in 1906, left Europe when Hitler rose. 'Since then,' he says, 'I've been a Jew not so much out of conviction as defiance.'

He owns one of Hollywood's finest art collections, which includes 'some Picassos'. His pictures are distributed 'all over the place'.

'Some hang on my walls, some in closets, some are with friends. Doesn't matter. When you're a real collector, it's no longer a question of wanting to look at your pictures all the time. It's enough to know you've got them. Like an alcoholic. He doesn't have to drink all the time. He just has to know there's a bottle around.'

So far Billy Wilder's movies have taken, altogether, more than £34 million at the box office.

'What are the great pictures?' he demanded, halting his marathon walk to respond to his own question. 'The great pictures are the pictures that most people pay to see. That's the business I'm in.'

5 FEBRUARY 1962

Billy Wilder lived into his mid-nineties, complaining bitterly that Hollywood studios would no longer employ him. Still, he continued to keep office hours. He sold part of his art collection, including many Picassos, for $30 million, explaining that 'We worried that the people in the apartment upstairs would let the bathtub overflow.' In his old age Wilder was heaped with lifetime achievement honours which he disparaged as 'Quick Before They Croak awards'. He also observed sourly that 'Awards are like haemorrhoids – sooner or later every asshole gets one.' Wilder, who married twice, died of pneumonia on 27 March 2002.

Nicol Williamson

CHAPTER 89

NICOL WILLIAMSON – BREAKING POINT

"I'll tell you the Big Secret about acting.
If you really listen, you come alive, and the play comes alive."

Nicol Williamson, an actor of genius, was a man of wildly divergent moods. What follows are excerpts two articles revealing him as a happy and fulfilled man and, secondly, as a tragic figure caught up in a kind of nightmare.

Alone next Sunday on the stage of a West End theatre the actor who sprang to world attention as a despairing lawyer in John Osborne's play *Inadmissible Evidence* will sing and dance a programme of poems and ballads. Nicol Williamson is looking forward to it with hope, pleasure and curiosity.

His offstage image has been that of a man with a low snapping point, to be approached with caution.

This forbidding picture of one of Britain's most distinguished actors (John Osborne called him 'the greatest actor since Marlon Brando') may once have been halfway true. But it wasn't at all true one afternoon this week when I met him in his cosy, well-swept little house in Chelsea, where Mr Williamson opened a bottle of good wine and shone with intelligence and a contagious sense of good will.

'I'm very happy,' he said, 'and I really wasn't very happy before. It's such a fortunate thing somehow to be able to do something.'

He was generously quick to ascribe his *joie de vivre* to his wife Jill, who at that very moment lay somewhere upstairs, a victim of the current flu epidemic.

'I'm no good at cocktail parties,' he said.

'Such a flimsy way to spend your time. Easier to buy some grub, get some friends round, find out what's in each other's heads, and shut up. That's what marriage has done for me. That's what Jill has done for me. Jill's got rid of that restless thing in me. In all truth I must say I feel terrific practically every moment of every day. I love being.'

Thin, fair and relaxed, Nicol Williamson talked about wine, divorce, critics, the theatre. He was never scornful except about grand actors who never give of their so-called best until the first night.

'The Dead Actors,' he calls them, 'who always work at quarter pace because rehearsals are such a bore. That's why they stumble and bluster about half the time. There are no rewards without work,' he said with emphasis.

> 'Unless you graft it's no good, it's no good. I find work excruciatingly pain-
> ful. I take it all away with me. I worry at dinner ... in bed ... when I
> get up in the morning. I can't let go. Then one day a light goes on, a
> door opens. These moments of discovery during rehearsals are the most
> exciting I've known in the theatre. The essential problem for an actor is to
> mould by painful process a character who is not himself, a separate crea-
> tion. The Dead Actors don't really care about this. Mostly they use the play
> to put themselves on an ego trip. Have you noticed how they never really
> listen to other actors in a play? How their eyes go dead when it's not their
> turn to speak? Listen, I'll tell you the Big Secret. If you really listen you
> come alive, and the play comes alive.'

About next Sunday's concert he says: 'I've done so many things in theatre that have been a slog. I just want to have some fun, too. My father used to say: "If you get knocked down by a bus you will never be run over by a tram." It was his way of saying "forget it, enjoy it!"'

8 DECEMBER 1972

Nicol Williamson was a lot unhappier when I met him again in Washington DC some six years later. He was one of the most brilliant actors of his age, but too tightly strung and self-judgemental to sustain a lifetime career on the stage. Besides, his marriage was heading for the rocks.

In 1976 I flew to Washington to meet Williamson who was appearing as Henry VIII at the Kennedy Center in Richard Rodgers's new musical Rex. *Next stop: Broadway! I expected to find an actor buoyed up by the challenge ahead.*

I found, instead, a man on the edge of a nervous breakdown, ready to snap, ready to quit.

Nicol Williamson is a man tormented by the realisation that he may have just made the great mistake of his career. Never an easy man, he is now like a tiger coiled to spring in unknown directions. He is taciturn and peppery, sleeping hardly at all. The sign on the door of Williamson's suite 702 of the Watergate Hotel read: Do Not Disturb.

'I feel as though I'm dying,' Williamson told me over lunch in Washington's Jockey Club. 'I'm absolutely beyond the point of no return.'

Emphasising that he was not concerned to criticise the musical *Rex* itself – which he described as 'a grand piece of confectionery, a mammoth juggernaut, resplendent to look at' – Williamson declared that he loathed being in a musical at all.

As an actor renowned for mastering giant roles like Hamlet, Macbeth and Uncle Vanya, he found the musical comedy form 'crushing' and 'diminishing'.

He said: 'You've got to drive it or it won't go. How can you be totally committed to something you hate doing? Every single moment is like being taken home in an ambulance…'

Williamson is on stage for almost all of the show's two hours and forty minutes. He sings in a true, full-bodied baritone voice. His authority is total. Nowhere in his performance is there a hint or clue to suggest his feelings of agony, anger, his fierce need for release.

'It was a mistake one can only find out by doing it,' he said. 'There's no way of predicting these things. I will never do another musical. Never again. Never!'

He lit a cigarette. 'I'm smoking like a chimney again after months off it. I could wind up a hundred-a-day man here. I'm not drinking. If I hit the bottle, I'll never set foot on that stage.'

Williamson, at thirty-eight, is one of those actors who never gives less than his best.

He said: 'I care for what I'm doing every minute of my life. I'm totally caught up in it. That's why people like me are not long for this planet.'

This is a man constantly at boiling point. He once walked out in the middle of a performance of *Hamlet* in Boston because he felt he wasn't giving his best.

'The most difficult thing in the theatre,' he said, 'is to maintain concentration and effort.'

'If you lose it, you're like a man who drives a train through a wall because he's been awake for forty-eight hours. I simply can't keep pumping that energy into *Rex*. I do possess a sense of honour and fairness. I don't want to damage the show or its fine company. What's more, if I quit the show it will put me on the deck financially. I may not even be able to salvage my new home in England. But I've got to protect myself. The prospect of doing the show for a year is killing. Today I looked at myself in the mirror. Every year the time goes faster. Every year it's harder to find the wind, to make the final track.'

'There's still nobody who can beat me,' he added fiercely. 'I'm burning myself out. That's why I won't last long on this earth. The only loser is me.'

8 MARCH 1976

As might have been expected, Nicol Williamson did snap during the brief run of Rex *on Broadway, slapping a fellow actor during a curtain call. A minor incident, no doubt, but it made news across the world for fifteen minutes.* Rex *on Broadway was a flop, folding after only fourteen previews and less than fifty regular performances – a rare instance of a Richard Rodgers failure. The show featured an unknown actress named Glenn Close in her first musical.*

Nicol Williamson died aged seventy-five on 16 December 2011, two years after being diagnosed with oesophageal cancer.

Nicol Williamson in a scene from *Laughter in the Dark*, 1969

Forest Yeo-Thomas

CHAPTER 90

FOREST YEO-THOMAS –
THE BRAVEST MAN I WILL EVER MEET

"I had it instilled in me that being British was the very finest thing
that could happen to anybody."

*Of all the heroes of the Second World War, none stands out more remarkably than
Wing-Commander Forest Yeo-Thomas, a British secret agent who thrice para-
chuted into Occupied France. Brutally tortured, he defied the Gestapo, escaped
repeatedly from custody, and lived on, much weakened by his wartime sufferings,
until 26 February 1964. He was the first secret agent of the Second World War
to be awarded the George Cross, the first to be commemorated by an English
Heritage blue plaque. One of his biographers, Mark Seaman, acknowledged that
the Yeo-Thomas story is 'more extraordinary than any fiction dreamed up by a
novelist or filmed by Hollywood'.*

He limped across the carpet and pulled back the lace curtains. 'That's
where they took me,' he said in a voice vacant of emotion. 'Over there
on those dirty steps.' We stared down into the Paris dusk, across the road
to the Metro station called Passy. Traffic horns barked nervously up at us
from the Rue des Eaux, a narrow street five floors down. He let the curtains
drop. Then, with some pain and difficulty, he took his seat again, crossed
his fingers beneath his chin and looked at me without a word. His eyes,
like his voice, seemed pale and flat and devoid of expression.

Wing-Commander F. F. E. Yeo-Thomas, when I met him in Paris,
was just out of hospital again. For sixteen years surgeons in Paris and
London have attended to the multiple agonies inflicted upon him
by the Gestapo when, on the self-same steps of Passy station, he was
captured as a spy.

Britain, in the testing time of the Second World War, produced many
men of daring and skill. But the story of Wing-Commander Yeo-Thomas

occupies a special place even in those archives of courage. Beaten, stran-
gled, half-drowned, suspended from chains from the ceiling like a carcass
in a butcher's window, Yeo-Thomas became, in a way, the incarnation of
all human suffering during the war.

He knew more than any man about the organisation and arms supplies
of the French Resistance Groups. But he never broke, he never spoke – not
even when the Germans chained his flayed body to a table-top and beat him
into insensibility, concentrating their heaviest blows beneath the belt.

Bruce Marshall has documented the story of Wing-Commander
Yeo-Thomas in film and biography, most famously in a best-selling book
called *The White Rabbit*. But there is another story that has not been told. It
has to do with the spirit that sustained him.

'I was brought up to believe,' Yeo-Thomas told me, 'that being British
was the very finest thing that could happen to anybody. I had instilled
in me ever since I can remember a sense of being special, privileged,
and better. It was a lesson I was never allowed to forget. And I never
did.'

Consider this. When Yeo-Thomas was growing up, his family had
already been settled in France for more than a century. Ever since 1885,
in fact, when the Wing-Commander's great-grandfather departed the
mines of his native Wales to start a coal depot in the French channel port
of Dieppe. Though the family never returned to Britain, it never forgot
that Britain was its fountainhead. This was the message, nourished by an
almost mystical devotion, passed on like a catechism from each generation to the next.

'We were so determined to remain British,' Yeo-Thomas said, 'that it
became a fixed family rule that the children, when they arrived, had to be
born in Britain.'

'As soon as I was old enough to stand up straight I remember how, every evening, our meals ended with family prayers and the singing of "God Save The
King". I joined in the singing almost before I knew what the words meant. It
was a mysterious thing. It was imbued in us like a faith … more than a faith,
for I am not a godly man. We had one large photograph, I recall, of King
Edward VII, which, when he died, was draped in black, and for weeks afterwards we were not allowed to talk above a whisper. I remember it very clearly.
And always my father saying: "Forest, you are British – remember that always."

So, you see, when the Germans were beating me up, I kept remind-
ing myself that I was British, as my father instructed that I should. I kept
remembering that I was better. I had grown up with this belief. It was in every

bone of my body. So I never gave up. I kept going like an athlete, like Gordon Pirie, I suppose. Get through the next few seconds … get through the next minute … I had to give an example. I couldn't let the side down…'

Such sentiments nowadays provide the seeds of popular satire, Jingo jokes and Colonel Blimp cartoons. The BBC's *Goon Show* ran riot on gags about the Union Jack and the unquestioning fidelity of the Light Brigade. But here in the Paris dusk, in the home of a hero, his words took on an almost forgotten dimension. I thought of four generations of a British family living in Dieppe, a small enclave of national pride in a foreign land, forging a faith so strong that it was eventually capable of withstanding even the most inhuman assaults on its foundations.

Wing-Commander Yeo-Thomas, as it grew darker, switched on the lights in his apartment. I saw for the first time, almost hidden in a corner, a framed photograph of General de Gaulle bearing an inscription in his own handwriting: 'To Forest – as a token of the faithful friendship (*d'attachement fidèle*) of his war comrade Charles de Gaulle.'

The photograph is the sole visible link with Yeo-Thomas's brave past, but the whole apartment is a link with Yeo-Thomas's years of courage. 'It was from this very room,' he said, 'that my father was taken by the Gestapo and sent to Fresnes prison. Only the other day, this fireplace collapsed and we found a concealed hole where my father had hidden his radio during the Occupation.'

Among the regular coded messages the old man would have heard broad-cast by the BBC was one that said simply: '*Le petit lapin blanc est rentier au clapier.*' ('The little white rabbit has returned to his hutch.') This was to inform the French Resistance that Yeo-Thomas had got back safely to London after his sorties in Nazi-held France.

In March 1944 the white rabbit did not return to his hutch. Betrayed by another agent at Passy station, Yeo-Thomas was captured by the jubilant Gestapo. Imagine this man, after repeated beatings, stripped and thrown into a bath of ice-cold water, his face forcibly pushed down until he was on the point of drowning, while all around the bath stood a crowd of German girls, Gestapo office workers, jeering at his nudity and agony.

Then consider again the almost absurdly simple reason for Yeo-Thomas's unbreakable will. 'I was British. I had to give an example. I couldn't let the side down.'

He filled and lit his pipe as Barbara Yeo-Thomas, the slim blonde he met in wartime London, entered the room with a very English tray of tea.

Before the war, Forest had been the manager of the Paris fashion house of Molyneux ('My God,' said an especially stupid brass hat in 1941, 'the RAF has sunk to employing a dress-maker!'). Today Yeo-Thomas is the representative in France of the Federation of British Industries.

He puffed at his pipe silently for a while. Then he said: 'The gilt has worn off the gingerbread ... I mean,' he said, 'it just hasn't happened, has it?'

> 'I look around me. I see a world which has returned to its old brutalities, and it hurts. I hear young people say that England has had it. Down the drain, I'm all right, Jack. It shakes me. Sometimes it hurts so much that I wish I could have died after my escape from Buchenwald in '45. It is not easy for me to tell you a thing like that. But it's true. I wish, sometimes, I had died then. We knew we had won the war. It was the most completely satisfying feeling I've had in all my life. I am, you must know, since you ask, a terribly disappointed man.'

Later, outside again, I watched the Parisians, huddled in their fur-collared overcoats, their faces chiselled by private ambition, jostling one another on the narrow pavements. I thought of a German named Rudi von Merode, chief and most odious of Yeo-Thomas's torturers, living today in the Spanish port of Bilbao, scot-free and fat with stolen wealth.

The steps of Passy station were covered by the dead leaves of autumn. I stood there for a moment, looking up for the last time at the window on the fifth floor of the apartment building in Rue des Eaux. Behind the window with his pipe and his memories, was the bravest and proudest man I had ever met – the white rabbit, who proved, when trapped, that he had the heart of a lion.

4 December 1961

The enterprise and courage of Forest Frederick Edward Yeo-Thomas GC, MC and Bar, Croix de Guerre (with palms), Commandeur de Legion d'Honneur, revealed itself early on. While still a teenager he faked his age, joined the Allied Forces in the First World War, fought with the Poles against the Russians, was taken prisoner for the first time and escaped execution by strangling a guard. At the time Yeo-Thomas was only eighteen. He died, aged sixty-one, in his Paris apartment on 26 February 1964, following a massive haemorrhage. He was cremated in Paris, his ashes interred in Brookwood cemetery, Surrey, England. His life is commemorated with an English Heritage plaque at his flat in Camden.

10 . 12 . 1961

Dear Mr Kretzmer,

Thanks very much for your letter and enclosures. I have since that received more letters sent to me direct to many fancy addresses, but thanks to the efficiency of the Post Office here, they have duly reached me. I have already replied to them all.

I want to thank you for the very able + authentic way you reported our interview and from the messages I have received, all those who read it were very impressed.

My wife and I both hope we shall have the pleasure of seeing you again one of these days, we enjoyed your company very much indeed.

With all our best wishes for Xmas + the New Year.

Yours sincerely

[signature]

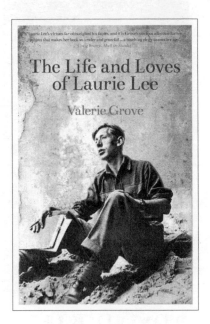